38- 4842

Y0-BDY-758

OTTO BRAHM
THE MAN AND THE CRITIC

OTTO BRAHM
THE MAN AND THE CRITIC

BY

MAXIM NEWMARK, Ph.D.

G. E. STECHERT & CO.

NEW YORK

LONDON   PARIS   LEIPZIG

1938

COPYRIGHT, 1938

MAXIM NEWMARK

Composed, Printed and Bound by
The Collegiate Press
George Banta Publishing Company
Menasha, Wisconsin

In Memory of My Grandfather
JOSHUA WOLLIN

FOREWORD

The following work represents the first attempt to gather and to classify within a single format the scattered materials which reflect Otto Brahm's total achievement as a critic of the drama and stage. Other writers have dealt with detached or isolated phases of Brahm's career, viewing him particularly as a theatre director, in which capacity he attained his greatest eminence. However, the present study proposes to emphasize Brahm's significance in the history of modern German literature, viewing him as the critic and man of letters rather than as the theatre practician.

I should like to acknowledge my debt of gratitude to Professor W. D. Zinnecker for his sympathetic criticism of those sections of the book dealing with the history of the German Theatre; to Professor H. W. Nordmeyer for suggestions concerning research technique and methodology; and to Professor H. B. Brennecke for his careful proof-reading of the manuscript.

TABLE OF CONTENTS

INTRODUCTION

Otto Brahm's career falls into two periods; one of philological preparation as a student and a critic, and one of practical activity as the director of various theatres in Berlin. Brahm is more remembered for his accomplishments of the second period because of its coincidence with the rise of naturalism and the evolution of the famous *Brahmstil*, which was the embodiment of naturalism in terms of the theatre. The unique cultural significance of Brahm's creation of a new technique in the theatre and his leadership of the Ibsen and Hauptmann campaign in the German theatre have tended to center the attention of historians of literature on this external phase of Brahm's work. But it must not be forgotten that the very fact of Brahm's recognition of these dramatists and his ability to interpret them in the one manner most subtly appropriate to their spirit and content was first of all due to his critical acumen.

To be sure, Otto Brahm's major contribution was in his second period, in the theatre rather than in the drama. His was ultimately a triumph of technique rather than imagination, of action rather than idea. Yet no one could have been more alive than he to the interdependence of these two sets of categories. In the most hectic days of the *Freie Bühne* and the *Deutsches Theater*, deluged by all the minutiae of theatre practice, Brahm never forgot that the theatre is but the formal means by which the drama is most effectively rendered articulate.

In his letters to Georg Hirschfeld Brahm expresses a growing resentment that the demands of the theatre leave him no time for literary work. In the midst of his greatest triumphs on the stage, going back to the theatre is for him a "Rückkehr zur Tretmühle" in which "—jedes Tagewerk ist auch ein Plagewerk."[1] Brahm's biography of Schiller and a projected work on Ibsen both remained fragments due to the exigencies of his work in the theatre. During the interim between his directorship of the *Deutsches Theater* and the *Lessingtheater* Brahm thought very seriously of going back to

[1] Letters to Georg Hirschfeld, Dec. 16, 1899; Feb. 13, 1900. Cf. *Otto Brahm, Briefe und Erinnerungen*, George Hirschfeld, Berlin, 1925.

his critical and literary life; so that, in spite of the success of Maeterlinck's *Monna Vanna* as his first offering in the *Lessing-theater*, Brahm was overcome by mixed feelings. Hirschfeld tells us:

Ganz wohl hat der Kritiker Brahm, der ja fast wieder zum Leben erwacht wäre, sich bei dieser goldenen Fülle nicht gefühlt.[2]

Such passages as these and the following leave no doubt as to the basic conflict in Brahm's career:

Eigentlich geht es mir gar nicht gut, innerlich, in diesen Frühlings-stürmen, die alles in einem aufrütteln. Ich bin unruhig und sehnsüch-tig. Wonach? Nach einem Lebensinhalt. . . . Auch lässt die Arbeit und die stets erneuerte Anforderung des Tages mich nicht recht zu mir selber kommen; zum Leben habe ich keine Zeit, nur zum Diri-gieren.[3]

Even up until the late summer of 1912, shortly before his death, Otto Brahm was still telling Arthur Eloesser that the theatre had robbed him of his health but that if he could once get back to his writing, everything would turn out for the best.[4]

It is important to remember that during the ten or twelve years preceding his directorship of the *Deutsches Theater* Brahm was the foremost dramatic critic of Berlin. Although his essays and reviews necessarily reflect a sort of journalistic terseness and a preoccupa-tion with externalities, they also show evidence of research and careful analysis. And if his writings are often more exact than pro-found, their very exactness offers us a detailed picture of the intel-lectual currents of the times. It is for this reason too, that a study of the dramatic criticism of Otto Brahm affords us a panorama of the German theatre and of German literature during the last twenty years of the nineteenth century. Brahm was in the very midst of the intellectual and social upheaval that ushered in the movement of naturalism. "Le Naturalisme au Théâtre" was to him what "Le Roman expérimental" had been to Michael Georg Conrad and Max Kretzer,—a new, inspiring catechism; but Brahm was objective enough in his appreciation of naturalism to forego

---

[2] *Op. cit.*, p. 208.
[3] Letters to Georg Hirschfeld, Mar. 25, 1897; April 10, 1897.
[4] "Das Theater hat mir die Gesundheit genommen. Aber wenn ich erst meine Ruhe wieder habe und ungestört an meinem Schreibtisch sitze, wird es noch eine Zeit-lang gehen." Quoted by Hirschfeld, *op. cit.*, p. 134.

the ridiculous extremes of the earlier Arno Holz and the other so-called "consistent" naturalists.

Otto Brahm's literary activity extends throughout the greater part of his life. His practical activities at the zenith of his career were: the directorship of the *Freie Bühne*, then that of the *Deutsches Theater* as the predecessor of Reinhardt, and finally, the directorship of the *Lessingtheater*. But even during this period of incessant work, Brahm continued writing. Concomitantly with his theatrical activities and during his period as a critic, Brahm was an indefatigable contributor to the *Nation*, the *Deutsche Rundschau*, the *Frankfurter Zeitung*, the *Vossische Zeitung*, and the periodical founded by him, *Freie Bühne für modernes Leben*, now known as the *Neue Rundschau*.

What, briefly, is the superficial content of Brahm's critical writings? In them we see how Brahm was among the first to champion Ibsen's cause in Germany. We see how Hauptmann, too, owed his first appearance to Brahm as director of the *Freie Bühne*. In critical appreciation and creative staging Brahm helped Hauptmann to recognition; and, subsequently, most of Hauptmann's dramas found their place in the repertory of the *Deutsches Theater*. We see how the remarkable significance of the troupe led by Duke Georg of Meiningen was immediately realized by Brahm long before they made their profound impression on Antoine and Stanislawski. Brahm's Kleist and Schiller biographies, his brochure on the *Ritterdrama* and his critical reviews were an indispensable prelude which culminated in his theatrical activity; and in his discussion of the Meininger's naturalistic technique we find a modified echo of his own dramaturgical theories.

The names of a host of younger dramatists run through Brahm's essays in a serried throng, evidence of a keen, receptive mind that could include the new as well as the old. He is interested in Antoine and offers him the hospitality of Berlin where the Frenchman is inspired by a performance of *Hanneles Himmelfahrt* which he is later to emulate in the "Théâtre libre." Brahm in turn takes over Becque and Maeterlinck from Antoine's repertoire. The younger Germans, Hauptmann, Sudermann, Halbe, Dreyer, Kretzer, Hartleben, Fulda, Hofmannsthal, Schnitzler, and Hirschfeld receive critical attention interspersed with the Anzengruber's, Fitger's, and Wildenbruch's. There are essays on Shakespeare, Molière, Grillparzer, Hebbel, Ludwig, Strindberg, and Tolstoi. Philological discussions, anecdote, history, aesthetics, politics, and sometimes mere journalese make up the body of the essays. Everything is sober and calculated. Brahm's personality very rarely seeps through except in such isolated instances as his open letter to Hauptmann on the latter's fiftieth birthday, or his commemorative essays on Wilhelm Scherer. Lyrical passages are prominent because of their rarity.

Brahm's literary background cannot be sufficiently emphasized in the evaluation of his contribution to the theatre. This literary tradition holds unbroken in the history of the German theatre from Goethe through Tieck, Immermann, and Laube. With the exception of the more florid days of Reinhardt, and during the post-war expressionistic orgy, this literary principle has held its ground. It provided a spiritual basis that lent aim and dignity to the mechanics of the theatre. The technical excellence of the German stage toward the end of the nineteenth century only served to bring into sharper relief the lack of such a basis. In a theatre that could only point to the classics and to an inept epigon drama for its lukewarm triumphs there could be no intellectual counterpart of contemporary life in the drama. It remained for such critics as Michael Georg Conrad, Maximilian Harden, and the Hart brothers, among others, to feel and to transmit to their compatriots the massive impact of Zola, Ibsen and Tolstoi, and thus prepare the ground for a new generation of authors whose themes and technique would be more in consonance with reality. It was as one of these critics that Otto Brahm made his initial contribution to the drama. To study Brahm's dramatic criticism is consequently no mere drawing of academic distinctions or quibbling misplacement of emphasis.[5]

There is yet another reason why Otto Brahm is so important as a critic. It is as a critic rather than as a man of the theatre that Brahm shows us his most articulate and therefore most permanent

---

[5] "Brahm hat der Bühne das literarische Gewissen zurückgegeben." Arthur Eloesser. Quoted by Hirschfeld, *op. cit.*, p. 131.

self. In the technique of the theatre we necessarily deal with the impermanent and irretrievable.[6] A system of the theatre no less than a single performance in the theatre has no well-defined or permanent significance until its vital principles have been recorded in writing. In practice these principles invariably change. How long would it take for the still living essence of the Moscow Art Theatre in its heyday to become a confused echo of hearsay and intangible fame if Stanislawski had not written his "Life in Art?" And even so, such records constitute the basis of imperfect re-constructions at best, particularly when we consider the limitations of verbal expression in regard to a plastic and dynamic medium, and how much the theatre owes to the unpredictable and non-recurrent accidents of genius and the times.

In tracing Otto Brahm's intellectual antecedents and development, it will be necessary to resort to biographical material. Brahm's critical sense was neither universal nor absolute. Its limits were defined by his specialized literary training, by certain intellectual influences, the whole singularly confirmed by a very pronounced native temperament. It shall be the purpose of the following chapter to show the formative influences in Brahm's life and to discuss briefly those of his writings which, in a strict sense, belong outside the sphere of his dramatic criticism, but which are nonetheless important in his development.

I. *A Literary Biography of Brahm*

When Otto Brahm (b. 5. Feb. 1856) died on the 28th of November, 1912, it was astonishing to note the number of lives into which he had entered so intimately. In the mourning ceremonies, in the expressions of condolence to his brother, Ludwig, and in the flood of periodical and newspaper necrologies there was revealed, as never during his lifetime, how deeply this diminutive and unassuming man had struck root into the innermost cultural life of

---

[6] Cf. Lessing's memorable statement of this truism: "Die Rechtfertigung des Dichters kann jederzeit angetreten werden; sein Werk bleibt da und kann uns immer wieder vor die Augen gelegt werden. Aber die Kunst des Schauspielers ist in ihren Werken transitorisch. Sein Gutes und Schlimmes rauscht gleich schnell vorbei." *Hamburgische Dramaturgie*, Ankündigung.

his time.[1] Gerhart Hauptmann,Walther Rathenau, Erich Schmidt, Arthur Schnitzler, Paul Cassirer, Theodore Wolff, Hermann Sudermann, Alfred Kerr, Max Reinhardt, Arthur Eloesser, Hermann Bahr, Ludwig Ganghofer, Otto Ernst, Björn Björnson, Heinrich Mann, Hugo von Hofmannsthal, Ludwig Fulda, Max Dreyer, Max Halbe, Georg Hirschfeld, Paul Schlenther, and a host of others in one way or another gave expression to the sense of personal bereavement which Brahm's death had brought them.

Nor were all of these merely formal or impersonal utterances such as we usually associate with the death-notice of a celebrity. Gerhart Hauptmann spoke of the inseparable bond that had united him with Brahm during twenty-five years of work and friendship. He praised Brahm for his idealism and *Treue*. He dwelt upon the remarkable interfusion of the practical and the ideal in Brahm's character and went on to show how Brahm had reclaimed the theatre from its esoteric aloofness.[2] Schlenther elaborated upon his friend's aesthetic creed. He showed how Brahm had shunned the dogmatic all his life, believing in a free development rather than in any hard and fast finalities.[3] Schnitzler contributed some personal reminiscences that revealed how much he and others owed to Brahm as an encouraging guide and mentor.[4] An insight into Brahm's character as a benevolent despot of the theatre was afforded by one of the famous "Brahm Ensemble," Emanuel Reicher, when he mentioned the informal nature that placed no great stock in title and outward dignity but was rather an adviser and helper to those who had once penetrated behind his mask of apparent inscrutability.[5]

[1] The letters of condolence, death notices, commemorative essays, and a detailed account of the elaborate funeral ceremonies are contained in: *Otto Brahm, Kundgebungen zu seinem Gedenken*, edited by Willi Simon, Berl. 1913.

[2] "Wir waren verbunden durch eine verwandte Innerlichkeit und durch äussere Umstände. Das Werk dieses Mannes war zum Teil mein Werk, und mein Werk war zum Teil das Werk dieses Mannes. . . . Dieser Mensch, Mann und Freund war deutscher Idealist in reinstem Sinne. . . . Ich glaube nicht, dass in der Geschichte des deutschen Theaters eine solche Verbindung von praktischer Kraft jemals vor ihm dagewesen ist. . . . Es (Brahm's work) hat auf einer gewissen Ebene die Einheit von Kunst und Volk zum Ereignis gemacht. Das Theater ist in ihm gleichsam zum Atmungsorgan der Volksseele geworden. Er gab dem Abseitigen, eigentlich Volks- und Weltfremden die schlichte Kraft einer naturnotwendigen Funktion." Gerhart Hauptmann, *op. cit.*, p. 8ff.

[3] *Op. cit.*, p. 12ff.   [4] *Ibid.*, p. 11f.   [5] *Ibid.*, p. 12.

A few days later, at the memorial services in the *Lessingtheater*, Ernst Hardt delivered a poetic peroration in which he characterized Otto Brahm as:

> Unbeugsam ehrlich! Grausam ehrlich um
> Der Heiligkeit des Dinges willen.[6]

Kerr then spoke of Brahm as the "Paulus Henrik Ibsens" and traced his historical position in the European theatre, showing how Stanislawski had learned from Brahm just as Checkov had learned from Hauptmann.[7]

But not all of the citations were laudatory. There were others who tried to do justice to the memory of Otto Brahm in the reverse direction, balancing the picture, as it were. A great deal was said about his inflexibility, his coldness, his hyperobjectivity. But even those who had fallen out with him during his lifetime admitted his positive as well as negative qualities. Max Reinhardt acknowledged Brahm as a teacher and friend who had decisively influenced his career and whom he loved and felt gratitude for, even though later years had distanced them from each other.[8] Kerr also wrote in his characteristic manner:

> Ich war die letzten vierzehn Jahre mit ihm verfeindet; wir grüssten uns nicht—aber ich habe keinen meiner Freunde mehr geliebt.[9]

As late as 1929, Maximilian Harden, still smarting from a personal *contretemps* by which he had dissociated himself from the founders of the *Freie Bühne* (and thus also from its later glory), dismissed Brahm from serious consideration by reproaching him with a lack of vision at having lost the services of Max Reinhardt and Gordon Craig, who had been under contract to him. Yet even he had to concede Brahm's human qualities.[10]

It is evident from these tributes and strictures that we are dealing with a man who, whatever else may be said about him, was imbued with high principle and whose personal integrity impressed enemies as well as friends. "Er lebt ganz für ein Prinzip, und das wird ihm eine spätere Zeit noch anrechnen," wrote

---

[6] *Ibid.*, p. 17.
[7] *Ibid.*, p. 21ff.
[8] *Ibid.*, p. 142.
[9] *Ibid.*, p. 101.
[10] In *Die Scene*, Apr. 1929, p. 108f.

Theodor Fontane about Brahm.[11] And Hermann Bahr expressed the opinion of a select circle of Vienna friends when he said: "Brahm, das ist die Treue, das ist die Zuverlässigkeit."[12]

A. *Early Education*

Otto Brahm was born in Hamburg into a lower middle-class family. His father (Julius Abrahamsohn, d. 1888) was a business man who barely managed to provide a modest existence for his family and who, in spite of a lifetime's efforts, never succeeded in attaining easy circumstances. Otto attended the *Bürgerschule* conducted by Dr. Anton Rée in Hamburg, and graduated at the age of twelve; but he remained for another year because he was too young to enter business. Since he showed an inclination for study, he was sent off to the *Realschule* in Perleberg where, among other subjects, his favorite studies were English and Latin. His reactions to the War of 1870 while in Perleberg resulted in his first literary effort, an essay on the advantages of war, which was read by his teacher to the class. At the age of fifteen he graduated from the *Realschule* and returned to Hamburg. Since, for pecuniary reasons, it was impossible for him to enter a university, he spent the following three years as a bank clerk in Hamburg. Brahm was not a brilliant success as a business man but he gained valuable experience in business and accounting which he was later to utilize as a theatre director.

In 1875, without any warning, Otto Brahm suddenly left his position with the banking firm, having decided to become a writer. He obtained his father's consent to this break from family tradition only after an essay which he had written had been submitted to Julius Rodenberg, editor of the *Deutsche Rundschau*, and had been returned with a favorable opinion as to the literary promise of the author. There followed a year of autodidactic activity during which Brahm studied to compensate for the deficiencies of his *Realschule* education. The main subjects upon which he concentrated at this time in preparation for university entrance were Latin, Greek, history and literature. In 1876 he entered the University of Berlin.

[11] Letter to Karl Zöllner, Sept. 6, 1894.   [12] Willi Simon, *op. cit.*, p. 63.

B. *The Hamburg Influence*

Before proceeding, it would be interesting at this point to show the influence which Hamburg exercised on Brahm during these early, formative years. As a bank clerk he had often visited the Thalia theatre with its venerable Lessing-Ekhof-Schröder tradition. As the place where the first grandiose conception of a German national theatre had leaped past political realities into the imagination of Germany's greatest critic, Hamburg undoubtedly left the mark of its literary and theatrical associations on Otto Brahm. Schlenther tells us that Otto Brahm both as a critic and director was the continuator of the Hamburg School that is so important in the history of the German theatre. He suggests that there is a direct line of descent from Lessing to Brahm, transplanted by the latter to Berlin.[13]

There is still another aspect from which the importance of Hamburg in regard to Brahm may be conceived. Hirschfeld points out that Hamburg as the largest harbor on the continent presents such social contrasts, with poverty and deprivation on the one hand and superfluity on the other, that this glaring disparity prepared Brahm for the social criticism of Ibsen and of *The Weavers*.[14]

C. *Friendship with Schlenther*

When Otto Brahm arrived in Berlin at the age of twenty he presented the appearance of a small, stout, beardless, but not always smooth-shaven, young man. His short-sightedness made him tilt his head forward as though with curiosity. The large, gold-rimmed glasses that he wore concealed a pair of shrewd but candid brown eyes. His forehead, mouth, and nose were the most prominent features in a broad, mature-looking countenance. In Berlin Brahm spent a good deal of time visiting the museums and art salons. At the University he religiously attended the lectures

---

[13] "Otto Brahm bewährte als Kritiker und besonders als Direktor die 'Hamburger Schule,' die in der deutschen Theatergeschichte von grösster Bedeutung ist. Es geht eine Stammbaumlinie von Lessing bis zu Brahm. Er verpflanzte sie von Hamburg nach Berlin." *Schriften der Gesellschaft für Theatergeschichte*, Band 40, Berl. 1930, p. 62.

[14] *Op. cit.*, p. 18.

of Hermann Grimm and Wilhelm Scherer and, in addition, visited
a great many others. His list of courses at Berlin included Harms
on Logic, Wagner on Socialism, Treitschke on Political Theory,
Du Bois-Reymond on Anthropology, Curtius on the History of
Greek Art, Erdmann on Philosophy, and Zoller on Literary
Criticism.

In 1877 Brahm went to the University of Heidelberg, but returned to Berlin the following semester, bringing with him his new
friend, Paul Schlenther. At Heidelberg Brahm had made few
friends, his predominant seriousness and the lack of money having
excluded him from the escapades and revelry of Schlenther's set.
It was characteristic of Brahm that he preferred the scientific and
factual methods of Grimm and Scherer to the rhetoric of Kuno
Fischer, Schlenther's Heidelberg idol. And it was on this issue that
Brahm and Schlenther began their life-long friendship.

In 1912, shortly after Brahm's death, Schlenther pored through
all the letters he had received from his friend since 1878. What he
found was an amazing degree of reticence. Brahm was always
complaining of how much better he could express himself by word
of mouth.

Nirgends fällt ein Wort der Leidenschaft, nirgends entladet sich
ein Erguss des Herzens. Aber im Zusammenhange spürt man ein
zähes Festhalten an Ideen, ein Zielsicheres Bestreben, Ideale in Wirklichkeit zu verwandeln. . . . Es weht eine kühle, herbe Luft durch
diese Korrespondenz.[15]

And this to his oldest and closest friend!

There was a laconic quality in Brahm's style, a sort of saturnine
acerbity that distorted genuine emotion into an ironic smirk.
Later commentators on Brahm's critical writings were to compare
him with Börne and Heine. In Brahm's correspondence with
Georg Hirschfeld, momentous events were jotted down with an
imperturbable, factual air. Epigrams and puns, nondescript wit-
ticisms, and even doggerel intersperse Brahm's letters; in short,
all those verbal detours and evasions that bespeak the subjective
and problematic individual. A most striking characterization of

[15] *Berliner Tageblatt*, Dec. 1, 1912.

Brahm's style was made by Alfred Kerr who called it "a form of silence."[16]

Schlenther was obliged to supplement these noncommittal letters with his memories of the man. He recalled their meetings in Heidelberg and later in Scherer's Seminar, and their long walks and excursions together. Here he had found an Otto Brahm who was sensitive to nature, a warm, human friend, a brilliant conversationalist and dialectician. They both learned a great deal from each other and developed themselves mutually in their long conversations. Brahm had an abrupt, sovereign manner of passing judgment that fairly challenged contradiction. In the middle of the nineties, during their impecunious, uphill struggle, Brahm and Schlenther lived together, and the story went round that they had only one pair of shoes between them so that when one went out the other had to remain at home.[17] Yet in appearance and disposition they were opposites; Schlenther elegant, almost aristocratic, with a Van Dyke beard, Slavic features, ears flat against the skull, the bulging neck and close-cropped head so typical of the Prussian; Brahm small, almost frail, with protruding ears, the broad aquiline nose, sensual lips, and high forehead of the Jewish intellectual. The total impression of Schlenther's appearance was that of a portly, porcine (not in the derogatory sense) dignity; whereas Brahm had a haughty, brooding seriousness accentuated by a myopic frown and a hard, supercilious cast about the mouth.[18] Such was the famous *Voltairelächeln* that his contemporaries constantly remarked about. Although they were both reared in the tradition of Berlin rationalism, in temperament Schlenther was the more extrovertive and enthusiastic of the two, Brahm the more deliberative and sedate. If Schiller's overworked distinction between the *naïve* and *sentimental* may once more be invoked, Schlenther would represent the former and Brahm the latter. Schlenther's verbal portrait of his friend in those early days illuminates the distinction between the two.

[16] In reference to the laconic conclusion of Brahm's biography of Kleist. "Es war eine Form des Schweigens, Tragisches durch sich selber wirken zu lassen." *Pan*, Dec. 6, 1912.

[17] The anecdote is related by Schlenther, *op. cit.*, p. 51.

[18] Photo portraits of both men appear in Soergel's *Dichtung und Dichter der Zeit*, Leipzig, 1928[21]; Brahm on p. 175; Schlenther on p. 177.

... er blieb in seinem Ausdruck scharf, hart und schroff, wickelte nichts in Watte, beschönigte nichts und goss mit Vorliebe über jugendlichen Überschwang eiskalte Duschen. Die geistige Unerschrockenheit dieses kleinen Menschen imponierte, und man empfand sehr bald, dass von diesem verneinenden Geiste zur Klärung der Begriffe und Anschauungen sehr viel zu profitieren war. . . . Dieser geborene Kritiker erzog sich und andere zur Kritik.[19]

Together these friends participated in the rejuvenation of German letters after the barren days of the *Gründerjahre*. Naturalism, Ibsen and Hauptmann, the *Freie Bühne*, then Brahm at the *Deutsches Theater* and Schlenther at the *Burgtheater*, such were the various stages and the culminations of their common spiritual Odyssey.

On the 8th of December, 1878, Brahm wrote to Schlenther from Strassburg:

So laut wie möglich rufe ich Ihnen zu, suchen Sie in ein Verhältnis zu Scherer zu kommen, wenn Sie es noch nicht sind. Sie haben den unglaublichsten Nutzen davon. Ich habe das Glück gehabt, in Hamburg ihm nahezukommen; ich würde, wenn es nicht trivial klänge, die Tage, die ich mit ihm verleben durfte, als die schönsten, die ich erlebt, bezeichnen.[20]

D. *The Scherer Student*

Needless to say, Brahm succeeded in convincing his friend that intellectual salvation lay with Wilhelm Scherer in Berlin. Later, the Brahm-Schlenther combination was to leave its imprint on German letters and journalism as the most famous issue—the "illegitimate issue" Bab calls them[21]—of the Scherer School, assiduously propagating the inspiration of a great teacher and scholar. It was the inception of what the humorist, Julius Stettenheim, was to call "eine verbrahmte und verschlentherte Zeit."[22]

Wilhelm Scherer (1841–86), himself a pupil of Jakob Grimm and Karl Müllenhoff, was at this time approaching the apogee of his career. Germanist and historian of literature at the Universities of Vienna, Strassburg, and finally Berlin, he exerted a profound influence on innumerable colleagues, pupils, and men of letters by

[19] *Op. cit.*, p. 50.   [20] *Ibid.*, p. 53.
[21] In *Das Deutsche Drama*, ed. by Robert F. Arnold, München, 1925; section 6, *Die Lebenden*, by Julius Bab, p. 666.
[22] Quoted by Max Osborn, *Berliner Zeitung*, Nov. 29, 1912.

reason of his specialized scientific method, his robust and masterful literary style, and the powerful appeal of his personality. Completely immersed in the latter 19th century atmosphere of scientific positivism, an energetic protagonist of the Comte-Taine-Buckle tradition, Scherer attempted to apply the inductive principles of the natural sciences to research in linguistics and literature. The resultant method was somewhat in the nature of an anatomy of the literary product in terms of its causative and developmental elements. Literary research became an elaborate process of probing for all conceivable biographical correlatives to the literary work. The question of inter-influences and counter-influences was followed out in all its labyrinthine aspects. A veritable detective system was instituted in order to ferret out related motifs, literature types, characters, plots, sentence and verse structures, rhyme and vocabulary idiosyncrasies, and the like,—and all of these not only within the one work under scrutiny but as compared with all the other works of the same author, the same school, and world literature in general. Having laid bare the conditioning influence under which a literary work originates, the Scherer method then traced its development with the same minute and exhaustive care. Here is where the whole laborious apparatus of variant texts had to be set up and then brought into play. Texts were compared, manuscripts checked against manuscripts, then against editions, and finally editions against editions. Notebooks, diaries, recorded and reputed utterances, evidence of every shape and description was collected. Since the idea, as in science, was to suspend judgment until all the facts had been collected, it can readily be seen that the collection of facts became such an infinite process, that it easily seemed an end in itself; and final judgments were indefinitely postponed.

The advantages of the Scherer method are its objectivity and factual preciseness. It has often served as a disciplinary check upon students and so-called "intuitive" methods. Its severest critics have never tried to supplant it entirely but have insisted upon its preliminary character, as Gundolf, for example, who used the results of the Scherer method upon which to base interpretation. Nevertheless, the Scherer method was so atomic that no concept of a whole could predominate; the wood could not be seen for the trees.[23]

All of this mechanical grubbing might be justified in the study and reconstruction of ancient and fragmentary literary remains; and there is no doubt but that a great deal of the procedure originated in the important work of Lachmann and his successors, appropriated by Scherer for his own uses. But the severe limitations of such dissection are immediately apparent—just as in biology it cannot be successfully applied to the living uni-cellular organism without death resulting. In all due fairness to Scherer, it should be said that the method was not the man; and that his shortcomings achieved a disproportionate prominence because they were the easiest part of him for his pupils to inherit. The remarkable power of synthesis and essential genius of the man—he died at the age of forty-five—can be seen above all in his *Geschichte der deutschen Literatur* (1883) and in his fragmentary *Poetik* (posthumously published, 1888). We shall see presently how this basic fault of the Scherer School also marred most of Otto Brahm's earlier criticism.

Otto Brahm soon became a close friend of Scherer. The teacher's unmetaphysical nature found a kindred response in the pupil. In the seminar, in the *Germanistenkneipe*, and at the home of his teacher,[24] Otto Brahm received friendship, advice, and intellectual stimulation such as were to prove the turning-point in his career. It was Scherer who suggested the *Deutsche Ritterdrama* as the theme for Brahm's dissertation. On Scherer's advice Brahm went to the University of Strassburg in 1878, warmly recommended to Erich Schmidt who had succeeded Scherer at that place.[25] The

---

[23] An evaluation of the Scherer method in its historical and ideological perspective is contained in Benda's *Der gegenwärtige Stand der deutschen Literaturwissenschaft,* Wien-Leipzig, 1928.

[24] A reminiscence of Brahm as a family friend of the Scherers echoes from Mary Scherer's (Wilhelm Scherer's widow) letter of condolence to Ludwig Brahm: "Sie wissen wie nahe er meinem Manne stand, wie sehr er sich stets als sein Schüler fühlte und nie aufhörte, ihm die rührendste Treue zu bewähren." In Willi Simon, *op. cit.,* p. 146.

[25] Erich Schmidt's essay on Brahm at the latter's death reveals how Brahm also endeared himself to the most famous Scherer student: "Als ich ihn 1879 in Strassburg kennen lernte, war ich ein sehr grüner Dozent, er ein sehr reifer Student, der seine unjugendliche Überlegenheit gern ironisch offenbarte, aber sich so gescheit, so selbständig

spring of 1879 found Brahm in Jena under Eduard Sievers; and on the 13th of June of that year, he passed his doctoral examination *cum laude* on the strength of his methodical and exemplary dissertation on the *Ritterdrama*.[26]

For Otto Brahm the degree was nothing more than a formality, a means to an end. An academic career, even if it had been possible, did not attract him. From the beginning his entire university education had been deliberately designed to prepare him for critical journalism. Here once again Scherer's advice and influence proved decisive. Scherer recommended Brahm to the *National-zeitung* and to the *Augsburger Allgemeine*, and Brahm's first critical articles appeared in the latter under the pseudonym of Otto Anders. The idea of a pseudonym had also come from Scherer. Because of the prevalent antisemitism Scherer had advised his pupil to abbreviate his family name, Abrahamsohn, and thus originated the name of Brahm.[27]

Scherer's was undoubtedly the most thoroughgoing single intellectual influence in Otto Brahm's life.[28] A characteristically terse

---

anregend, so wahrhaft und tüchtig, auch bei aller scheinbaren Kühle so warm und anhänglich erwies, dass ich ihn bald lieb gewann und seitdem in ungetrübter Freundschaft mit ihm gelebt habe." Erich Schmidt, *Dt. Rdsch.*, Jan. 1913.

[26] *Das Deutsche Ritterdrama des 18ten Jahrhunderts*, Strassburg, 1880. It is an exhaustive study of the imitators of Goethe's *Götz*, particularly Görring, Babo, Klinger, Leisewitz, Hahn, and Maier. Brahm distinguishes five stages of development in the *Ritterdrama* on the basis of styles, motifs, themes, characters, etc. *Götz* is the prototype; then came the *Sturm und Drang Ritterdramen* of Babo, Klinger and Leisewitz; Görring with his *Agnes Bernauerinn* (1780) rises above the mediocrity of the others; the Bavarian patriots, Hahn and Maier start a series of plays on Bavarian history; and finally the *Ritterdrama* as a hackneyed type receives its quietus through the individual genius of Kleist, Hebbel and Ludwig. Shakespeare's influence is uncovered throughout, and Schiller's relationship to the *Ritterdrama* is also analyzed. The minute analysis and statistical charts make Brahm's dissertation unreadable except for the research specialist. Nevertheless, it still remains the definitive treatment of an obscure period in German literature.

[27] Antisemitism became a political shibboleth at the time of the financial crises and industrial depressions following upon the *Gründerjahre* (1873ff.). Wilhelm Scherer, filled with the classical ideals of humanity, repudiated race persecution even though it brought a rift into his friendship with Müllenhoff and Treitschke. Cf. Brahm, *Schriften*, II, p. 300. Brahm later had his name legally changed. Cf. Schlenther, *op. cit.*, p. 66.

[28] The complete sway which Scherer's method had over Brahm in his early period is accurately described by Schlenther in discussing Brahm's essay on Keller: "Auch Scherer pflegte so etwas ganz anders zu machen als der Scherer-schüler, der noch im seminaristischen Banne seiner Doktorarbeit stand und Scherer überschererte." *Op. cit.*, p. 73.

and unembellished quotation by Brahm serves admirably to summarize all that Wilhelm Scherer meant to him: ". . . für meine geistige und menschliche Bildung danke ich ihm mehr, als ich jemals aussprechen könnte."[29] Acknowledgment of this gratitude emanates from every page of Brahm's essays on the death of his teacher. Teeming with fine insights and evaluations, these essays are masterpieces of intimate characterization. An approximate formulation of Brahm's debt to Scherer would include, in addition to habits of intellectual discipline, a deeply-implanted regard for the *Humanitäts-* and *Bildungsideale* of the great German classicists and also somewhat of their subservience of all utilitarian and ethical criteria to an idealistic aestheticism.

E. *Friendship with Fontane*

In 1881 Brahm was engaged by the *Vossische Zeitung* as a dramatic critic. His senior colleague was Theodore Fontane, (1819–98) who was belatedly rounding out a lengthy career by writing novels and incidentally reporting the performances in the *Königliches Schauspielhaus.*[30] Brahm's duties consisted in covering the performances of the private theatres in Berlin. Here once again we have an instance of permanent friendship between men of disparate origin and view.

Between the sixty-two-year-old rejuvenated belletrist and the twenty-five-year-old precocious cub-reporter there developed a reciprocal relationship that had its roots in their opposite yet complementary temperaments. Mild and congenial, Fontane looked forward to Brahm's visits and the proddings of his keen, polemical mind. "Auf Harmonie der Gesinnungen und Auffassungen kam es ihnen weniger an, als Klingen zu kreuzen," wrote Schlenther, who was often present at their stirring intellectual duels.[31] Georg Hirschfeld, also a friend and observer of the two, notes this about their relationship:

[29] *Schriften,* II, 296.

[30] Fontane's most representative reviews were collected and edited by Paul Schlenther: *Causerien über Theater von Theodor Fontane,* Berlin, 1905. A critical treatment of this phase of Fontane's writing is afforded by a Columbia University dissertation: *Theodor Fontane as a Critic of the Drama,* Bertha E. Trebein, N. Y., 1916. Cf. p. 43–54 for the relations between Fontane and Brahm.

[31] *Op. cit.,* p. 68f.

Brahms Verhältnis zu dem alten Dichter hatte eine tiefe Anmut. In ihm war unbedingte, wenn auch schalkhafte, verhüllte Ehrfurcht, während Fontane über den 'kleinen Brahm' lächelte, aber ihn zugleich als Felsen der Zuverlässigkeit empfand. . . . Mit innigem Vergnügen kam er zu den Gesellschaften Otto Brahms am Luisenplatz. Das war etwas für ihn—hier fand er eine saubere, launige, funkelnde Geisteswelt.[32]

Brahm, with his innate aversion for informal writing, preferred to express himself in person, whereas Fontane was a brilliant and voluminous epistolarian. In Fontane's correspondence we have a reflection of Brahm's character and philosophy of life that can be illuminated in no better way than by quotation with emendatory comment.

Fontane's first letter to Otto Brahm was in acknowledgment of receipt of the latter's extended essay on Paul Heyse (1830–1914). To Brahm's generation Heyse represented the resuscitation of Goethean classicism. His impeccable form and style were lent a superficial aura of modernity by his invective against conventional ethics (*Kinder der Welt*). But Heyse's flight from Berlin to Munich symbolically accounts for his exaggerated popularity. His was the embodied consciousness of the German Middle Classes then embroiled in the throes of an industrialization that violated the lulling dream of a feudal past. Heyse's aestheticism, his squeezing of the social question into a narrow corner of the erotic realm, his pessimistic individualism (many of his heroines commit suicide on matters of principle),—and above all, his legendary and historic themes,—all corresponded to the frustrated "escapist" criticism directed against an increasingly materialistic reality.

Brahm was at that time—and had been all during his youth—an ardent admirer of Heyse. In 1880 he had visited his idol and the above-mentioned essay resulted.[33] Brahm's admiration and reverence for the "master" are candidly outspoken, yet his manner of treatment is so supremely objective that all of the above strictures —written from the superior perspective of the present—are implicitly contained in it. The diminutive disciple of Wilhelm

---

[32] *Op. cit.*, p. 115.
[33] *Ein Besuch bei Paul Heyse, Dt. Montagsbl.* 15. März, 1880. The essay on Heyse appeared in *Westermanns Monatshefte*, Nov. 1882. Cf. Schr. II, p. 86–135.

Scherer had written better than he knew. It was a case of an objective method revealing all the pertinent factors of a situation.

Now, exactly what had Brahm done in his Heyse essay? For one thing, he had schematized the whole gamut of Heyse's literary achievement. He had divided his life and work into periods and had gone into the statistics of the literature-types, themes, motifs, and characters which defined these periods. With impressive quotations of verse and chapter, he disingeniously disclosed the paucity of ideas and the uniform frequency of their repetition. The whole concept of Heyse was boiled down to three ideas:

Drei Momente sind es, die als charakteristisch in Heyses Dichten erscheinen. Der Glaube an die allgemeine Menschensehnsucht nach dem Glück, das sich in der Welt verwirklicht, ist das erste; das zweite die Gleichsetzung von Liebe und Kultus des Schönen, der einen romantischen Gegensatz zu der Wirklichkeit in sich schliesst; das dritte der Kultus der Persönlichkeit, der Selbstherrlichkeit und Ganzheit des Individuums, welcher zu Darstellung gestörter Harmonien, verlorener Ganzheit anreizt.[34]

Nothing could have been better designed than this breaking down into least common denominators as a means of showing up the pretentious and inessential. No wonder Heyse's and Brahm's friendship went into a sudden decline at about that time. How terrifying to see one's spiritual barrenness starkly outlined in an inexorably definite intellectual formula! Not that Brahm was fully aware of what he had done. He had simply gone about erecting a monument of glory with laborious devotion and with the best means at his disposal. If the result resembled a tombstone, we can only refer to the unconscious, divinatory sharpness of his observation.

Fontane recognized Brahm's critical power but was exasperated at his lukewarm, Olympian objectivity. This noncommittal weighing of pro's and con's left one with a feeling of anticlimax. What Fontane wanted was praise or damnation, a definite personal and moral stand in the matter. His letter deserves quotation, bearing as it does on a trait in Brahm that may be viewed either as a virtue or as a limitation, depending on one's orientation:

[34] Schr. II, p. 93.

Sie sind wie zum Kritiker geboren: scharf, klar, fein und was bei dieser glücklichen Dreiheit kaum ausbleiben kann, ein brillanter Stilist. Alles was Sie schreiben, les' ich mit Vergnügen, wie man einen klugen Menschen gern sprechen hört . . .

Sie haben unseren Freund sorgfältig untersucht und der im Nebenzimmer ängstlich wartenden Familie das mitgeteilt, was diese— pardon—schon wusste. Ja, er fiebert, die Zunge ist belegt, der eine Leberlappen ist etwas angeschwollen, das Herz hat keinen regelmässigen Schlag; aber die Schlüsse daraus haben Sie nicht gezogen und haben der Familie nicht mitgeteilt, ob er leben oder sterben muss . . .

Sie nehmen persönlich keine Stellung zu der Erzählung, Sie finden sie weder wundervoll noch wundersam, weder zu glorifizieren noch zu stigmatisieren. Sie sagen nur einfach: seht her, so ist sie. Das ist zu wenig. Wer sich an diesen Dichter ‚ranmacht', kann es nur tun in Liebe oder Hass. In Ihrem Aufsatz ist nicht Liebe, nicht Hass. . . .[35]

F. *Gottfried Keller*

In his essay on Gottfried Keller (1819–1890) Otto Brahm attempted his first exhaustive study of a famous contemporary.[36] Based on personal conversations with the old Swiss poet and raconteur and also on a minutely intimate acquaintance with his works, this 20,000 word appreciation is a masterpiece of rational analysis. It is eloquent of the finest of what can be achieved by the Scherer method when applied by an ingenious pupil, but it also displays the glaring inadequacy typical of the whole school. Some premonition of the futility of his procedure must have invaded Brahm's consciousness toward the end, but in the very wording of this premonition we have a clear indication that he was unaware of his cardinal fallacy; for he merely believed that his failure to do justice to Keller was quantitative rather than qualitative. In other words, he thought this exhaustive study was not exhaustive enough! That the essence of Keller's many-facetted, intuitive genius could never be epitomized in an abstract, conceptual system never dawned upon Brahm. Towards the conclusion of the essay he wrote:

Allein alles, was sich durch abstrakte Begriffe zur Bezeichnung dieser durch und durch konkreten Art sagen liesse, reichte nicht aus,

---

[35] *Theodor Fontane-Briefe*, hrsg. Pniower und Schlenther, 2 Bde., Berl. 1910. Letter dated 29. Okt. 1882.
[36] Schr. II, p. 135–235. *Dt. Rdsch.*, Juni, 1882.

die Sache, auf die es ankommt, auch wirklich deckend zu bezeichnen. Man müsste, um ihrem Geheimnis auf die Spur zu kommen, in einer methodischen Untersuchung den ganzen Bau nachkonstruieren. Man müsste wiederum von ihren malerischen Qualitäten, von den Bildern und Vergleichen sprechen, die dem Dichter in unerhörter Neuheit, aus der wirklichen und der vorgestellten Welt, von der platten Erde und vom höchsten Himmel zuströmen, und sie in ein System zu bringen suchen.[37]

There is no point in going into all the details of this essay, as though Brahm's sins could be condoned by doing to him what he had done to Keller. Our purpose is served by indicating in gross outline the scope of the essay and its method of treatment.

True to his notion that criticism consisted of an interpretative reconstruction of the creative process with the aim of bringing it into a system, and also imbued with the ideal of portraying and understanding rather than judging,[38] Brahm defined three periods in Keller's life: a subjective period into which fall the early poems, the first version of *Der Grüne Heinrich*, and the earlier *Novellen;* a pedagogical and didactic period in which subjectivism is largely overcome and to which belong *Romeo und Julia auf dem Dorfe*, the *Seldwyla Novellen*, and the *Sieben Legenden;* and finally a period of realism interspersed with romantic irony, in which belong the *Züricher Novellen*, the second version of *Der Grüne Heinrich*, and the *Sinngedicht*.[39] Brahm not only showed how each of Keller's works fits ideologically into these periods but also showed how the characteristics of one period filter through into the other periods. He constantly points out analogies, influences, biographical parallels, sources and prototypes, character-groupings, vocabulary idiosyncracies (*e.g.* the word *seltsam*), and the like. He pounces upon favorite motifs and character-types, showing for example how often Keller's women take the initiative, how often declara-

---

[37] *Ibid.*, p. 210.

[38] "An diesen ersten Poesien Kellers eine nachträgliche Kritik zu üben, wäre unangebracht hier, wo es mehr auf das Darstellen als auf das Urteilen abgesehen ist." *Ibid.*, p. 147. " . . . nicht beurteilend, sondern begreifend, in den Werdeprozess der Umschmelzung einzudringen," in reference to the two versions of *Der Grüne Heinrich*. *Ibid.*, p. 155.

[39] *Martin Salander* was not published until 1886 and hence was not included in this essay of 1882. Cf. Schr. II, p. 211–217 (*Nationalztg*. 9. Dez. 1886) for Brahm's review of *Martin Salander*.

tions of love occur with accidental spontaneity, the significant manner in which certain characters laugh, etc. After a deprecation of Hegelian aesthetics and the ingrained German predilection for symbolical interpretations, Brahm naïvely proceeds to discuss the symbolism in Keller's works according to an "objective" scheme of his own. A notion of the validity of his scheme is gained when we perceive that he discusses not only actual, literary symbolism that is immediately apparent and was obviously meant to be so by the author, but also dwells upon possible and presumable symbolism.

Undoubtedly the Scherer influence is most virulent in Brahm's analysis of *Der Grüne Heinrich*. Keller's *Bildungsroman* was first completed in 1855 and then revised in 1880. Brahm proceeded to compare the two versions and laid bare inconsistencies and loose ends in the second version that made it appear less organic than the first.[40] Not content with this criticism, in itself sufficiently devastating, Brahm calmly advised the author where and how the changes should have been made in order to improve the novel as a work of art and to alter it so that it would coincide with the author's altered philosophy of life. When we consider that in addition Brahm had unkind things to say about the vacillatory and almost pathologically unaccountable hero (a largely autobiographical figure!), that he ferreted out innumerable parallels to Jean Paul Richter's *Titan* and to Goethe's *Wilhelm Meister*, that he unmercifully uncovered the digressive padding (*Beiwerk*) of the novel and showed how it obscured the central problem; and when we consider further that all this was done with adamant objectivity, no judgment being advanced without a ponderous muster of proof in the way of actual quotations from characters, from Keller's introductions and letters, and the like, we are not surprised at the harassed old poet's reaction.[41]

[40] Note particularly the change to the first person (*Ich-Form*) and then the poorly motivated reversion to objective narrative in the third person. Note also the new ending on a note of resignation which replaces the older tragic ending while the foreshadowing of a tragic conclusion still remains and is also implicit in the very character of the hero. Cf. Schr. II, 149ff.

[41] Keller was so intent upon erasing the memory of the earlier *Grüner Heinrich* that he bought out the remaining copies from the publisher and burned them. Cf. Emil Ermatinger, *Gottfried Kellers Leben, Briefe, und Tagebücher*, 3 Bde., Berl. 1915–19, Bd. I, p. 586.

Der Verfasser des bewussten Artikels (he wrote to a friend) ist aus der Schule des Professors Wilhelm Scherer, welche uns arme Lebende historisch-realistisch behandelt und mit saurer Mühe überall nur Erlebtes ausspürt und mehr davon wissen will, als man selbst weiss.

As though to reassure his friend that his words are not entirely prompted by pique, Keller continues:

Dieser Otto Brahm ist übrigens ein feines und gescheites Jüdchen und voll reinen Wohlwollens, wie die berühmten Juden des vorigen Jahrhunderts. Er hat sich nach verübter Tat neulich bei mir vorgestellt.[42]

To be dissected alive, to be subjected to the presumptuous scrutiny of a bumptious upstart was all the more disturbing because of his naïvely reverent air. When an honest admirer exercises such sweeping criticism, the effect is all the more painful. In a letter to another friend there is a querulous reference to "Brahm, der das Buch mit philologischem Apparate untersucht und das Gras darin wachsen hört,. . . "[43] Keller intuitively hit upon the very point at issue in Brahm's shortcomings and those of the Scherer School in a letter to Julius Rodenberg in which he discusses the philological method as applied to living authors.

Es liegt hierin ein tiefgehendes Missverständnis der kritischen Aufgaben, welches sich gelegentlich wohl aufklären wird, wenn der Vorgang selbst eine kompetente kritische Untersuchung erfährt.[44]

In regard to the fallacy of biographical analogies as drawn between his life and *Der Grüne Heinrich*, Keller writes to Theodor Storm apropos of Brahm's essay:

Der Kritiker in der ,Rundschau' hat mir gerade nicht zugesagt. Derselbe (Otto Brahm) hat an anderer Stelle die philologische Methode noch verkehrter angewendet, indem er die alte und die neue Ausgabe meines Buches mit A und B bezeichnete wie alte zu vergleichende Codices, um meine Selbstverballhornung nachzuweisen, während er die Hauptfrage der Form: Biographie oder nicht? gar nicht berührte oder dieselbe ignorierte. Diese Frage umfasst nämlich auch die andern nicht stilgerechten epischen Formen: Briefform, Tagebuchform, und die Vermischungen derselben, in welchen nicht der objektive Dichter und Erzähler spricht, sondern dessen Figuren-

[42] To Marie von Frisch, 13. Aug. 1882.
[43] To Wilhelm Petersen, 21. Apr. 1881.
[44] 2. Dez. 1880.

kram, und zwar mittels Tinte und Feder. Hier ist der Punkt, wo die Kritik einzuspringen hat und der Schreiber den formalen Handel verliert. Diese Untersuchung ist aber nicht eine (dazu unwichtige) textkritliche, sondern eine reine ästhetische Sache und Arbeit und führt zu anderen Gesichtspunkten, etc.[45]

When the essay had finally appeared in its entirety in the *Deutsche Rundschau* Keller once more wrote to Rodenberg, the editor, expressing his thanks to Otto Brahm. Again it is the loose, haphazard biographical method and the futile probing for imaginary or non-existent sources that aroused his spirit of contradiction:

Zu Brahms in gutem Sinne gegebene Kritik muss ich mich indessen auch etwas kritisch verhalten, wie das so menschlicher Brauch ist. Das Prinzip, aus zusammengerafften oder vermuteten Personalien die Charakteristik eines poetischen Werkes aufzubauen und alles so viel möglich auf Erlebtes zurückzuführen, solange der Hervorbringer sein Leben nicht selbst geschlossen hat, ist, abgesehen von den Inkonvenienzen, die daran entstehen können, nicht richtig, schon weil der fern stehende auf blosses Hörensagen, auf Klatsch und flaches Kombinieren hin arbeiten muss und darüber das freie Urteil über das Werk, wie es vor ihm liegt, beeinträchtigt oder ganz verliert. So werden namentlich mittelst solcher Methode die verschiedenen Stoffmotive geradezu unrichtig behandelt und auf nicht existierende Quellen zurückgeführt. . . .

Once again, to show that the fundamental difference of opinion was not motivated by his personal feelings in the matter, Keller concluded:

Doch genug mit diesem undankbaren Genörgel! Mit Ihnen glaube ich, dass der feurig belebte, geistvolle und von gesunder Gesinnung beseelte junge Mann ein schöne Zukunft hat.[46]

G. *Miscellaneous Essays*

From 1881 to 1885 Brahm continued his work with the *Vossische Zeitung*. An adverse commentary on the state of the German theatre in the capital city emanates from the very subject matter he was obliged to review. The box-office successes of those years were Dumas, Meilhac and Halévy, Sardou, Labiche, Delacour, Scribe, Augier, Ohnet, Pailleron, Daudet, and their lesser German

[45] 11. Apr. 1881.   [46] 22. Juli, 1882.

translators and imitators, Lindau, Lubliner, and L'Arronge. Such occasions as the performance of the Meininger in Berlin[47] provided an only too infrequent relief from the monotonous drudgery of reporting the inanities of the theatre. Small wonder that he turned to literary projects of his own as balm for his self-respect. In 1882 he wrote a series of essays on such diverse figures as Dorothea Mendelssohn, Berthold Auerbach, and Friedrich Spielhagen, the latter two related in that they were proponents of a realism that had emerged much earlier in the narrative field than in the drama.[48]

In Auerbach he admired the *"scheinbar tendenzfreie"* element, the virtue of organically interweaving *Tendenz* with the narrative so that the latter exists as an independent work of art and the former does not appear to be artificially superimposed. Auerbach's *Diethelm von Buchenberg* represented for him the forerunner of Freytag's *Soll und Haben* and Otto Ludwig's *Zwischen Himmel und Erde*, the beginning of a realistic treatment of German business and economic life, showing among other things the conflict between urban and agrarian interests, and how bankruptcy in the modern business world can replace the nemesis of classical tragedy. There is also a note of personal kinship in his admiration of the way in which Auerbach, the Spinozist, deserted the chafing confines of the synagogue for a *konfessionslose* pantheism that encompassed all religions.

What elicited his admiration in Dorothea Mendelssohn were her feminine, submissive qualities, her modesty and womanliness, her unquestioning loyalty to Friedrich Schlegel. He dwelt especially on her unsophisticated style, her tact and sensitivity as contrasted with Caroline Schlegel who, he wrote, had more genius but was less *sympathisch*. Not the least of the traits which commended Dorothea to Brahm was her worship of Goethe.

The Spielhagen essay was largely a criticism and appreciation of the novelist's theoretical work, *Beiträge zur Theorie und Technik des Romans*, in which Brahm tested Spielhagen's theories against his own novels, to the detriment of the former.

[47] Schr. I, 10ff.
[48] Schr. II, pp. 1, 39, 77.

H. *Biography of Kleist*

In 1883, amidst the plethora of daily reviews, extensive essays
on Conrad Ferdinand Meyer, Turgeniew, Anzengruber, and others
stand out.[49] And in 1884 comes the first widespread recognition
from the republic of letters that one, Otto Brahm, had attained
significance as a critic. In this year his biography of Heinrich von
Kleist was awarded first prize by the *Verein für Deutsche Literatur*.[50]
Dedicated to Erich Schmidt, the comparatively short and emi-
nently readable work enjoyed an enthusiastic reception and had
gone through five editions when Brahm revised it in 1911. Fontane,
with the humorous malice of a free-lance author, wrote to Brahm:

> Viertausend Mark sind kein Pappenstiel, und wenn schon das
> Geld was bedeutet, so die Ehre noch mehr. . . . Als Kollege habe
> ich—und mit mir gewiss viele—noch die Spezialfreude gehabt, dass
> ein Schriftsteller den ersten und ein Professor erst den zweiten Preis
> errungen hat. Es ist recht gut, dass wir Professoren und Geheimräte
> haben, aber ihre Alleinherrschaft dann und wann gebrochen zu sehen,
> ist doch eine Wonne, weil ein gelegentlicher Triumph von Gerechtig-
> keit und *bon sens*.[51]

In his preface to the first edition of the Kleist biography[52]
Brahm renders acknowledgment to Scherer's inspiration and influence. His dedicatory gesture to Erich Schmidt was an exhortation to realize the plan of a definitive critical edition of Kleist's
works. Brahm is thus still entirely under the sway of a school and
a method. What he was striving for was an historical understanding of Kleist and his writings. In line with this cardinal aim he
proposed to study and discuss Kleist's style and poetic technique;
and in the analysis of characters he further proposed to trace all
single aspects back to decisive characteristics; and finally to align
these characteristics with general tendencies of the time. We observe once more the rationalistic drive to reduce the multiformity
of his subject matter into a systematic pattern. In order to appeal
to as large a public as possible he omitted the pedantic *impedi-*

---

[49] Schr. II, pp. 236, 311; I, 36.
[50] Scherer was one of the three professors of the University of Berlin who officiated
as judges.
[51] *Op. cit.* The letter is dated 2. Jan. 1884.
[52] *Heinrich von Kleist*, Berl. 1884.

menta of foot-notes and cross-references, contenting himself with
a short bibliography of the most important literature on Kleist
up to 1884, the date of publication.

Brahm's method of procedure is clearly indicated at the beginning of his discussion of Kleist's first drama, *Die Familie Schroffenstein*. He writes:

. . . . wir dringen in der Erkenntniss des Dichters entscheidend vor,
wenn wir ihr (Kleist's drama) Entstehen in seiner Seele, ihr Werden
und Wachsen Schritt für Schritt begleiten.[53]

This aim places a well-nigh insuperable onus of exhaustiveness and
detail upon the biographer. Let us try to realize what must be done
in order to follow step by step the origin, development and growth
of the work in the mind of the author. The work must be conned
for all conceivable sources and influences. The letters and other
writings of the poet, and those of his friends and contemporaries
must be gleaned for corroboratory information. Complicated
hypotheses involving comparative psychology must be erected.
Variant texts must be compared and the resulting conclusions
drawn. Works must be definitely dated if their general mood is to
be identified with the mood of a specific time.

Brahm plunges into the Gargantuan task with long-winded
deliberation. Each work, each incident receives its painstaking
due. The chapters are integrated according to the following
method: First the biographical prolegomena leading to the real
and presumable origins of the theme are traced. Then follows a
selective paraphrase of the story or contents. Plays are discussed
technically as to characterization and action, both measured by
the criteria of verisimilitude, inner consistency, logical motivation,
and organic unity. Inconsistencies, defective or weak motivations,
uneconomic diffusion of effect are explained as much as possible
on a psychological basis, *i.e.* the conflict of sources, the confusion
of aims, the personal deficiencies and pathological states of the
author as induced by external and internal factors. Corroboratory
material is introduced in minute detail, and pointed commentary
follows the intricate course of argument. An evaluation of technique and style is concluded, for the most part, atomically, *i.e.*

[53] *Ibid.*, p. 73.

motion and color words, economy of dialogue, inter-connection of scenes, effect-creating devices, etc. Finally comes a discussion as to how the work was received by contemporaries of note and on the stage, followed out historically to the then present time. The whole generally ends on a note of either criticism or appreciation, with an attempt being made to align the work with the literary currents of the times and to foreshadow the future course of the author.

The almost literal repetition of this procedure with every successive play makes for monotonous reading, and in the first edition of this book Brahm lays himself open to the charge of conscientious dullness. But defects graver still detract from the unquestionably deserving aspects of the book. Julius Bab flays the inherent myopia of a rationalistic approach to the *demonic* quality in Kleist, when he writes:

... aber von dem Dämon, der die Seele dieses rasend Leidenschaftlichen mit mystischem Dunkel umhüllte, hat Brahm wenig gespürt. Nichts charackteristischer, als dass er bei Betrachtung des *Amphitryon*, dessen mystischer Aufschwung ihm genau so unsympatisch war wie seinem Lehrer Scherer, mit philologischer Treue zu untersuchen anfängt, auf was für Einflüssen die pantheistische Wendung in der Gestaltung des Zeus hier beruhe. Als ob nicht das erschütternde Gefühl von der ständigen Gegenwart eines allvereinenden Geistes das Grunderlebnis wäre, von dem überhaupt jede künstlerische Existenz zehrt![54]

Anyone who reads a few pages at random in Brahm's Kleist biography is immediately struck by the aptness of Julius Bab's criticism. Everywhere the attempt to crowd an infinite amount of material into finite categories results in the dissipation of an organic view. It is as though every possible aspect of the subject is discussed but never the subject itself. In a sense Brahm's procedure might be called an escape from criticism. His forte is exegesis rather than an imaginative re-creation of the work under critical scrutiny.

Nevertheless the work was not without its merits. As the first considerable biography since Adolf Wilbrandt's *Heinrich von Kleist* had appeared in 1863, Brahm's work incorporated the new

[54] In Robert Arnold, *Das Deutsche Drama*, München, 1925, p. 666.

material that had accrued in the interim: new light on Kleist's
relationship to Wilhelmine von Zenge, his dealings with Cotta, the
strife surrounding the *Abendblätter*, Kleist's last days, newly discovered essays, variant versions of the *Familie Schroffenstein, Der
Zerbrochne Krug*, information culled from the publication of
Fouqué's, Brentano's, and Körner's letters with their memoranda
on Kleist, etc. The biography was also significant in that it
centered attention once more upon a tragic and lonesome figure
whose doom was predestined by the indifference and shortsighted-
ness of a material environment of national expansionism. Kleist
dreamed of a new category in the drama. He was intent upon a wild
self-assertion of the individual in the face of an oppressive social
and spiritual milieu. This revolutionary element in Kleist it may
have been that attracted Brahm to the writing of his biography.
That Brahm, then under the Goethe-Scherer influence, rejected
much of Heinrich von Kleist was nothing to be marvelled at. That
he could accept Kleist as a whole was the strange and significant
fact. Kleist's psychological realism was also a decisive point of
attraction to Brahm.[55]

1. *Comparison of the Two Editions*

At the hundredth anniversary of Kleist's death Brahm subjected his biography to a thoroughgoing revision.[56] A quarter of a
century had elapsed since the book's initial appearance. Brahm
was then—unknown to himself—approaching the end of a stormy
career. He could look back upon his literary origins with the
maturer air of one who had long ago superseded them. New ideals
and the naturalist revolution had intervened to create an entirely
different Otto Brahm. His personal association with living poets
and artists had given him a real insight into the mysteries of
creative genius. And his own struggles against philistine indifference and hostility, his strife-ridden attempt to educate the

---

[55] The biography was reviewed by Fontane in the *Vossische Zeitung*, by Frenzel in
the *Nationalzeitung*, and by Schlenther in the *Frankfurter Zeitung* (Jan. 1884). Concerning Brahm's style Frenzel wrote: "So innig hat sich Brahm in die Werke seines Helden
eingelebt, dass selbst seine Darstellung zuweilen Kleistisch berührt. . . . ". Schlenther
also remarked on the peculiarity: ". . . . über Kleist im Kleistschen Stile zu sprechen. . . . ".

[56] The revised fifth edition appeared in 1911, the centennial of Kleist's death.

Berlin public had undoubtedly aroused a heartfelt sympathy for
the lone artist striving to have his creations prevail against the
inertia of the mob. Schlenther tells us:

Es liegt eine feine symbolische Absicht darin, dass er die Vorrede
zur neuen Ausgabe gerade in Gerhart Hauptmanns Agnetendorfer
Villa schrieb.[56a]

And indeed there is in Brahm's new preface a vivid awareness of
having outgrown the narrow, pedantic spirit of his earlier years.

Als ich das Buch zum ersten Mal schrieb (he writes) kam ich eben
aus der Scherer-Schule her, an die ich mit warmem Dank mich stets
erinnere; aber neue Ideale, als der Schüler Geselle ward, entstanden
ihm, und die Literaturrevolution von 1889 machte dumpf Emp-
fundenes frei, das kein Germanist hätte lehren können. Die festen
Massstäbe, mit denen eine ältere Zeit an das Kunstwerk herantrat,
zerbrachen, das Urrecht geschlossener Persönlichkeiten ward wieder
entdeckt; und gerade das Schicksal Kleists enthüllte sich der neuen
Erkenntnis, die den unendlichen Streit aufdeckte zwischen dem Genie
und dem Bann seines Milieus.

This confession offers a clue to the changes in the revised edition
which we may follow out in some detail, calling the 1884 edition
"A" and the 1911 edition "B."[57] The changes are so manifold that
one might almost say that Brahm used *A* merely as an outline
sketch for the writing of a new book, if the spirit of the old had not
been so completely retained. There are stylistic changes on almost
every page; new material is included; there are more copious
quotations from Kleist's works and letters. The purely speculative
sections of *A*, written apparently to fill in the gaps of information,
were deleted in *B*. Transitions from paragraph to paragraph and
from chapter to chapter were made more unobtrusive and graceful.
The revised edition has a more assured and even tempo; it flows,
whereas *A* alternately flounders in a turbid sea of facts or spurts

[56a] *Op. cit.*, p. 10.
[57] The comparison shows Brahm's development during the period from 1884 to 1911
and is thus necessitated by the very aim of this biographical chapter. It is interesting
to note that the present study is the first realization of Schlenther's forecast: "Aber
eben dadurch, dass er sich selbst vom rein philologischen Betrieb der Literaturwissenschaft bewusst abkehrte, gab er künftigen jungen Germanisten einen dankbaren Unter-
suchungsstoff. Wie er selbst einst zu Kellers Schrecken die alte und die neue Ausgabe
des 'Grünen Heinrich' verglichen hatte, so würde er jetzt selbst eine Parallele zwischen
seinen beiden Kleistbüchern vom Seminare dulden müssen." *Op. cit.*, p. 75.

forward where these are absent. Whole sections of *A* become casual
references in *B* or are deleted altogether; and the converse is also
true. Mere suggestive phrases or suppositions are expanded into
miniature disquisitions. In general it can be said that in *B* there is
a vastly more integrated development because the beginning has
been written with a knowledge of the end. *B* is synoptic and organic whereas *A* advances from stage to stage, each stage largely
independent of the other. In *A* the sequence is mechanically
chronological; in *B* there is a sequence based on mood and poetical
development. *B* looks both forward and backward; *A* looks only
backward. B is a much more humanized and psychologized docu-
ment, whereas *A* is more factual and formalistic. In *B* elaborations
of the obvious and platitudinous, generalizations, tautologies, and
rhetorical padding are mercilessly deleted. *B* also lays more stress,
in the early chapters, upon the influences of music and nature in
Kleist's awakening to his poetic mission.

The shortest and simplest way to illustrate these changes is to
juxtapose typical words and phrases from corresponding positions
in the two versions and to note the general tendency of the
changes.

I. *Examples of a more profound insight into Kleist's creative genius,
this insight leading to sympathy and tolerance:*

A-p. 49, die stete Abhängigkeit, in der er Wilhelmine hält, scheint ihn
   nicht zu drücken, becomes, die stete Abhängigkeit, in der er
   Wilhelmine hält, empfindet der ganz von seinem innern Dämon
   Hingenommene nicht, B-p. 53.
A-p.63, krankhaft, becomes, masslos, B-p.68
A82, verderblich—gefährlich, B90
A104, krankhafte Vorstellung—tiefe Verstimmung, B114
A109, der wahnwitzige Vorsatz—der verzweifelte Vorsatz, B120
A130, in einer zunehmenden Gemütskrankheit—getrieben von jener
   selben Furie des Ehrgeizes, B145
A193, Schwächen—Eigenheiten, B217
A208, fangen wir an zu zweifeln—fangen wir an zweifelnd zu erstau-
   nen, B234
A285, unkünstlerisch—gewaltsam, B321

II. *Examples of stylistic changes:*

1. *literal to figurative*

A91, concipirt—empfangen, B101

A97, schwankend—wankend, B106
A98, in Besitz genommen hat—in Fesseln geschlagen hat, B106
A109, in dieser schlimmen Stunde—in dieser düsteren Stunde, B119
A131, die Stimmung dieser traurigen Zeit—die Stimmung dieser schwarzen Zeit, B145
A143, Dichten—Schaffen, B163
A150, eine Vorstudie zum Kätchen von Heilbronn—eine Schwester des Kätchen von Heilbronn, B171

2. *general to particular*

A89, Verbrechen—Mord, B98
A90, Kunst—Poesie, B100
A92, Arbeit—Werk, B101
A93, das Stück—die Schroffensteiner, B103
A101, Auch dem alten Wieland nicht, zu dem er bald in ein freundliches Verhältnis gekommen war—Auch dem alten Wieland nicht, der ihn, wie einen Sohn aufgenommen hatte, B111

3. *superlative to positive*

A146, das Lustspiel *Amphitryon* und die Tragödie *Penthesilea* entziehen sich der Darstellung gänzlich—entfernen sich kühn den Bedingungen der Szene, B165
A162, die gewaltigste deutsche Novelle—seine gewaltigste Novelle, B183
A177, das unerreichte Muster des deutschen Charakterlustspiels—ein deutsches Charakterlustspiel, B200
A206, die unverletzlichen dramatischen Gesetze—die Forderungen des Theaters, B232

4. *pedantic to informal*[57a]

A108, das postscriptum—die Nachschrift, B118
A139, wie er hier *pro domo* redet—wie hier seine eigene Erfahrung redet, B151

A great many deletions from *A* to *B* can be traced to the modern spirit of relativism in matters ethical, and to the more refined insight into human motives and psycho-physical processes gained by modern psychology, particularly in the field of psychoanalysis. To the former can be attributed the deletion of an ethical judgment on the *Marquise von O . . .* from *A*165; to the latter the deletion from *A* of a fanciful interpretation of Kleist's mysterious journey to Würzburg and the insertion in *B* of the explanation now currently accepted. To the psychoanalytic approach is also due a

[57a] But note *Oxymoron*, A87–B97 and A139–B159.

profounder appreciation of *Penthesilea*.[58] Similarly, where in *A*139 the *Prinz von Homburg* had been given as the example of Kleist's most individual style, in *B*160 this example is changed to *Penthesilea*. In like vein, the famous letter in which Kleist ecstasizes on his feelings of friendship for Pfuel, and which did not appear in *A*, is quoted verbatim in *B*150–153. The factual terms in which this friendship had been referred to in *A* are pitched in a more mellifluous key. The poetic interpretation which Brahm interpolates is notable for the tact and delicacy of its phrasing.

The sections most thoroughly re-written rather than merely changed are those dealing with the journey mentioned above, and particularly, those concerning Kleist's latter years in Berlin. Steig's much-disputed *Kleists Berliner Kämpfe* (1901) with its mass of new material and perspectives on this period in Kleist's career was undoubtedly the inspiration and source for Brahm's almost complete revision of this part of the book, even though he pejoratively refers to Steig as "ein Düntzer der Kleistforschung."[59] In general, Brahm's new material and new points of view were inevitably included after the appearance of the compendious works of Steig, Servaes, Meyer-Benfey, and Herzog. Treitschke's essay on Kleist is also listed in Brahm's enlarged bibliography in *B*. And finally, the monumental critical edition by Erich Schmidt and his collaborators, Steig, and particularly Minde-Pouet—who was responsible for the fifth volume, Kleist's letters—undoubtedly played an important role in affording a wholeness of view over Kleist's entire life and the sum of his creative achievement.

For all the vast detail of change between *A* and *B*, it is doubtful whether the total spirit of *A* has been appreciably altered. As seen from the above analysis, the difference between *A* and *B* was created mainly by superficial changes such as those of style, increased objectivity, conformity with newly-discovered material; and only incidentally by changes due to a new philosophical and aesthetic outlook. This new outlook was present but Brahm would have had to write an entirely different book in order to make it manifest. And this was impossible owing to the exigencies of his

[58] Cf. biographical parallels to *Penthesilea* in *B*, p. 223–4.
[59] Cf. Vorwort to *B*.

career in the theatre and the demands of his publishers. In the few months at his disposal during the summer, while suffering from the premonitory twinges of the illness that was to snuff out his life, Brahm was obliged to content himself with changes that required the least time and research.[60]

Brahm's biography of Kleist offers a trustworthy and reliable introduction to Kleist's life and works seen in their interrelationship and in their further connection with the literary and sociopolitical currents of his time. All the sources and motifs, the biographical parallels, the variant texts, in brief, all the preliminary material upon which one might base an interpretative biography of Kleist are faithfully and even interestingly set down. The literary-historical emphasis of the book, as Erich Schmidt points out,[61] is invaluable. What Brahm has written on the similarities and differences between Kleist and the *Sturm und Drang*, the Rousseauan influence, the *Schicksalstragödie*, the poets of the Wars of Liberation, even if literally conceived, is valid and indispensable to the student of Kleist. But for the revolutionary significance of Kleist (compare the intensity of his patriotic ideals with those of the *Freiheitsdichter*), for the mystical, Dionysian strain that runs through his most significant works, for his frenzied idealism, Brahm (he rejected Wedekind)[62] may have had a vague awareness, but certainly no profound inner understanding.

I. *From the Vossische Zeitung to the Nation*

The period between 1881 and 1885 had been one of unremitting belletristic activity for Otto Brahm. His essays in the *Deutsche Rundschau* and his Kleist biography compensated in some measure

[60] From letters to Georg Hirschfeld dated 30. 1. 1911 and 22. 7. 1911, we learn that Brahm was in a sanatarium in Semmering near Vienna and thus, perforce, had leisure to work at the revision. But his illness was so painful (intestinal ulcers) that of the six months at his disposal he spent only from eight to ten weeks in actual work. Hirschfeld, *op. cit.*, p. 264.

[61] " . . . Otto Brahms durch Klarheit der literarhistorischen Analyse ausgezeichnetes Buch . . . "; Erich Schmidt, *H. v. Kleists Werke*, 6 Bde. Leipzig, 1904 ff. Bd. I, Einleitung, p. 45, footnote.

[62] Max Liebermann tells of the hilarity which greeted the most tragic passages of Wedekind's *Erdgeist* when read by the author to Otto Brahm and the board of directors of the *Freie Bühne*. *Das Wedekindbuch*, ed. by Joachim Friedenthal, München und Leipzig, 1914, p. 213.

for his daily reviews in the *Vossische Zeitung*. It shall be the purpose of subsequent chapters to deal in detail with these latter. Meanwhile, the year 1885 saw a severance of Brahm's connection with the*Vossische Zeitung*, under rather malodorous circumstances. The entire episode is one of triviality and petty recrimination. Those who are curious as to its details may consult Schlenther.[63] Suffice it to say that Brahm contracted the enmity of many theatrical small-fry by his trenchant criticism. Turning an incorruptible beam of logic on theatrical conditions had once proved too much even for a Lessing. In Otto Brahm's instance, it cost him his position. An adverse criticism of Lebrun, director of the *Wallnertheater*, unleashed a whole series of unpleasant consequences that hounded Brahm out of the offices of an ultra-conservative newspaper that glossed over the real fact of its obsequious, mollifying response to an advertiser's displeasure with an ironic show of indignation at an incident conveniently interpreted as a threatened blot on its own lily-white escutcheon. The loss was the newspaper's and not Brahm's. Thenceforth he was relieved from the stultifying pressure of daily journalism and became an editorial contributor to the *Nation*, a weekly. Here his essays took on a more unharried, more profound quality. And, perhaps most important of all in the light of subsequent events, it was here that he learned the business of editing a periodical.

He remained with the *Nation* until 1890 when the first numbers of the *Freie Bühne für modernes Leben* began to appear under his editorship. This was the consummate stage of his journalistic existence. Here he reached the most decisive turning-point in his career, the transition from critic to man of the theatre. The body of this essay will order and evaluate Brahm's dramatic criticism in the *Vossische Zeitung*, the *Nation*, and the *"Freie Bühne."* In this chapter, however, only the history of his more extensive and independently-published works is being considered.

J. *Ibsenerlebnis*

The next new perspective in Brahm's intellectual horizon was conceived under the sign of a strange, eccentric, but dominating

---

[63] *Op. cit.*, pp. 69ff.

personality: Julius Hoffory, a Dane who had become a naturalized
German citizen and who was Professor of Old Norse philology and
phonetics at the University of Berlin. Brahm's first meeting with
Hoffory dated back to his student days when he and so many other
aspiring Germanists had foregathered at the brilliant *Germanisten-*
kneipe presided over by Wilhelm Scherer. The fact that they dwelt
at the same *Pension* cemented their friendship. Hoffory was a peculiar and highly individual sort of person. He was a great admirer
and devotee of Ibsen and Zola, a champion of Bismarck and, con-
tradictorily enough, of Social Democracy; and his chief pleasure
was to go off into ranting denunciations of the traditionally sacro-
sanct. Schiller and Heyse were his pet aversions. In short, he was
a literary and social radical to young innocents such as Brahm and
Schlenther, a sort of Socratic gad-fly whose sharp sting fretted
convention-bound mentalities into irritable and ultimately vital
response. Capricious and self-centered as he was, a man of domineering nature and ill-considered extremes, Hoffory could not
exercise permanent sway over Brahm; but for a brief and fateful
period he exerted the most potent influence that anyone had ever
had upon the impressionable student of Germanics. Together with
Schlenther, Brahm assiduously studied Danish under Hoffory's
tutelage in order to be able to read Ibsen in the original.[64] To
Hoffory can be credited that profound *Ibsenerlebnis* that thenceforth became a salient part of Brahm's consciousness. Brahm
became a German crusader in Ibsen's cause. For years he in-
cessantly propagandized for the acceptance of a poetic force which,
he felt, was the necessary antidote to the queasy aestheticism into
which German literature had lapsed. In 1887 when Ibsen was
merely an opprobrious name to the form and beauty obsessed
beaux esprits of German letters—Heyse spoke with disgust of the
"*Spitalpoesie*" of *Ghosts*—Brahm published a modestly thin little
volume that rebelliously sang the praise of the great social poet-
dramatist from the North. The dedication to Professor Julius
Hoffory leaves no doubt as to the inspiration for the essay.[65]

---

[64] "Damals lernten wir zwei bei Hoffory dänisch, um das grosse Werk (*Ghosts*) in
der Ursprache lesen zu können." Schlenther, *op. cit.*, p. 80.

[65] *Henrik Ibsen: Ein Essay*, Berl. 1887.

In this paean of appreciation, among the first of its kind in Germany,[66] Brahm described his meeting with the lonely old playwright in Rome in the spring of 1885. Ibsen spoke of his humanistic belief in the free development of the personality, picturing society as the arch offender and breeder of evil, and not the hapless individual. Pondering on these utterances, Brahm was moved to inquire into the causes which had given rise to such a *Weltanschauung:*

... wie hat eine so ausgeprägte Persönlichkeit sich entwickeln können? Unter welchen Bedingungen ist sie gross geworden, welche Erlebnisse haben ihr Richtung gegeben?[67]

His positivistic conception of viewing the individual as developing out of the context of an environment and being molded by experience, still follows Scherer's wholesome precept of *Ererbtes, Erlebtes, und Erlerntes.*[68] So much of this essay is a clear anticipation of Brahm's subsequent development that it proves the deliberateness and self-awareness with which he pursued his way. For that reason, the import of the Ibsen essay will be integrated in detail, together with Brahm's other dramatic criticism, into the larger and more abstract context of the following chapters. In this biographical section, a gross outline will suffice.

Of the seventy pages constituting the brochure more than forty deal with Ibsen's contemporary social dramas. *Brand, Peer Gynt,* and the historical dramas in verse receive perfunctory notice. By far the bulk of discussion centers on those of Ibsen's plays which are naturalistic in technique, those that deal with questions of the day. Here Brahm was in his element, for it was precisely in his social significance that Ibsen appealed to Brahm's generation. Ibsen's great individualists, his relentless questioners, his men and women of indomitable social will and conscience—the Brands, the Stockmans, the Noras—these were figures of tremendous immediacy and pertinence in the Germany of the latter eighties. And Ibsen's themes: social hypocrisy, family strife, heredity, feminism, psychological conflict, were all framed in the bright

---

[66] For an account of Ibsen's reception in Germany cf. W. H. Eller, *Ibsen in Germany,* Boston, 1918.

[67] *Op. cit.,* p. 7.   [68] Quoted by Benda, *op. cit.,* p. 10.

attractive aura of contemporaneity. Nora represented to Brahm at that time the highest peak of Ibsen's artistic development. Our critic of the drama very acutely sensed here a profounder turn to the former love and marriage dramas with conflicts originating in the disparity of social station. Here the conflict was one of disparate outlook and sensibility, in other words, a subtler conflict on a socio-psychological level. Brahm's essay very significantly reaches its climax in the chapter on *Ghosts*. The points which Brahm makes with regard to naturalism, Ibsen's revolutionary optimism (sic!), the evolution of poetic forms, and above all, the confession of his aesthetic creed in an exalted epilogue which, incidentally, is one of the finest stylistic passages that Brahm ever penned, are all treated, as has already been intimated, in following chapters.

A word on Brahm's method. The search for literary influences and biographical parallels still wages unabated even though Brahm admits that Ibsen has denied such influences and in spite of the fact that the objective nature of Ibsen's naturalistic works makes the tracing of biographical parallels a maze of conjecture. Parallelisms in characters, problems, and motifs are followed from play to play. Following the corollary precept to *Ererbtes, Erlebtes und Erlerntes* (in the analysis of the poet), namely, *Logik, Ethik, und Ästhetik* (in the analysis of the work), Brahm concludes with an inquiry into the aesthetics of dramatic form and the creative process. For Ibsen creation was induced essentially under the impact of experience. Literary composition was for him, somewhat as for Goethe, an act of liberation, of intellectual and spiritual catharsis. However, Brahm shows the preponderance of the ethical element in Ibsen as compared to Goethe. Goethe's self-expression was purely as an artist. Ibsen wishes to cure; he is a *Seelenarzt*, an *Ethiker*, the Nordic Christian who sees through the dark spectacles of the reformer; whereas Goethe sees things directly, through his *Sonnenaugen*.[69]

Otto Brahm's essay on Ibsen was a pioneer, proselyting effort designed to produce a salutary effect on moribund German letters and on the languishing German stage. Accurately foreshadowing

[69] *Op. cit.*, p. 68–9.

a task which was to be carried out by none other than himself,
Brahm wrote:

Noch zwar hat die schöne Pflicht Niemand eingelöst: ein ganzes
Publikum in planmässigem Zusammenhang in den Gedankengang
des Dichters einzuführen, und durch eine Darstellung seiner modernen Schauspiele, vom ‚Bund der Jugend' an gerechnet, auch die
deutschen Theaterbesucher ibsenreif zu machen![70]

K. *Last Days with Fontane*

1. *Differences in Regard to Ibsen*

An interesting contrast to Brahm's unmitigated enthusiasm for
Ibsen is afforded by Fontane's antithetical position in regard to
the dramatist. Fontane's political liberalism and ethical con-
servatism are too well known to require further comment here.[71]
In a series of letters to various friends and also to Brahm himself,
Fontane repeatedly asserts the moral reservations with which he
accepts Ibsen. His appreciation of Ibsen as a dramatic technician
is unbounded. As always, with his artistic liberalism, he intuitively
recognizes genius even when its purport runs counter to his own
convictions. But he is unequivocally true to his subjective attitude
by his decisive *"Ablehnung unter Bewunderung."*[72] He writes concerning his admiration of Ibsen as compared with that of the
younger generation:

Wenn ich mir da meine jungen Freunde ansehe, die Brahm, die
Schlenther und andere, von denen ich ausserordentlich eingenommen
bin und zwar nicht bloss redensartlich, sondern wirklich,—eines haben
sie nicht: die Reife. Ich bin auch scharf Ibsenianer mit siebzig, die
andern mit fünfunddreissig und—unverheiratet. Daher das Eingehen
auf den Ibsenschen Eheblödsinn.[73]

Fontane recognizes Ibsen's technical virtuosity, his creation of
new types, and his envisagement of new problems. He realizes that

---

[70] *Ibid.,* p. 70.

[71] Thomas Mann throws some interesting light on Fontane's sympathy with Social
Democracy: *Theodor Fontane: Ausgewählte Werke,* Leipzig, 1928. Cf. Einleitung von
Thomas Mann.

[72] Cf. Fontane's letter to Otto Brahm, 14. Jan. 1895; and Brahm's essay: *Freie
Bühne,* Schr. I, p. 465, in which Brahm recalls the 'Gespenster'—Matinee of January,
1887: "Ich sehe mich noch mit dem alten Weisen Theodore Fontane streitend durch die
Strassen irren, um das Residenztheater herum."

[73] Letter to Guido Weiss, 14. Aug. 1889.

Ibsen represents the beginning of a new world that makes the old seem dated and boring. But that does not prevent him from disagreeing categorically with the ideas and the philosophy which Ibsen's plays embody: (*"Alles, was da von Lebensanschauungen und Doktrinen mit drunterläuft, ist der reine Unsinn."*)[74]

The central theme of Fontane's novels—his *L'Adultera, Irrungen Wirrungen, Effi Briest,* and others—revolves about the institution of marriage; and in the circumscribed bourgeois world of these novels, the fate of those who transgress against this institution is invariably dire. In Fontane's scheme of things, which faithfully reflected the sentiments and practice of Prussian middle-class society, the *summum bonum* of existence is not happiness but orderliness; and, as his Major Botho in *Irrungen Wirrungen* lugubriously concludes, *"Ordnung ist Ehe."* In the light of this we can readily understand why Fontane, from the secure citadel of his own impeccable and orderly family life, could look down upon Brahm's admiration of Ibsen and loftily ascribe it to the former's dangerous state of celibacy. On this one point Fontane's championship of the younger literary generation clashed with his personal views and thus placed him in the line of fire between two camps. Querulously he writes to his daughter:

Man muss unverheiratet sein, wie unsere jungen Freunde, um auf diesen Zopf von Ehe, freier Liebe, Selbstbestimmung, Verantwortlichkeit, usw. anzubeissen. Alles verrückt und manches auch noch sehr unangenehm, wie z.B. in ,Rosmersholm,' was glaub ich, der kleine Brahm ganz besonders schön findet. Ich in meiner Eigenschaft als zwischen zwei Stühlen Sitzender bin schlimm dran. Keinem kann ich's recht machen.[75]

The essence of what Fontane meant to Otto Brahm is contained in an address delivered by Brahm at the Fontane memorial ceremony of the *Freie Bühne*.[76] In this address Brahm touched upon the high points of their long association, from the days of the *Vossische Zeitung* through the eventful inception of the *Freie Bühne,* down to the triumph of Hauptmann at the *Deutsches Theater*. Brahm told how he had made the fateful decision to pre-

---

[74] Letter to Fr. Stephany, 30. Sept. 1889.   [75] *Ibid.*
[76] "Rede gehalten bei der Fontane-Feier der Freien Bühne", repr. in *Neue Rdsch.,* Bd. 10 (1899) pp. 42–52.

sent *Vor Sonnenaufgang* and had already sent an enthusiastic article on Hauptmann off to the printers, when he received the famous letter written on Hauptmann's behalf by Fontane.[77] He recalled Fontane's article on the *Freie Bühne* in the *Vossische Zeitung*,[78] applauding the idea of an experimental theatre for the presentation of plays that could get no hearing elsewhere. Fontane quoted the motto of *"wage zu irren"* as appropriate to the new enterprise, for he was confident that it would bravely grope its way to artistic truth and beauty. The old "Wanderer through Mark Brandenburg" was remarkable for his youth and understanding, and achieved new fame through his recognition of and identification with the naturalists. But Brahm takes pains to point out the wideness of his and Fontane's concept of naturalist·

. . . wobei wir unter einem Naturalisten den verstehen, der, jedem Regelzwange feind, frei dem Treibe seiner eigensten Natur folgt.[79]

Fontane was primarily an artist, not a critic. He relied upon his personal feeling rather than upon objective, factual judgments. He was essentially subjective in his critical appraisals and, strange to say, often unerringly right. When Brahm sent him his review of *Irrungen Wirrungen*, Fontane gratefully answered in a letter which is quoted here verbatim because of its significance and because it seems to be missing from Fontane's collected letters.

Ich danke Ihnen herzlich. Sie können sich unmöglich eine Vorstellung davon machen, wie einem alten Knopf, um den sich 68 Jahre lang eigentlich niemand, oder höchstens eine Partei-Mediocrität (bei Gelegenheit der Wanderungen etc.) gekümmert hat, wie solchem *vieux* zu Mute wird, wenn er sich, in seinem vielleicht letzten Lebenssemester, erstens überhaupt noch beachtet und dann *so* liebevoll betrachtet sieht.

Dass in meinem Ibsen-Aufsatz und in ‚Irrungen Wirrungen' dieselbe

---

[77] Schlenther confirms the fact that Brahm had accepted the play before receiving Fontane's letter of recommendation, a flattering reflection on Brahm's literary acumen not always recognized in histories of literature: "Als Brahm das Stück las, hatte er Fontane's Empfehlung noch nicht erhalten. Er war bald entschieden, das Stück aufzuführen. Erst nachdem dieser Beschluss endgültig gefasst war, erfuhr er zu seiner Freude, dass damit zugleich ein Wunsch seines alten Gönners und Freundes erfüllt werden sollte." Schlenther, Paul, *Gerhart Hauptmann. Leben und Werke*, revised ed., Berl. 1912, p. 63.

[78] In *Causerien über Theater*, ed. by P. Schlenther, Berl. 1905.

[79] *Op. cit.*, p. 44.

Tendenz lebt: ,Ehe ist Ordnung', ist mir erst durch Ihre Kritik zu Gemüte geführt. Und diese Tendenz selbst,—ja das ist ein weites Thema, das man eigentlich nur behandeln kann, wenn man an einem schönen Sommerabend zwölf Mal um den Kroll'schen Platz herumgeht. ,Du sollst nicht Ehebrechen', das ist die Norm und wohl dem, der, nicht in Versuchung und nicht in Kämpfe geführt, dieser Norm entspricht; aber der Compliciertheiten modernen Lebens sind so viele, dass das Gesetz jeden Tag und jede Stunde durchlöchert wird, weil es durchlöchert werden muss, wodurch wir, wollend oder nicht, unsere Stellung zur Schuldfrage beständigen Wandlungen unterworfen sehen. Das zugleich ein Ideal verkörpernde Gesetz, es bleibt, aber seine Strafandrohungen und Strafbemessungen, auch die bloss gesellschaftlichen, ändern sich nach der veränderten Schuldanschauung, und die Zeit kann kommen, wo das Gesetz selbst darüber zusammenbricht. Vielleicht, wenn wir vier achten schreiben, 8888. Aber noch ist es da.[80]

Brahm, in his dialectic appreciation of Fontane, by no means viewed him as an out and out conservative. He spoke of his polar qualities. Although a believer in law and order and in traditional institutions, Fontane was nevertheless aware of the principle of eternal change: ("Beständig wechseln die Anschauungen, auch die sittlichen . . . ");[81] and he also harbored a sympathy for, if not condonement of, the claims of passion (*L'Adultera—Effi Briest*). Brahm compared Melanie, the heroine of *L'Adultera*, to Ibsen's Nora, because of a certain similarity in their power of moral decision. And thus he was able to show an implied coincidence of ideas between the morally straitlaced but humanly lovable old novelist so resolutely opposed to all ethical revolutionism, and his apparent antithesis, Ibsen.

2. *Karl Stauffer-Bern*

The identical spirit of moral constraint albeit relieved by aesthetic acceptance underlies Fontane's objection to Brahm's sympathetic study of an ill-starred artist, Karl Stauffer-Bern.[82] Stauffer-Bern was a tortured being whose life was a perpetual

---

[80] *Ibid.*, p. 45, Fontane's letter to Brahm is dated 21. Apr. 1888.
[81] In a letter to Brahm, 29. Okt. 1882, quoted by Brahm at the Fontane-Feier, *op. cit.*, p. 44.
[82] *Karl Stauffer-Bern, Sein Leben, Seine Briefe, Seine Gedichte, dargestellt von Otto Brahm*, Berl. 1892–1911.[12]

Sturm und Drang. He was embroiled in an incessant struggle to
find himself both in his calling and in his personal relations. His
was an ideal-obsessed soul restlessly shifting from medium to
medium in art, concocting grandiose artistic and literary projects,
a strange composite of stern, ascetic power of concentration when
working on some portrait or etching, and as extreme a weakness
and instability when that work had not measured up to his fabu-
lous expectations. A Hölderlin-like figure, Stauffer-Bern seduced
his Diotima, Frau Lydia Escher-Welti, the wife of his wealthy
patron, and ran off to Rome with her, taking with him a sum of
money which the husband had left in his trust. The Swiss artist
showed signs of unmistakable mental derangement, and his condition became hopelessly confirmed when he was subsequently
thrown into prison as a result of the legal redress which his betrayed friend had obtained. Brahm belonged to Stauffer-Bern's
Berlin circle and, upon the tragic death of his friend, published his
reminiscences of the unfortunate man together with some of his
letters. Shortly thereafter, Lydia Escher sent him a packet of
Stauffer-Bern's letters with her permission to publish them. Such
was the accidental impetus to a work that appears anomalous in
the main body of Otto Brahm's writings, otherwise almost exclusively devoted to literature and the theatre.

Brahm's biographical introduction and explanatory interpolations can in no sense be called the conscious revindication of a
reprobate. But his objective fairness and, above all, the beautiful
idealistic temper of the letters themselves evoke a sympathetic
mood, a tender impression that mitigates the sordidness of
Stauffer-Bern's tragedy and arouses pity rather than censure. *"Es
zählt zu dem Schönsten und Wirkungsvollsten, das Sie geschrieben,"*
. . . wrote Fontane to Brahm;[83] and in another letter he echoes
Frau Fontane's opinion that the book belongs at the head of all
of Brahm's works.[84] He thinks that the high artistic plane of the
book is due to the fact that Brahm has had virgin soil in writing
on Bern. (*"Ich weiss aus Erfahrung, dass einem dies Bewusstsein
die Flügel wachsen lässt."*)[85]

[83] 30. Dez. 1891.   [84] 22. Okt. 1892.
[85] *Ibid.*

But Fontane had no patience with a passion in the grand manner, a love that conquered all and stood above moral considerations. He relegated such unconscionable sentiments to the gods, not to mortals, and was inclined to minimize the emotional justification for Bern's sin and to magnify his tragic weakness. Fontane's hidebound standards in the matter of love and convention inexorably stigmatized such irregularities.

Stauffer war doch wunderlich gemischt, (he writes to Brahm) und wer ihn bloss nach seinen ganz wundervollen Briefen beurteilen will, der, glaube ich, leistet mehr der Freundschaft als der historischen Wahrheit einen Dienst.[86]

His moral indignation is even more scathingly expressed in an earlier letter:

Mein Degout gegen solche Geschöpfe Gottes—ich nehme dies letzten an, weil der Vater Prediger war—bleibt. Solche Genies sollten gar nicht existieren, und wenn das ‚Genietum' so was fordert, so bin ich für Leineweber.[87]

The biography of Karl Stauffer-Bern discloses unexpected facets in Brahm's interests and critical powers. There is an urbanity and delicacy to his style never before attained. His sentences teem with subtle aesthetic observations in the analysis of Bern's paintings. He shows the essentially plastic genius of Bern even in his painting and etching, and thus bares the cause for that devastating sense of self-deficiency which we now see to have been inevitable in an artist who has been working in the wrong medium. In this unusually keen and sensitive study Brahm no doubt availed himself of the stored-up knowledge of art acquired in his early courses at the University of Berlin, his visits to the art galleries, and his friendship with artists. No doubt his knowledge of art was later to be an important factor in his success as a theatre director. In a sense it is to be regretted that Brahm's practical activities in the theatre precluded any further writing on aesthetics, for there is scarcely any doubt—in view of the twelve printings of the book by 1911—that he would have achieved eminence in this field as well.

---

[86] 30. Dez. 1801.   [87] 8. Feb. 1891.

3. *Fontane's Death*

The last chapters in Brahm's friendship with Fontane can now be skimmed through rapidly, dipping into Fontane's correspondence here and there. The close association goes on uninterruptedly until Fontane's death in 1898. Otto Brahm invites his friend to a private dinner after the première of *Hedda Gabler* in the *Lessingtheater*, for the purpose of having him meet the author. Fontane declines with an excuse that seems a trifle too specious when we remember his opinion of Ibsen.[88] Fontane, in letters to friends, longs to travel to Lugano where Brahm is vacationing.(*"Wo Brahm sich immer wieder kriegsfertig macht, muss eine gesunde Luft wehn."*)[89] A copy of *Jenny Treibel* arrives at Otto Brahm's with a request to grant it a few friendly words.[90] When Brahm makes his speech of welcome to Antoine at the première of Hauptmann's *Hannele*, Fontane congratulates him on his successful handling of a delicate situation.[91] On the occasion of Brahm's first failures in the *Deutsches Theater*, Fontane writes:

> Mir tut Brahm leid, denn er ist besser als sein Ruf und hat jenen eigentümlichen Idealzug, der sich bei den Juden, auch wenn sie noch so scharf und bissig und selbst noch so happig sind, so häufig findet. Er lebt ganz für ein Prinzip, und das wird ihm eine spätere Zeit mal anrechnen.[92]

Notes of congratulation come regularly at the milestones in Brahm's career: at the triumph of the first performance of the *Weber*,[93] after the bitter struggles against censorship. Long discussions follow, on the performances of *Klein Eyolf*,[94] on *Florian Geyer*,[95] and on *Die Versunkene Glocke*.[96] A reminiscence of Brahm's habit of punning echoes from a note to Schlenther: *"Vor ein paar Tagen kam Brahm zu uns in ziemlich guter Stimmung und wortspiel-produktiv."*[97] There are several references to dramatic readings at

---

[88] *Ibid.*

[89] To Hans Hertz, 14. Apr. 1891; to Wilhelm Hertz, 26. Mai, 1891.

[90] 22. Okt. 1892.

[91] "Ich finde es alles sehr gut, doppelt gut, wenn ich bedenke, wie schwierig die Situation war. Deutsch sein und patriotisch und sich nichts vergeben und zugleich doch wieder artig und huldigend." 3. Dez. 1893.

[92] To Karl Zöllner, 6. Sept. 1894.

[93] 27. Sept. 1894.

[94] 14. Jan. 1895.

[95] März, 1896.

[96] 17. Dez. 1896.

[97] 6. Dez. 1894.

Brahm's home which Fontane attended.[98] The last letter to Brahm was written by Fontane from the suburbs of Dresden on the tenth of June, 1898, the year of his death. In his address at the *Fontane-Feier*, Otto Brahm spoke of his last days with Fontane and then concluded with these reverent words:

Am anderen Tag, um die Mittagsstunde, führte mich seine Tochter an sein Totenlager: ruhig war er gestorben, und in sanfter Ruhe lag er auch da, das schöne Greisenantlitz nur wenig gesenkt, keine Spur von Kampf oder Schmerz in der Miene, Philosoph noch im Tode. Die Augen geschlossen für immer, die so leuchtend lächeln, so blau blitzen konnten, leicht gefaltet die feinen emsigen Hände, der Mund verstummt, der mit so viel Charme zu plaudern wusste und mit so echter Anmut. Ein überreiches Leben geendet, das durch so viel Wandlungen deutscher Literatur geschritten war als ihre persönlichste Persönlichkeit, sich selber treu und der Heimat, im Nächsten wurzelnd, und im Vertrautesten, und aufsteigend von ihm zu lichten Höhen des Dichtens und Gestaltens. . . .[99]

L. *Biography of Schiller*

Otto Brahm's last extensive work—before the success of the *Freie Bühne* put an end to any further sustained literary effort on his part—was his biography of Schiller, which remained uncompleted for reasons already made obvious.[100] It appeared in a decade which witnessed the beginning of two other Schiller biographies, those of Weltrich and Minor, beside which Brahm's *Schiller* takes its place; and singularly enough, because of the high ideals of accuracy and exhaustiveness which inspired all these works, none of them was ever completed. Yet each one remains a permanent monument no less to the memory of the classic figure it describes than to the time in which it was written. As the varying spiritual temper of subsequent eras can be traced in varying judgments on the Ancients, on Shakespeare, and on Goethe, so in Otto Brahm's Schiller we have a faithful commentary on Brahm's own time. Brahm's reinterpretation was a spiritual necessity in an age that realized the meaninglessness of eternal idealism amidst the clamor of temporal existence. The times demanded substantial

[98] Fontane to Paula Schlenther-Conrad, 12. Apr. 1895.
[99] *Op. cit.*, p. 51.
[100] *Schiller*, Berl., 1. Bd. 1888, 2. Bd. 1892 (unvollendet).

ideals and for the most part neglected formal ones. The divorcement of spiritual expression from real life was reflected in the plethora of Schiller-epigons who continued to posture and verbalize in an antedated form. The result was a brittle shell of rhetoric and bathos. And as often happens in such cases, the resentment against the epigons was transferred to their great prototype in one of those egregious identifications of a genuine entity with its shadow, many times removed.

This attitude of his time was shared by the younger Brahm.

Als Student war ich Schillerhasser (he confesses in his foreword). Dies Bekenntnis schicke ich voraus, nicht weil ich ihm eine persönliche Bedeutung beilegte, sondern weil ich umgekehrt in meiner Anschauung eine für unsere Tage typische zu erkennen glaube.

But with increasing maturity Brahm was impelled to revise his judgment, and in this biography he intended to atone for his youthful sin. Yet he was firm in his desire to remain free from all prejudice and false reverence in determining the exact significance of Schiller as judged from contemporary standards. His intention, as he rightly observed, not only fulfilled a personal need, but one which was typical of the time. What Brahm's contemporaries thought of the significance of his work is exemplified by Fontane who wrote of it as revealing "the real Schiller" ("*der eigentliche Schiller, der Brahmsche*").[101]

The Schiller biography had first been suggested to Brahm by Scherer in the summer of 1879, but it was not until 1885 that he was able to apply himself to it seriously. Scherer was already dead when the first volume appeared in 1888; and appropriately enough, the work was dedicated to its spiritual godfather. Although twelve folios of the second volume had been lying in print at his publishers since November 1889, the second volume was not published until 1892. It was twenty years from this date to Brahm's death, yet the work was never completed. When we consider that important parts of the second volume were written between 1889 and 1892 in the very midst of the most hectic days of the *Freie Bühne*— a period that is unequalled in all of Brahm's career for the intensity of his journalistic and theatrical activity—we are compelled to

[101] Letter to Schlenther, 20. Sept. 1887.

seek for other causes besides the mere pressure of affairs to account for the non-completion of the work. What has been said of Brahm's desire to revaluate Schiller in contemporary terms undoubtedly affords significant evidence to account for a slackening of interest on his part. Brahm's fragment dwells with great love of detail on Schiller's early period: Schiller as the harbinger of social justice; the restive Schiller of *Karlschule* days; the wild revolutionary of *Die Räuber;* the critic of social disparity in *Kabale und Liebe;* and, above all, the idealistic champion of intellectual freedom and the implacable enemy of secular and ecclesiastical despotism in *Don Carlos.* It is the Schiller of the *Sturm und Drang* and the Age of Enlightenment, the Schiller imbued with Rousseauan social idealism that spoke to Brahm's spirit in understandable accents. Here were tangible points of reference with the social criticism of 19th century naturalism. In his foreword he tells us:

Durch hergebrachten Massstab nicht mehr gebunden, erkennen wir die Grenzen in Schillers Kunstübung, welche die Zeit und die eigene Individualität ihm gesteckt haben; und finden freudig seine hinreissendsten Wirkungen da, wo er mit dem realistischen Prinzip unserer Tage zusammentrifft.

The social interpretation of Schiller receives extended treatment in Brahm's work. What he says of Schiller's early naturalism and the social idealism of the Marquis von Posa, not in favor but in criticism of these, is wholly conceived in the atmosphere of social criticism which was so typical of the movement of naturalism. The faults of the Scherer School emerge most glaringly in Brahm's chapter on *Die Räuber,*[102] which is largely a genetic treatment of sources, parallels, motifs, and text revisions, but which tells us nothing of the completed play in its totality.

Brahm, as was natural in a dramatic critic, displayed an unusually keen interest in the technical side of Schiller's dramas considered as stage-plays. It was from this point of view that he could appreciate Schiller most. Whether Brahm ever really achieved more than an intellectual respect for the subject of his biography is a moot possibility; the man who had been a "Schiller-hater" probably never entirely outgrew the indelible impressions of youth.

[102] *Op. cit.*, 1. Bd. pp. 111–141.

For one thing, there was the eternal contrast with Goethe; for another, Brahm's whole reticent and rationally-inclined temperament shrank from anything that smacked of theatrical rhetoric. His contribution to the German theatre represented the naturalistic, subdued, and matter-of-fact technique both of writing and acting. Although he was the creator of an integrated style that stands as one of the unique and indisputably great achievements of the German theatre, there was absolutely no room in it for what is known as "the grand manner." The historic failure of Brahm's presentation of *Kabale und Liebe* at the *Deutsches Theater* symbolizes Brahm's inner remoteness from Schiller.[103]

M. *The Man of the Theatre*

The culminating period in Otto Brahm's career must perforce be slighted in this biographical sketch. The years from 1889 on in Brahm's life, vital as they are in the history of the German theatre, lie beyond the province of the present discussion. Only their broader significance can be briefly indicated here. Otto Brahm's career, from this point on, is retold in detail in every standard work on the history of the German theatre. It would be supererogatory to attempt to expatiate on the excellent accounts about Brahm and his achievement which are to be found in such compendious works as those of Bab,[104] Winds,[105] and Hagemann,[106] to mention only the more considerable ones.

In a sense, the acid test of the dramatic critic comes when he graduates from the theoretical, sheltered, and often irresponsible cathedra of judgment into the practical sphere of creation. If he is identified with the life of his time in a broad sense, if his day by day study of the contemporary theatre has resulted in an organic view or a unified program, some conscious realization will come over him of the direction which theatrical reform must take. And this is especially true if his whole maturer criticism has been based on some such program. It follows then that the higher validity of his agitation and propaganda can only be affirmed in practice.

---

[103] For Brahm's apologia concerning this failure cf. Schr. I, p. 475.
[104] *Das Theater der Gegenwart*, Leipzig, 1928.
[105] *Geschichte der Regie*, Stuttgart, 1925.
[106] *Regie*, Berlin, 1921.

Unfortunately, few critics, especially journalistic critics, are ever able to manage their own theatres. There are myriad conceivable reasons why this is so: Goethes, Immermanns, and Laubes have been few and far between. To this illustrious company of critic-managers Otto Brahm belongs. His critical writings were the natural prelude to his work in the theatre.

1. *Naturalism on the Stage*

The school of naturalism in German letters found its perfect exponent in Brahm. As the animating spirit of the *Freie Bühne*—one of the many European theatres inspired by Antoine's *Théâtre libre*—Brahm gave Ibsen, Hauptmann, Tolstoi, Strindberg, Holz and Schlaf, Zola, Becque, Hartleben, and Fulda their first genuine introduction to the German theatrical public. From the *Freie Bühne*—as was the case with new dramatists in the entire independent and experimental theatre movement in Europe and in the United States—these dramatists graduated to the established theatres of Germany. Such actors as Agnes Sorma, Kainz, Reicher, Rittner, and Else Lehmann, among others, achieved their greatest fame in Brahm's ensemble. The final triumph of naturalism was celebrated when Brahm took over the *Deutsches Theater* (1894) from L'Arronge. Here Hauptmann, Dreyer, Hirschfeld, Schnitzler, and Sudermann came into their own, interpreted in a spirit in complete harmony with their works. What Brahm created on the stage was an ultimate in naturalistic technique. Brahm was not so much theatrical as he was literary, and that within the limits of the literary movement with which he was identified. His actors were no longer masks, mimes, imitators of characters; they actually were those characters themselves, living, palpitating human creatures, speaking, gesticulating, and moving with all the halting, dumb articulation, the casualness and half-tone restraint of conversational figures in life-situations. Brahm's settings were also conceived in this spirit; subdued, naturalistic, unobtrusively but powerfully evocative of milieu. As Michael puts it:

Hier aber war zwischen naturalistischer Weltanschauung und Bühnenatmosphäre eine künstlerische Einheit, wie sie vorher nur auf der Weimarer Goethebühne zwischen dem hohen Stil der Tragödie und der statuarischen Haltung der Schauspieler gewaltet hatte.[107]

2. Brahm and Reinhardt

With the passing of the extreme naturalistic phase and the coming of a neo-romantic and impressionistic interlude, Brahm's style was outmoded. The new spirit demanded more color, more sensuous mood, more unrestrained, imaginative appeal. Brahm's inflexible literary conscience proved unadjustable to the expansive needs of the day, and Max Reinhardt, discovered by Brahm and an actor in his ensemble, became his successor.[108] Michael contrasts them with great felicity when he says:

Bei Brahm war Stil. Reinhardt stilisierte. Brahm war Literat, einseitig, ein Charakter. Reinhardt war Schauspieler, wandelbar, ein Charakterspieler. Weil das naturalistische Drama nicht einem allgemeinen Weltgefühl entsprach und seine Dichter selbst ihm bald untreu wurden, konnte der Naturalist Brahm nicht das Theater der Zeit schaffen. Der Schauspieler Reinhardt konnte es, weil bei ihm der Wille zum Theater der Zeit nicht durch ein aussertheatralisches literarisches Gewissen gehemmt wurde. Der echte Komödiant ist in jeder Rolle ein anderer, der Schauspielerregisseur Reinhardt war es in jedem Stück. Bei allem Unterscheidenden war Reinhardt doch darin Brahm verwandt, dass er nicht aus der Idee, sondern aus dem Milieu, der Atmosphäre des Dramas gestaltete. Der grössere Reichtum der Töne bei Reinhardt ergab sich aus dem grösseren Instrument des vielseitigen Repertoires; der Anschlag war der gleiche, aber die Hand griff vollere Akkorde.[109]

3. Word Portraits of Brahm

The full spiritual stature of Otto Brahm will one day be revealed when all of his letters are available. Until Schnitzler's *Nachlass* is completely published[110] and until Hauptmann releases Brahm's

---

[107] *Deutsches Theater*, Breslau, 1923, p. 90.

[108] Schlenther writes concerning the break between Brahm and Reinhardt: "Brahm hat in seinem Berufsleben wohl nie etwas schmerzlicher empfunden, als diese Sezession eines jungen Freundes, auf dessen Dank er Anspruch zu haben glaubte." *Op. cit.*, p. 90.

[109] *Op. cit.*, p. 80.

[110] Cf. O. P. Schinnerer, *Arthur Schnitzler's "Nachlass,"* Germanic Review, 8 (1933), pp. 114-123; cf. particularly p. 121-2. Jakob Wassermann, in his reminiscences of Schnitzler, relates the following. "Ich entsinne mich eines hitzigen Wortgefechts zwischen Hofmannsthal und Brahm, von dem Schnitzler nachher mit seiner hübschen Selbstironie bemerkte, einen so pointenreichen Dialog habe keine Szene seine Dramas aufzuweisen." (*N. Rdsch.* 43 (1932), p. 7f.)

letters to the general public, we shall have to remain unenlightened as to Brahm's precise influence on the dramatic production of these two, and on many other, playwrights. That this influence was not inconsiderable we know from the letters which Hirschfeld has published and which contain innumerable references to an almost daily companionship with Hauptmann. There are also technical discussions of the genesis of Hauptmann's plays. To follow out this influence in greater detail will some day be the task of a student interested in Hauptmann's practical dramaturgy.

I can think of no better way of giving this biographical chapter some semblance of dealing with a real flesh and blood character than by appending a few verbal portraits of Otto Brahm, written by men who knew him intimately. Fontane, who always referred affectionately to *"der kleine Brahm"* once jocosely remarked of Brahm's appearance:

Es ist nicht wahrscheinlich, dass er für einen verkappten preussischen Offizier gehalten wird; selbst als Fusilier würde er immer noch eine Extrastellung am linken Flügel der 12. Kompanie bedürfen.[111]

Hirschfeld's account of a visit to Brahm is a delightful portrait of a famous man in an informal moment, *en pantoufles*, as it were:

. . . wenn man die Klingel an seiner Tür zog, öffnete er selbst, ein bartloses Männchen mit dem fahlen Gesicht des Stubengelehrten, unbeirrbare Klugheit, Güte, die sich hinter Ironie verschanzte, in den scharfen Zügen. Der künftige Herr des Deutschen Theaters steckte in einem alten Schlafrock, und die Formen des Mannes waren so schmucklos wie nur möglich. Ein dünnes ,Guten Tag' gewann er sich eben ab, und den Schlapphut behielt er auf dem Kopf, weil es ihm wichtiger war, an eine mögliche Erkältung zu denken als an die Begrüssung des Besuches.[112]

And finally, Kerr, with his strange gift for terse and profound characterization, describes Brahm as:

. . . still, mit vornehmer Zurückhaltung des äusseren Wesens, scheinbar voll Ruhe; und doch steckte hinter dieser Ruhe eine stark konzentrierte Anteilnahme. Geschlossene Lippen; er machte kein Aufhebens. Alles Pathos lag ihm fern: alle Nachgiebigkeit auch.[113]

[111] In a letter to his son, Theodor, 9. Mai, 1888; *Theodor Fontane—Briefe an seine Familie*, 2 Bde. Berl. 1924.

[112] *Op. cit.*, p. 20.   [113] *Pan*, 6. Dez. 1912.

27516

THE MATERIALS

II. *Naturalism in the Drama*

A. *Naumann's Analysis of Modern German Literature*

Otto Brahm's dramatic criticism extends through the latter decades of the 19th century. In the history of literature the customary terms used to designate the various phases of this period are: realism, naturalism, impressionism, and expressionism. That these literary terms are more expedient than exact need not be emphasized. It is important to realize that side by side with 19th century realism there runs a strain of epigon classicism; that waves of neo-romanticism and expressionism accompany the flow of realism and naturalism. And furthermore, when it is taken into account that this progression and alternation of movements proceed at such a rapid tempo that they often occur within the same individual artist, a broader and more inclusive perspective becomes necessary so that some logical order may be filtered out of an apparent welter of literary currents and counter-currents. The growing realization among historians of literature that the history of all art, and therefore of literature as well, is ultimately inseparable from the history of thought, presents a fruitful solution to the quest for order.[1] If, as Naumann among others suggests,[2] we view the myriad literary currents of our time as varying phases of the same larger counter-currents of realism and romanticism, then the movements of naturalism and impressionism—our major concern here—appear to be identified with the picture of a rational, objective, and scientific universe such as has been an integral part of European thought since the Age of Enlightenment. It is this same spirit, interrupted on occasion by a romantic *Sturm*

[1] Hans Naumann in his *Die Deutsche Dichtung der Gegenwart*, Stuttgart, 1931, p. 2, expresses this notion concisely: "Immer und so auch in unserer Epoche ist die Kunst, und so auch die Dichtung, der feinste und früheste Ausdruck des Zeitgeistes allgemein, von diesem im Grunde untrennbar, und Literaturgeschichte also zuletzt nichts anderes als Geistesgeschichte überhaupt."

[2] Wilhelm Dilthey's collection of essays: *Das Erlebnis und die Dichtung*, Leipzig und Berlin, 1906ff., has remained a classic example of literary interpretation as ingrated with the history of thought. Cf. Oskar Benda, *op. cit.*, p. 10.

und Drang and idealistically tempered and corrected by classicism, which reached its apogee in the epoch of natural science, technics, and materialism: the 19th century. The creative as well as the critical spirit manifested in this tradition is rationalistic and materialistic in its philosophy, sceptical and humanistic in its religion, relativistic in its ethics, and individualistic in its social outlook. The spirit of realism—to continue Naumann's thesis— is furthermore characterized by a certain sluggishness and atrophy of the emotions with a corresponding hypertrophy of the intellect. Its feeling for form is calm, lucid, and sensuous; and it is possessed of a capacity for the deliberative and contemplative in aesthetic norms.

Naumann goes on to delineate the respective contrary traits of expressionism as over against naturalism and impressionism. The altered intellectual universe of expressionism is metaphysical and idealistic rather than scientific. Moral relativism gives way to moral decisiveness. There is an inspiring leaven of faith, religiosity and emotionalism interfusing all thought and conduct. A primitive, ecstatic spirituality becomes manifest in all creative effort; and the former contemplative, lucid aesthetics is now shot through with restless movement and mystic exaltation. Symbolism becomes a recurrent motif in the new literature. And finally, the former social individualism is transposed into a broader collective consciousness.

To view the development of modern German literature from this broader perspective is not necessarily an over-simplification, especially when the current terms of naturalism, impressionism and expressionism are also taken into account for whatever critical significance they may possess. Naumann, furthermore, examines these literary movements in reference to their attitudes toward certain typical problems which literature repeatedly raises: the problem of art and nature, and the problem of the purpose of art. Because the spirit of the times and the fluctuating attitudes toward these problems are nowhere better mirrored than in the dominant problem of form, Naumann studies his men and movements against a background of literary forms: the drama, the novel, and the lyric.

The intention of this chapter and of those following is to present the materials of Brahm's criticism and to adapt the above scheme of literary study, wherever feasible, to the compass of the present theme. We are interested in classifying various judgments on the history of the German drama as expressed in the critical writings of Otto Brahm. This classification should prove a sound basis for a subsequent theoretical analysis. We must not expect the same plenitude of discussion in regard to expressionism as in regard to the movements of naturalism and impressionism because Brahm was no longer a critical force when expressionism arrived and could only display a feeble, half-aware petulance at its first premonitory symptoms.[3] The rubrics to be observed later are predicated on Naumann's procedure; among them will be: Naturalism in the Drama (*Kunst und Natur*), and The Function of Criticism (*Zweck der Kunst*).

B. *The Naturalist Movement*

Before entering upon an abstract analysis of Brahm's ideas dealing with naturalism in the drama, it would be well to outline briefly the literary-historical development in Germany which culminated in the movement of naturalism. During the latter part of the 19th century the unprecedented development of the natural sciences and the accelerated industrialization of Germany resulted in a materialist view of the universe and an intensification of social stresses that was mirrored in the creative life. As a result of this, the entire drift of literary production in its most vital and representative manifestations veered increasingly towards the direction of realism. The striving for truth—always an avowed ideal of all poets and literary schools—now became the striving for a realistic truth, a truth undistorted by preconceived idealistic notions and social prejudices, but shaped to conform with the real, objective world. One who reads the innumerable programs, manifestoes, campaign tracts, and theoretical works by the various writers emerging in the middle of the 1880's cannot help being struck by the unremitting recurrence of the word *Wahrheit*. From all the

[3] Cf. Arthur Kutscher's *Frank Wedekind: Sein Leben und seine Werke*, 3 Bde., München, 1922–27–31, Bd. II, pp. 1, 77, 220, for Brahm's miscomprehension and rejection of Wedekind.

naturalist theoreticians there resounds a mighty antiphonal chorus of *Wahrheit, Natur, Wirklichkeit, Naturwissenschaft, Gegenwart, Gesellschaft*, etc. These catchwords and slogans indicate exactly what the younger writers were agitating for. "Der Bannerspruch der neuen Kunst," wrote Brahm in the program of his new periodical, "mit goldenen Lettern von den führenden Geistern aufgezeichnet, ist das Wort: Wahrheit; und Wahrheit, Wahrheit auf jedem Lebenspfade ist es, die auch wir erstreben und fordern."[4]

What the naturalists aimed at was truth, in the sense explained above, truth based on the exact observation of life and conceived in the spirit of the dispassionate scientist observing a laboratory experiment. Furthermore, it was to be a truth that was living and contemporary, a reaction against the life-falsifying drama of the idealistic epigons, against the mechanically deft but essentially unreal French *Salonstück*, and against the ivory-tower *Goldschnittlyrik* of the beauty-cultists. The German moderns of the 1880's turned to the contemporary scene, to life as it was currently being lived in all classes of society, particularly the neglected classes. Although the decisive catalytic influences came from abroad— from Zola, Ibsen, and Tolstoi—there was an indigenous German tradition leading to naturalism. Marie von Ebner-Eschenbach and Ludwig Anzengruber may be considered among the forerunners of naturalism. Other forerunners such as Freytag and Spielhagen, in their choice of contemporary themes and in their realistic technique, show the continuity of this development within Germany itself. The so-called "poetic realists" such as Hebbel (*Maria Magdalene*) and Ludwig (*Der Erbförster*) may also be considered, at least in a technical sense, as having influenced the dramatic writers of the new movement.

The short-lived history of naturalism may be traced in the following works and dates: In 1882 there appeared in Berlin the *Kritische Waffengänge*, edited by the Hart Brothers. In 1884 a lyrical anthology with prefaces by Conradi and Henckell was compiled by Arent under the title of *Moderne Dichtercharaktere*. 1885 saw the founding in Munich of Michael Georg Conrad's periodical: *Die Gesellschaft*. In the same year Bleibtreu published his

[4] Schr. I, p. 285.

tract: *Die Revolution der Literatur*. 1889 witnessed the appearance
of Otto Brahm's periodical: *Freie Bühne für modernes Leben* (now
the *Neue Rundschau*). In 1890 Arno Holz published the first part
of *Die Kunst, ihr Wesen und ihre Gesetze*. And finally, in 1891, we
have the first conscious and organized realization that the movement, in its narrower sense, was at an end: Hermann Bahr's *Die
Überwindung des Naturalismus*.

I have confined myself to the theoretical works as delineating
most accurately the course of the naturalist movement which was
singularly sparse in its creative production. In fact, it has often
been said that, with the possible exception of the earlier Hauptmann, the one writer of the period whose works still live and who
best realized on a creative plane what the naturalists were groping
for, was Theodore Fontane who, although he was the friend of
many of the younger writers, never belonged to any naturalist
school. As for the remaining creative productions of any significance, there were Max Kretzer's novels, Holz and Schlaf's technically interesting dramatic sketches entitled *Papa Hamlet* (1889),
and their drama, *Die Familie Selicke* (1890), Schlaf's drama,
Meister Oelze (1892), and Hauptmann's first dramas up to and
including *Die Weber* (1892). Wildenbruch's concessions to the new
spirit of the times may also be mentioned, even though he was
mainly representative of a tradition that was anathema to the
naturalists. In *Die Quitzows* (1888), *Meister Balzer* (1892), and
Die Haubenlerche (1890) we have examples of at least an external
conformity with naturalist doctrine.

1. *The Creative Impasse*

The vogue of naturalism was as brief as it was stormy. Its own
adherents—even assuming the debatable premise that they ever
were really and wholly identified with "consistent naturalism"—
soon developed in a direction away from it. We realize the inevitability of this change when we consider that the deterministic
Weltanschauung upon which the movement was based soon led to
a creative impasse. In a technical sense, the method of docu-
mentation and the attempted recording of reality in its minutest

details (*Sekundenstil*) resulted, when consistently applied, in an inartistic monotony and sordidness. The functions of the artist were debased into a mechanical technique of exhaustive observation and passive recording.

Determinism, however, depressed the creative spirit most profoundly in the social sphere. Viewing the individual as the impotent product of heredity and environment resulted in moral fatalism (the denial of free will) and precluded the possibility of social melioration. The social criticism of the naturalists (the movement was intimately bound up with Social Democracy) confined itself to the exposure of social evils, to compassion for the "victims of society," and to a vague denunciation of conditions. But naturalistic determinism and the passive will could not point to a way out of these conditions. The result was social pessimism.

Although naturalism made the stage a political tribunal for a short space of time, Marxist critics now point out this element of social pessimism as a factor leading to the creative barrenness of the movement. Except for the later novels of Zola, none of the naturalist works envisions a society of the future to supplant the present order. Like Ibsen, the German naturalists never got beyond a querulous burst of despair at the exposure of social hypocrisy.[5]

Naturalism was also attacked from the right. Theoreticians such as Paul Ernst saw in the destruction of free will and in the resultant dissolution of a set frame of moral values (moral relativism) the death of great tragedy. Another objection to the subject matter of naturalism came from the plutocratic notion that the proletariat is an amorphous and nondescript class and is thus unsuitable for the materials of great tragedy.[6]

With the realization that naturalism as a consistent principle did not jibe with the reality of artistic creation, that the colors, shades, and overtones of reality are not eternal absolutes but vary in accordance with the perspective and insight of the artist, who can thus only reproduce subjective and momentary impressions at

[5] Cf. Erwin Piscator, *Das Politische Theater*, Berl. 1929, p. 30.
[6] *Der Weg zur Form*, München, 1928f., pp. 30–49; cf. the refutation of Ernst's social bias in Johannes Volkelt, *Ästhetik des Tragischen*, München, 1917f., p. 34f. and p. 76.

best—the naturalist inevitably turned to impressionism as a more unconstrained creative technique.[7]

We shall now see in Otto Brahm's critical essays this limited cyclorama of figures and movements unroll before our eyes, cannily recognized in all their significance and colored by an individual personality that conceived them not only as objective "chroniclers of the times" but mainly as convenient vehicles for the promulgation of a set of literary and dramatico-cultural principles.

C. *Wildenbruch and Heyse*

From his very first days with the *Vossische Zeitung* Brahm turns his critical attention to those writers of the older tradition in whom he sees, in one way or another, traits which deserve to be saved and which can be used as a bridge to modernity. We need not be surprised, therefore, that his first protagonists are the very ones against whom he is to turn later on. There is a preponderance of discussion on routine matters of the theatre in these first essays, for the modern German drama has not yet been born and the demand of the hour for a pioneer critic is to clear away the suffocating pall of outworn ideas and conventions which impede progress. Drama, the most social of the arts, is singularly dependent upon a sympathetic and open-minded theatre and audience before it can so much as be given a hearing; otherwise it eddies into the stagnant and ineffectual backwaters of an impotent closet drama. Thus we see that Brahm's sympathetic criticism of such writers as Wildenbruch and Heyse is not so much a positive preachment of their virtues as it is the negative arraignment of theatrical entrepreneurs who do not give them a hearing or who do not visualize their modern implications.

Whatever shortcomings he discerns in Wildenbruch's *Karolinger* he attributes to the fact that the author has written the play as a book drama without the expectation of its ever being performed. He praises Wildenbruch as representative of a virile Prussian spirit and as a master of dynamic action, but points out at the

---

[7] Alfred Kleinberg shows the inevitable transition from naturalism to impressionism under the influence of the French theory of impressionism in painting in his stimulating work: *Die Deutsche Dichtung in ihren sozialen, zeit- und geistesgeschichtlichen Bedingungen,* Berl. 1927, p. 373.

same time his technical deficiencies and his haziness in the matters
of motivation and character portrayal. "Wir sind noch nicht reich
genug an dramatischen Autoren, um eine Kraft, wie Wildenbruch
sie offenbart hat, geringschätzen zu dürfen";[8] he writes with
rather lukewarm and apologetic praise; but his emotional interest
in the performance of the *Karolinger* is not so much the drama
itself as the indignation against a tendency which has prevented
it from being seen. He seizes the opportunity to imprecate against
the enemies of theatrical progress, and caustically observes:

> Dass ein Autor, dem diese Fähigkeit in so hohem Masse eigen ist,
> erst nach jahrelangen Mühen mit dem lebendigen Theater in ein
> Verhältnis kommen konnte, wirft ein schlimmes Licht auf unsere
> Theaterdirektionen . . .[9]

In much the same fashion Brahm defends Heyse who had
attempted to turn from his established and successful medium of
the novel to the stage. Brahm realizes that Heyse is no dramatist
of the first water; nonetheless he is a Protean artist whose versatility and mastery of style deserve intelligent notice. Once again
his faint praise recognizes a desideratum rather than a fulfilment
when he writes:

> Sind wir denn so reich an dramatischer Produktion in dieser Zeit,
> dass wir nicht zugleich dieses vornehmen und unermüdlichen Talents,
> dieser allseitigen, reichlich ausfliessenden Begabung froh sein soll-
> ten?[10]

A good deal of Brahm's high opinion of Heyse may be attributed
to the latter's literary background; it can be noted in general that
Brahm judges the theatre primarily from the point of view of
literature. He is concerned with the promulgation of ideas through
the medium of literature and, as we shall later see, views the stage
as the most effective medium of literary agitation. Consequently
he seizes upon his review of Heyse's *Die Weisheit Salomos* as an
occasion to excoriate the enemies of the literary movement which
he is promoting.

The unwitting irony of using Heyse, an avowed enemy of naturalism, as a foil against the other enemies of naturalism is an

8 Schr. I, 5.   9 *Ibid.*
10 Schr. I, 155.

indication of Brahm's unilateral view and intensity of purpose. His messianic zeal blinds him to the inconsistencies of his position. With the combative urge of a Lessing, the soul of polemical ardor in refuting an opponent, Brahm drives along towards his goal and does not disdain the use of his enemies' own weapons. This time the "enemy" is the general run of critics who have attacked Heyse for his lack of realism: "Dieselben Leute, welche sonst vor dem modernen Realismus im Drama schaudernd ihr Haupt verhüllen, klagen nun Heyse ob seines mangelnden Realismus peinlich an," he writes.[11] What has been proved by showing that Heyse is neither a Flaubert nor an Ibsen, as some of these critics had pusillanimously done? Heyse represented a positive entity not to be measured mechanically by foreign standards:

In meines Vaters Hause sind viele Wohnungen; und eine in ihrer Individulität so bestimmt ausgeprägte und so anziehende Persönlichkeit wie Heyse will nicht nach fremdem Massstab, nur nach ihrem eigenen gemessen sein.[12]

In scrutinizing the drama for traits and motifs typical of the new spirit Brahm characteristically found the culminating point of Wildenbruch's art in *Die Quitzows*. He recognized the technical and contentual faults of the drama, particularly the weak dualism of its style; it attempts to be a dramatized history of the Shakespearean type, yet lacking the genius of the Briton, Wildenbruch is overwhelmed by a mass of irrelevant historical detail; he fails to translate historic events into dramatic action; but *Die Quitzows* also attempts to be a Schiller tragedy, with all its expansive pathos and poetic idealization. This underlying dualism is reflected and confirmed in all the aspects of the play: the forms—prose and iambics; the language—literary High German and Berlin dialect (often spoken by the same character); the characters—an historically true, individualistic fighter, Dietrich Quitzow, and his opposite brother, Konrad, whose idealistic patriotism is absolutely unhistorical and counterfeit. Of this spurious character who, in a versified prophecy, oracles the future glory of the Hohenzollern, Brahm writes:

Und all diese schönen, tönenden Worte in den Mund gelegt einem

[11] *Ibid.*   [12] *Op. cit.*, p. 156.

märkischen Junker des Jahres 1411, dem Kinde einer Zeit, welcher der Begriff der Nation, des Vaterlandes in unserem Sinne so fremd sein musste, wie die loyale Bewunderung für einen süddeutschen Herrn, der um hunderttausend ungarischer Goldgulden willen ins Land gekommen war![13]

The suspect dualism and false pathos of Wildenbruch's drama notwithstanding, Brahm is jubilant at its appearance because it raises the central problem of realism as regards the historical drama. The dualism itself is not necessarily an unfavorable symptom because it bespeaks a transitional style in which the new has not yet been able to free itself from the accretions of the old. The new realistic departure in Wildenbruch's dramatic art is greeted with approbation:

... es kennzeichnet die literarische Richtung dieser Zeit, wenn gerade Wildenbruch jetzt einen Schritt über sein bisheriges Schaffen hinaus versucht hat, einen Schritt auf den modernen Realismus zu.[14]

Brahm proceeds to enumerate and dwell upon the modern realistic facets of the play: the precise factual details, the life-like, accidental incidents, the individual genuineness of the character portrayal, the employment of prose and modern dialect in order to bring a past age to life and thus achieve a palpitating reality rather than archaeological correctness. Brahm even finds a suggestion of social tendency in the sympathy expressed in the play for the sufferings of the poverty-stricken of the Mark Brandenburg in the year 1411, an indelible signature of the fact that this play has been written in an era of social reform.

Thus we see the shaping of an attitude toward the historical *genre;* it, too, must express the spirit of the times, must not do violence to the broader spirit of the past but must reinterpret it in a language and technique comprehensible to the theatre-goer of the present. Brahm is still speaking of a non-existent drama, the drama of the future. Wildenbruch's *Quitzows* is not as significant to him for what it is as for what it might be. For Brahm the prophecy of a new historical *genre* was later fulfilled in Hauptmann's *Florian Geyer*. But meanwhile his faith in the future and the following prediction of a coming development are testimonials

---

[13] Schr. I, 222.   [14] *Op. cit.*, p. 223.

of a superior insight and of the confidence of one who is engaged
in the daily struggle to make his prediction come true:

Wenn nun aber dieses Moderne in Gehalt und Form, wenn stärker
oder schwächer soziale Tendenzen, Realismus, Dialekt, Prosa selbst
in das höhere Drama vordringen—kann die Entwicklung an diesem
Punkte stehen bleiben? Je empfindlicher der Widerspruch zwischen
dem Stil dieser Szenen und dem mehr konventionellen Pathos der
anderen bemerkbar wird, desto mehr muss das Neue Herr werden
über das Alte, desto mehr müssen die Ausdrucksmittel unserer
Zeit die schönen Überlieferungen einer gewesenen zurückstossen:
und auch in der historischen Tragödie wird der Realismus siegen, wie
er gesiegt hat in der modernen.[15]

D. *The French Influence*

As we have seen, Heyse and Wildenbruch represent negative
enthusiasms to Brahm. He greets their plays with many reservations. Their transitional drama marches with indecisive, faltering
steps towards the goal he is striving for; but he never labors under
any illusions concerning their limited significance from his point
of view. Before going on to discuss those dramatists whom Brahm
finally does accept as exemplary, for whom he comes out openly
and without any qualification, we must turn our attention to the
representatives of the French *pièce bien faite* school whose influence
on the German drama had been so considerable.

The Berlin theatre-going public that frequented the *Deutsches
Theater, Lessingtheater,* and *Wallnertheater* represented the middle
and upper classes whose tastes—or unconscious lack of them—
and interests were faithfully catered to by the choice of plays at
these private commercial theatres. And the *Vossische Zeitung*
(Brahm's employer), as the conservative organ of these classes
reflected the entire set-up, an important link in the hierarchy of
owners, subscribers, and advertisers who, in the last analysis, were
also the theatre-going public. The inveterate German francophilia
in things cultural once more exercised undisputed sway. The
French farce, the comedy of manners as incorporated in the *pièce
bien faite* school of Augier, Sardou and Scribe and their German
satellites, Lindau, Lubliner, L'Arronge, Blumenthal and Moser

---

[15] *Ibid.*

were now in their heyday in Germany. In France, the culminating expression of a *bourgeoisie* that had expanded powerfully since the Revolution, with all the advantages of tradition and technical schooling, this drama was an organic growth. Yet it found a sympathetic and responsive audience in Germany, too; which is, perhaps, a reflection of the essentially international tastes of the middle classes when undeterred by nationalism.

To Brahm, as to many of his more thoughtful contemporaries, the French influence was deleterious, not because such drama was French (Cp. Becque, the Goncourts, Zola) but because it was unreal. Later on we shall see a profounder objection to this type of French drama because its content—its treatment of love, for instance—is wholly Latin in conception and totally at variance with the Teutonic spirit. But right now his main objection is directed against its falsity, its suave adroitness, its neat plots and complications, all unravelled with dead mathematical precision in conformity with some preconceived scheme or thesis which the author has been trying to prove. There is no vital action flowing out of the nexus of character and situation, but a plot, creakingly unrolled by the all too visible *deus ex machina* of an author. The message is not implicit in the action of the characters and in an inevitable conclusion but is artificially expressed through the convenient mouthpiece of the author: the omniscient *raisonneur*. Since all this is the very antithesis of life, which presents no neatly solved plots but which buffets human beings around in a blind, fortuitous struggle like puppets whose strings are manipulated by chance and by environment, Brahm is inexorably opposed to it. This trend in the German theatre is just so much deadwood that must be chopped away if the living growth of truth and reality is to flourish. In this exposure and denunciation of the Augiers, the Scribes, the Sardous—to mention only the more considerable names—Brahm had already been preceded by Zola,[16] just as in the 18th century Lessing had had the example of Diderot in denouncing Crébillon, Voltaire, and the other epigons of French classical tragedy, and in establishing the *drame bourgeois*.

Brahm admires Sardou as a *"Kenner der Bühne"* who can treat

[16] Cf. *Le Naturalisme au Théâtre*, and *Nos Auteurs Dramatiques*, Paris, 1881.

the most scabrous subjects with Gallic levity. He marvels at the Frenchman's technical perfection but realizes that this "*französische gaieté*" is rather ponderous and heavy-footed in its German metamorphosis. For all of Sardou's gay insouciance and Aristophanic lack of nordic prudery, Brahm nevertheless refers to "*die nachlassende Erfindung und der bequeme Wortreichtum eines alternden Routiniers.*"[17] Scribe is epithetized as the "*Erfinder der raffinierten französischen Theatermache.*"[18] Brahm writes of Scribe:

... nach dem Höchsten hat auf keinem Gebiet der Mann mit dem nüchternen, schlauen Bourgeoisgesicht gestrebt, der das europäische Theater so lange Zeit hindurch beherrschte; aber was im Drama vom Übel war: die regulierende, mit Menschen wie mit Ziffern spielende Mechanik, die sich Technik nennt und die auf bloss symmetrische Wirkungen, auf die Effekte der Situationen, nicht der Charaktere abzielende Handwerksübung ....[19]

As to the German counterparts of this French *Salonstück* tradition, Brahm views them with utter contempt. He speaks of the plays of Moser and Blumenthal as "*leichte Tagesware.*"[20] These two, and the Lubliners and Schönthans, he pitilessly dismisses with the annihilating epithet of "*Macher.*" Even a more considerable figure than these, Paul Lindau, is eliminated from serious consideration by Brahm because of spiritual antecedents that are essentially French rather than German. Lindau's Latin traits are evident in his technique and in his form. Between the naturalistic social drama of a Hauptmann and the urbane comedy of manners of a Lindau there can be no reconciliation as far as Brahm is concerned. In Lindau he sees a "*Taktiker der Bühne*" rather than a poet realistically portraying life; he is merely a "*Theaterschriftsteller, der in Verkennung seiner Eigenart sein Talent in spanische Stiefel einschnürt und die poetische Wahrheit verfehlt.*"[21]

E. *Anzengruber*

When we come to the name of Ludwig Anzengruber in Brahm's writings, for the first time we see what unalloyed enthusiasm our critic is capable of. Anzengruber is to Brahm the playwright of

---

[17] Schr. I, 288.
[18] *Op. cit.*, p. 182.
[19] *Op. cit.*, pp. 179f.
[20] *Op. cit.*, p. 148.
[21] *Op. cit.*, p. 270.

profound folk-humor, *"der Shakespeare des Volksstückes,"*[22] whose artistic mastery he never ceases to admire. The *Kreuzelschreiber* he considers a genuine masterpiece rich in detail and vital contrasts, effortless in its unfolding of a typical picture of peasant life. Anzengruber's otherwise bitter and tendentious writing against the stultifying influence of the Church on naïve, simple-minded peasants is here dissolved into pure artistic humor, Brahm feels.[23] As a realistic portrayer of life Brahm compares Anzengruber with such diversified writers as Björnson and Kretzer.[24] The Austrian dramatist's great virtue is that his themes and moods are rooted in contemporaneity.

In the *Pfarrer von Kirchfeld* Brahm admires the intellectual integrity of the author who has had the courage to end his play with what is generally known as an "unsatisfactory solution." For Brahm, this sort of ending is real because life itself does not offer any neat, conclusive solutions to most of its profounder problems. It is in this respect that Anzengruber is more modern than Björnson in his *Fallissement* which does have a happy ending. On the subject of endings and artistic reality Brahm writes:

Ein leichtes Lustspiel mag man wohl mit Verlobung und dem Duft von Hochzeitskuchen beendigen; aber wenn ein ernster Poet zu uns gesprochen hat in wahren Gestalten, empfinden wir solche Abflachung um so stärker als ein Zerreissen der Illusion. Auch das Leben unserer Zeit gewährt die runden Abschlüsse nicht, welche eine bloss äusserliche Kunstbetrachtung fordern möchte; wie also soll die Poesie sie leisten, die realistische Poesie, welche Wahrheit geben will?[25]

Brahm traces the development of such so-called inconclusive endings, those famous Ibsenian question marks whose function is to make one think about the problems of a play long after the play itself is over. This thought-provoking power of a play is one of the most important signs of a vital drama to Brahm. It represents one of the definite characteristics of the modern drama as distinguished from the neat, made-to-order-even-at-the-cost-of-logic conclusions of the preceding drama. Brahm is later to use this kind of ending as a criterion to test the verisimilitude of a play. He speaks of

---

[22] *Op. cit.*, p. 330.
[24] *Op. cit.*, p. 211.
[23] *Op. cit.*, p. 99.
[25] *Op. cit.*, p. 213.

... jene unbestimmten Lösungen im Stile des ‚Pfarrers von Kirch-feld‘, jene vielbesprochenen Fragezeichen, welche in dem Theater-besucher noch ein eigenes Denken anregen, über die Stunden von 7 bis 10 hinaus, und die Erinnerung an tragische Gestalten um so tiefer in ihm nachklingen lassen.[26]

Brahm sees a resemblance between Anzengruber and the great Norwegian dramatists in the fact that he as well as they has no happy endings after grand emotional outbursts and no purely external tragedies in which chaotic problems are solved through the medium of a pistol-shot.[27]

Anzengruber is the first of the German dramatists whom Brahm takes under his wing as a defence against the frequently repeated charge that modern realism is not a German but a foreign product. Here at last is a German dramatist (*"denn man wird doch Anzen-gruber den Österreicher, noch nicht unter die argen Ausländer werfen müssen"*)[28] who can be pointed out as an exponent of realistic art and who derives from an indigenous tradition. Brahm sees that Anzengruber's power is due in great measure to the fact that he is the continuator of a tradition of long standing: the *Volksstück*. The thematic sphere of this type of play is rather limited, but within these limits, and because of his struggle against the en-slaving power of religious obscurantism, Anzengruber was able to select poetic motifs amenable to dramatic interpretation. In this respect, as we shall see, Anzengruber had a tremendous advantage over those dramatists whose portrayals were framed in modern urban life in its variform heterogeneity and who had no such closely-defined tradition to bolster them. It was for this reason that Anzengruber most naturally represented to Brahm a pioneer, although still transitional, dramatist.

In one of those necrologies in which Otto Brahm summed up the essence of what some deceased friend and author had meant to him and to his contemporaries there is a testimonial to the pioneer significance of Anzengruber in the movement of natural-ism.[29] Brahm recalls Anzengruber's theoretical prefaces to the *Dorfgänge* and the practical examples of his *Volksstücke*. Anzen-

[26] *Ibid.*
[28] *Op. cit.*, p. 218.
[27] *Ibid.*
[29] *Op. cit.*, pp. 325ff.

gruber was no petty local poet of Vienna; he was an indignant moralist of universal stature and also an indulgent judge who exposed the foibles and dissipations of his contemporaries; he was an enemy of all theatrical gloss and false idealization. Brahm quotes from the preface of the *Dorfgänge* lines which might have been written by himself. "Should not art be an idyllic sylvan glade, a sanctified temple, a merry tavern—in short, a place of refuge from life? What the public wants is soft pain and gentle tears." *"Ja, für die Verklärung des Lebens spricht alles und dagegen nur eines: die Wahrheit,"* wrote Anzengruber;[30] and he entreated the devotees of artistic truth to give ear to his opposition against conventional falsifications of life: *"Lasst mir den Realisten gelten! Lasst mich gelten!"*[31]

Brahm exposes the shallowness of public and critics and the oppressive force of censorship in the failure of Anzengruber's plays; fortunately, the succession of failures and reverses was exceeded only by Anzengruber's astonishing prolixity. The enemies of Anzengruber, and therefore of the theatre, as Brahm sees them now are the *Philister*, the *"hohe Polizei,"* and the *"ästhetisch Superklugen."*[32] Anzengruber also aroused a feeling of spiritual kinship in Brahm by his admiration of Ibsen and by his conscious preoccupation with aesthetic and social problems. Of the latter particularly, Anzengruber had much to say to Brahm in a conversation which Brahm reports.[33] The Austrian dramatist spoke of the social conditions which his Viennese *Volksstücke* reflect, of the remarkable transitional figures which separate *Alt-Wien* from *Neu-Wien*, of the menace of pauperism, and of the false atmosphere of *Gemütlichkeit*.

The ultimate gesture of Brahm's recognition of Anzengruber as a pioneer realist was the presentation of *Das Vierte Gebot* by the *Freie Bühne*.[34]

---

[30] Quoted by Brahm, Schr. I, 335.

[31] *Ibid.*

[32] *Op. cit.*, p. 341. Cf. Goethe's words on the subject: "Das Theater hat drei Hauptgegner, die es immer einzuschränken suchen: die Polizei, die Religion, und einen durch höhere sittliche Ansichten gereinigten Geschmack." *Deutsches Theater*, 1813.

[33] Schr. I, 344.

[34] 1890.

F. *Literarische Schutzzollpolitik*

We have seen Brahm's championship of Anzengruber partly because of the Austrian's own positive qualities as a realist and partly because he wished to offer some defence against "nationalist" critics. For the most part, however, Brahm had no patience with such narrow *Schutzzollpolitik*, as he called it. Without losing sight of his German identity, he is nevertheless vividly aware that certain aspects of genius and culture are international in their significance. German civilization incorporates into itself at every vital period in its development so much of foreign influence that an attempt to ignore this palpable fact is little short of willful self-delusion. Thus we see that Brahm is not mechanically opposed to foreign influences merely because they are foreign but because he considers certain of these influences destructive even within their own national context. How much more so must they be in their German transposition, if this is the case. Foreign influences are, consequently, not to be banned *per se;* they can be salutary as well, particularly if they help the Germans to a profounder realization of their own uniqueness. In regard to this myopic "nationalism" in the arts Brahm writes:

Hat es den Vätern unserer klassischen Literatur, den Lessing und Herder, von ihrem Ruhme ein Tüttelchen geraubt, dass sie in einer Zeit neuen Werdens und Gestaltens auf den Ausländer William Shakespeare enthusiastisch hinwiesen? Dass sie das Heil nicht von den deutschen Cronegk und Brawe, sondern von dem grossen Engländer kommen sahen? Und sind, in solchen Anschauungen wurzelnd, die Goethe und Schiller uns erwachsen, so wird uns heutige, in unserm engern Streben nach verwandten Zielen, der Unkenruf der neuen Gottschede nicht stören dürfen; und auch wir werden, indem wir die grossen Muster leuchtend hinstellen, allen sichtbar, auf die deutsche Produktion energischer wirken als durch eine schwächliche und künstliche Schutzzollpolitik. Wenn der Weizen im Osten kräftiger aufschiesst, so holen wir ihn eben aus Russland; und wenn man danach lernt, ihn auch bei uns besser und reichlicher anzubauen, so haben wir das Endziel unseres Strebens erreicht, und niemand wird froher sein als wir.[35]

Dramatic genius developed earlier in France and in Scandinavia where a freer intellectual atmosphere and a revolutionized theatre

[35] Schr. I, 254.

had facilitated its growth and emergence. Zola, the Goncourts, Björnson, Ibsen, and Strindberg are Brahm's new lodestars for the budding German drama. In these authors and playwrights he sees an international significance. Their emulation can only redound to the advantage of the emulators, in his estimation.

Since Zola's field is primarily the novel and his drama *Thérèse Raquin* merely a dramatization of a novel, Brahm shows the defects of its epic or narrative traits. In spite of Zola's agitation against the effete drawing-room drama of his dramatic compatriots, Brahm shows that he is still under the sway of their technical devices. In comparison with a play like Ibsen's *Rosmersholm*, with which it has many motifs in common, Zola's play is far inferior. The fact that sex (an adultery in this instance) is represented as the *primum mobile* of Zola's dramatic action reveals its essentially French orientation to Brahm. But Brahm does not dwell overlong on these formal defects. He writes enthusiastically:

> Aber doch wieviel unmittelbares Leben, scharf beobachtet und mit bewunderungswürdiger Konsequenz gestaltet tritt uns aus diesem Drama entgegen![36]

Zola's play evokes an entire world of petty, circumscribed existences; its fullness of circumstantial detail provides the proper background for an act that disrupts the sham equanimity of philistine life. Each single action provides a glimpse into the profounder underlying mainsprings of guilt and sin. Zola's genius is summed up for Brahm in his profound knowledge of human nature and in his intrepid laying bare of human motives:

> . . . ein Menschenkenner, dessen Unerschrockenheit so gross ist wie seine künstlerische Anschauung, spricht auf diesem eng begrenzten Boden, in dieser scheinbar so anstössigen ‚Mordgeschichte' echte psychologische Wahrheiten aus.[37]

Brahm detects somewhat of the same technical shortcoming (epic rather than dramatic) in the Goncourts' *Henriette Maréchal* which was presented as the third offering of the *Freie Bühne*. He justifies the choice of this play on the basis of the literary significance of the Goncourts, and also in the hope that its temperate or

---

[36] *Op. cit.*, p. 141.   [37] *Op. cit.*, p. 142.

modified naturalism would mollify the aesthetically and morally indignant. He also defends the play against the superficial criticism that it is no better than countless other plays of Sardou or Dumas which deal with the same theme of adultery: "... *nicht auf das Was des Stoffes, auf das Wie der poetischen Anschauung kommt es an,*"[38] Brahm writes, and goes on to show that the initial motif of adultery very swiftly changes into the subtler and more centripetal motif of a conflict between sexual love and maternal love. It is in the review of this play that Brahm expresses his credo that the stage is the most invaluable means of literary agitation: "*Das unschätzbarste Agitationsmittel in dem Kampf um eine neue Kunst.*"[39] Of this we shall hear more later.

Björnson's *Ein Falissement* was a dramatic commentary on the dangers of speculation in an era of commercial expansion. In Brahm's view it held up the sterner laws of business ethics as an admonition to the unwholesome *Gründertum* of the 70's and 80's, and showed the happy security which a quieter and more honest business practice on a more modest scale can afford. Not by any particular conflict in itself but by portrayal of living individuals does this drama achieve its effect. Björnson still strives for the complete solution of all conflicts at the end of his drama, and we see not only the fall of a dishonest business man but also his rehabilitation. To Brahm this represents a weakening of the dramatic tension:

... was in starken Szenen von dramatischer Spannung begonnen hat, endet so in einem rührsamen Idyll, welches von der platten Behaglichkeit deutscher Familienstücke nicht ganz fern ist.[40]

As we have already seen, Brahm holds up this sort of ending as the antithesis of the one in Anzengruber's *Pfarrer von Kirchfeld*.

G. *Björnson-Strindberg*

A problem which was touched upon in Ibsen's *Ghosts*—the dual standard of male and female morality—provides the central theme of Björnson's *Ein Handschuh*. The play has an interesting history which is reflected in its three different versions. The first and the

[38] *Op. cit.*, p. 275.   [39] *Op. cit.*. p. 274.
[40] *Op. cit.*. p. 212.

second versions are opposites, going from a conciliatory to a de-
fiant and inconclusive ending. Brahm showed the inartistic effects
of this change and attempted a fusion of the two previous versions
for the performance of the *Freie Bühne*. He retained the conclusion
of the first version but was at pains to point out that it is by no
means an expression of callow optimism when the heroine, Svava,
bows to circumstances and accepts the dissipated wooer whom her
father favors. Of this conclusion Brahm writes:

Sie enthält eine bittere Anklage und ein revolutionierendes Element,
und deutlich klingt in uns das Wort der Svava nach: ,So tief muss
man sich also beugen, um für das Leben zu passen!'[41]

The wide difference of opinion with which this play was received
confirmed Brahm's opinion of its vital power. The social import
of the play, its *Tendenz*, and its poetic problems were to him its
most salient qualities. The discussions which it aroused in the
press were gratifying in the extreme to Brahm, who was often more
happy over a grand failure than a moderate success. In Brahm's
opinion, the failure of a play of literary value is more often the
failure of the public and the critics.

The success of Strindberg's *Fräulein Julie* as a presentation of
the *Freie Bühne* inspired Brahm to a few cynical remarks about
the unaccountableness of the audience which had never given any
German naturalist the attention it here accorded to a Swedish
naturalist. Personal pique, however, does not blind him to the
greatness of the play. The importance of its theoretical preface,
which was read to the audience by Paul Schlenther, cannot be
sufficiently emphasized in problems of naturalistic technique.
With the exception of a single performance in Kopenhagen, this
was the first European showing, a tribute to Brahm's divinatory
realization of the play's significance. He justifies certain changes
in its manner of presentation by the *Freie Bühne* on the grounds
of adaptation to a German audience, and shows how these changes
in no way interfere with the spirit of the play.

The nuclear idea in this play to Brahm is the tragedy arising
out of the irreconcilable differences between persons of different
social strata. But this is no antedated Rousseauan conflict:

[41] *Op. cit.*, p. 278.

Nicht die äusseren Konvenienzen erscheinen als das Trennende, nicht Kabale tritt der Liebe entgegen, sondern das Innerste der Menschen trennt sie, Empfinden und sittliche Gewöhnung; und nicht der sozial Steigende, die Gefallene steht als Heldin zuletzt da; sie geht zum Sterben, und grosse Schuld büsst sie gross, er aber steht zitternd im Lakaienrocke da, gehorsam der Glocke des Grafen, eine robuste Knechtsnatur.[42]

Brahm speaks of the philosophical strain that runs through Strindberg's play beyond the actual scenes and characters themselves into the violent struggles of the times, pointing to a new morality and a new insight into social distinctions: the decadent nobility goes down and the more robust servant-class rises. Brahm sees the characters as types depicting the *Degenerierten* (Julie) and the *Aufstrebenden* (Jean); and there is also the indeterminate character of Christine, who represents the oblivious philistine type that remains static in the face of all social change, and dies as unobtrusively as it has lived.

H. *The Ibsen Campaign*

Before going on to the theories of naturalism in the drama as expounded in Brahm's criticism, there remain the two dramatists, Ibsen and Hauptmann, to discuss. As has already been indicated, to Brahm these two represented the highest point of perfection in the new dramatic art. Ibsen was the great master of form, the perfecter of an analytic drama reminiscent of the Greek tradition, the fearless iconoclast, the social critic and reformer. Hauptmann is considered at first as Ibsen's disciple but displays independent traits pointing to a strong individual genius. We know already about Brahm's pioneer work on Ibsen, the first in Germany to treat adequately of Ibsen as a man and as a dramatist.[43] We have pointed out the limited scope of Brahm's interest in Ibsen as confined mainly to his contemporary social plays in the realistic manner. We shall now see how Brahm regards Ibsen through the medium of critical reviews of the performances of his plays. Starting from the pioneering articles which prepare the ground for Ibsen audiences, actors, and directors, we shall see Brahm himself

[42] *Op. cit.*, p. 404.
[43] Cf. William Henri Eller's *Ibsen in Germany*, Boston, 1918, p. 50 et passim.

achieve what he has been agitating for as a proselyter in Ibsen's cause. The limited number of Ibsen's plays as first performed in Germany is gradually rounded out until we have model performances of entire cycles of these plays. There arises an Ibsen cult and an Ibsen tradition which affects all phases of the drama, the theatre, and the dramatic arts in general. This apotheosis of Ibsen was to a great extent Brahm's work. He it was who more than most German critics of the time carried on incessant journalistic and literary agitation to educate audiences, critics, actors, managers, and playwrights; and the practical examples of his personally directed Ibsen performances of the *Freie Bühne*, the *Deutsches Theater*, and the *Lessingtheater*, provided, as he says, a more powerful and widespread agitation than any amount of literary discussion possibly could. In this way he matured the Berlin theatre-going public to the point of being *ibsenreif*, to use his favorite term.

Brahm's Ibsen campaign begins in 1884 in the pages of the *Vossische Zeitung;* in other words, at the very beginning of his journalistic career. He has read *Ghosts*, and the realization of its dramatic power and moral fearlessness has overcome him with the possibilities it presents for a literary awakening in Germany. He asserts that the full dramatic impact of this drama can only be felt in a performance, for it is anything but a book-drama. He challenges the newly founded *Deutsches Theater* to present this play, and even goes so far as to suggest a possible cast for the various roles.[44]

Brahm continues his discussion of *Ghosts* shortly thereafter in the *Frankfurter Zeitung* and limns the play against the broader background of the country in which it was written and of the literary-social movements which accompanied its birth. He speaks with envy—as a German—of the unified literary movement with its full consciousness of aim in the Scandinavian countries: an aim pursued with adamantine fearlessness and directed toward the liberation of the spirit from the darkness of tradition. Ibsen, Björnson, and Brandes are the leaders of "young Scandinavia" in its fight against the medieval oppressiveness that clouded the

[44] Schr. I, 73f.

spirit in these ecclesiastically ruled countries. Little Denmark, which had remained bogged in the reactionism following the Wars of Liberation, had long been isolated from the main stream of European culture. Brandes was the critical force who had reëstablished contact with a freer Europe and thus ushered in a more enlightened epoch for Scandinavia. Social satire, the modern *Tendenzdrama*, and a leaning towards naturalism characterized this movement.

The most outstanding trait in the Scandinavian renascence as Brahm sees it is its proclivity for subordinating *Poesie* or *Form* to *Tendenz*.[45] Bound up obsessively in their earnestness for social reform in all its immediate phases, these young Scandinavians used literature merely as a means to an end. The fact that in Brahm's eyes this was heresy and irreverence towards the idealistic muse of the liberal Goethean tradition in which he had been nurtured, is readily understandable. To the aloof, disinterested muse of German classicism, poetry, in its more sublime phase, is an end in itself. Form, the eternal perspective, emphasis on the universally human were all fused in the conception of "pure" poetry. To permit burning questions of the day to invade this rarefied Elysium too abruptly would be tantamount to contamination. Such is the intellectual origin of that irreconcilable dualism between form and content—or expressed in other categories—the dualism between poetry and propaganda which is an essential component of Brahm's make-up. We shall discuss this problem more fully in connection with Brahm's critical method. Of the problem of *Tendenz* in connection with the literature of Scandinavia he writes:

Tendenz—das ist das entscheidendste Merkmal dieser Bewegung. Tendenz im guten und im üblen Sinne, Tendenz, die künstlerisch verwirklicht ist zu Gestalten und Situationen, und Tendenz, die neben dem Kunstwork herläuft und trotz allem Bellen doch nicht in das Gefährt aufgenommen werden kann. Für diesen tief greifenden Unterschied hat der Kritiker der Schule, Brandes, nicht immer den Sinn; ihm ist der geistige Gehalt so wichtig, dass er darüber die Form geringer achtet; und er und seine Jünger fühlen sich so sehr als Kämpfer für die Sache der Freiheit, dass ihnen die Poesie oft nur Mittel zum Zweck, nicht Selbstzweck ist.[46]

[45] *Op. cit.*, p. 75.   [46] *Ibid.*

Brahm does not uphold the same position expressed in the above lines throughout his career. We shall read similar statements of his, but couched in a modified vein, at the end of his critical life. At this early stage, his approach to the problem is simplistic, because it emphasizes a dualism which he later finds irrelevant, as we shall see in our subsequent discussion of this subject. However, one of his legitimate objections to a bald *Tendenzdichtung* from the perspective of the permanency of great art, is stated thus:

Es ist das natürliche Los solcher Dichtungen, dass ihre Dauer die kürzeste ist: denn wenn nun diese Fragen einmal gelöst sind, wer wird jene Werke noch lesen wollen? Sie bleiben zurück, wie der Sandsack, wenn die Festung erstürmt ist: mit geplatzten Nähten.[47]

It is in the spirit of the above dualism between *Tendenz* and *Poesie* that Brahm first views Ibsen's *Ghosts*. The primary aim of the young Scandinavians in their drama was to instigate discussion on various pressing social, intellectual, and moral problems. And it is as the embodiment of the problem of heredity and social hypocrisy that Brahm visualizes *Ghosts;* to be sure, a problem presented with much greater subtlety and mastery of artistic technique than the ordinary, run-of-the-mill *Tendenzdrama.* Brahm gives a detailed technical analysis of the play, discusses the problem of Ibsen's pessimism as over against his activism, of society against the individual, and speculates concerning the symbolic implications of the play.

We must bear in mind the fact that so far Brahm is merely laying the first interpretative foundations for the reception of Ibsen's *Ghosts*. He concludes with a challenge: *"Wird kein deutsches Theater den Mut finden, es auf die Szene zu stellen?"*[48] Three years later, he triumphantly recalls this challenge when reviewing a private performance of *Ghosts*, the first in Berlin.[49] The play in printed form had already sold 5,000 copies, an astonishing phenomenon when we consider that, exclusive of a narrow literary circle, playgoers as a rule do not buy plays but go to see them. The reactions of the audience prompted Brahm to a great many reflections on audience psychology. The play was a success and

[47] *Ibid.*   [48] *Op. cit.*, p. 81.
[49] In the Residenztheater, 9. Jan. 1887.

Ibsen was called out from back-stage to receive personally the plaudits of the enthusiastic audience. But afterwards, when the effects of the excitement had worn off, there were adverse comments. "How revolting!" was the general remark that Brahm heard from the lips of the departing audience. Brahm is indignant at this sort of extraneous, and to him irrelevant, criticism.

> Der Inhalt des Schauspiels allein, nicht seine Form ist es, was hier die Entscheidung bestimmte; aber kann man es wirklich künstlerisch urteilen heissen, wenn nur das Thema einer Dichtung, nicht ihre poetische Behandlung den Massstab hergibt?[50]

The fallacious principle underlying this sort of criticism impels Brahm to an expression of his *"ästhetisches Glaubensbekenntnis"* of which we shall hear more in connection with the problem of naturalism. Meanwhile, Brahm bewails the limits of his journalistic medium in doing justice to a masterpiece that reveals new and astonishing facets to him at every repeated reading:*". . . denn dies Werk, als ein echtes Kunstwerk, ist unerschöpflich wie das Leben, wie die Welt."*[51]

It is almost three years later, at the opening of the *Freie Bühne*, that *Ghosts* comes to Berlin again as the first offering of the newly founded theatrical society. Significantly enough, Brahm is at the head of this society. The presentation of *Ghosts* was an additional testimony to the exemplary influence of Ibsen in the new German drama. The play is still under the ban of censorship in Berlin, and its choice is a foregone conclusion in view of the aim of the *Freie Bühne* to present plays inaccessible to the established theatre for reasons of censorship or audience prejudice. Brahm scarifies the stupid arbitrariness of a local censorship that is incomprehensible even to the critical opponents of Ibsen's *Ghosts*. In Frankfort-am-Main, in Danzig, and in Königsberg the play has been given public performances, but in Berlin it has been banned. The proscription of the play is viewed as an affront to civic liberty: *". . . vor dem Gesetz sind alle Staatsbürger gleich, aber vor der Zensur, scheint es, nicht."*[52] He appeals to some liberal and artistically minded representative in the Prussian *Landtag* to champion the cause of literary freedom.

[50] Schr. I, 106.   [51] *Op. cit.*, p. 109.
[52] *Op. cit.*, p. 253.

With the performance by the *Freie Bühne*, the artistic battle
for the acceptance of Ibsen's *Ghosts* has been won. Ibsen is an
established dramatist in Germany, and there are only the police
authorities who remain to be convinced of the fact. Of this performance of *Ghosts* Brahm writes many years later:

Die Wirkung der ‚Gespenster' war tief und stark wiederum, jedoch
einheitlicher als das erste mal; niemand verkannte mehr die über-
ragende Grösse des Werkes.[53]

We have traced Brahm's championship of Ibsen and his final
triumph as typically exemplified in the destinies of *Ghosts*. Brahm
reviews the Berlin *premières* of practically all the other plays of
Ibsen: *Der Volksfeind, Rosmersholm, Die Wildente, Ein Puppenheim, Die Frau vom Meere, Stützen der Gesellschaft, Hedda Gabler*,
and others. In addition, he was responsible as a director for the
production of all of Ibsen's plays, from the first dramas in verse
down to the last play, *Wenn Wir Toten Erwachen*.[54]

Ibsen's *Volksfeind*, in addition to its mastery of individual
characterization in the person of the truth-obsessed Dr. Stockmann, offers Brahm an opportunity to refute once more the narrow nationalism of certain critics—*die Superklugen*, he calls them
—whose factual reasons for opposing Ibsen are so slight that they
must needs go out of their way to stress the foreign character of
Ibsen's work. Brahm has nothing but scorn for these carping
critics:

... dieselben Leute, welche die Vorherrschaft der Franzosen auf
unserer Bühne so lange geduldet haben, verweigern nun, in plötzlich
aufwallender patriotischer Entrüstung, dem norwegischen Dichter
die Gastfreundschaft der deutschen Bühne.[55]

To Brahm, on the contrary, nothing could be more Teutonic in
spirit and more wholly in harmony with the great masterpieces of
German literature and drama than Ibsen's works. He sees in
Ibsen's *Volksfeind*, the obstinate, self-willed individual who,
dauntlessly confident of his own power and the righteousness of
the cause he is championing, braves the opposition of an entire

---

[53] *Op. cit.*, p. 454.
[54] Cf. Herbert Henze's dissertation: *Otto Brahm und das "Deutsche Theater" in Berlin*, Berl. 1930.
[55] Schr. I, 127.

world. Brahm sees in Dr. Stockmann a spiritual prototype of Kleist's *Michael Kohlhaas* and Otto Ludwig's *Erbförster*. The *Enemy of the People* represents the tragedy of an inexorable self-will in the same German tradition as Goethe's *Götz* and Schiller's *Karl Moor*. In the same tradition Brahm views the other relentless Ibsenian individualists: Rebecca West, Nora, Gregers Werle, and Hedda Gabler—women of daemonic will reminiscent of a Lady Macbeth or of Goethe's Adelheid, and men of passionate, indomitable idealism.

We can best estimate Brahm's appreciation of Ibsen by recalling the constant parallels which he draws between Ibsen's dramas and the traditions of Greek classical tragedy. *Ghosts* was to Brahm an analytic drama in which past occurences are revealed, but translated into a present dramatic action. It follows the unities of time, place, and action. The events are concentrated and the dialogue involves a limited number of persons. Heredity and the suffocating onus of social hypocrisy represent the relentless *Nemesis* or dark *Moira* of fate from which there is no escape.[56]

In the same way Brahm recalls Hegel's tragic category of antagonistic yet equally righteous and equally justified characters in Greek tragedy, and draws a parallel between this type of Greek tragedy and Ibsen's *Volksfeind:*

> Hegel und die Ästhetiker aus seiner Schule haben viel von einer Tragödie der gleichen Berechtigungen gesprochen und als ein Musterbeispiel dafür Antigone und Kreon angesehen, in denen freier Herzensdrang und Staatsräson einander gegenüberstehen, zwei grosse, bestimmende Lebensmächte; der nämliche typische Gegensatz, in ganz modernen Daseinsformen, prägt sich in dem Badearzt und dem Bürgermeister des ‚Volksfeindes‘ aus; zwar die Sympathie des Dichters gehört jenem, nicht diesem, so gut wie die Sympathie des griechischen Tragikers der Antigone, nicht dem Kreon zufiel.[57]

In conclusion, Brahm's own historical summarization of the influence of Ibsen upon himself, his contemporaries, and upon the German drama and stage may be paraphrased from his two commemorative essays: *Henrik Ibsen in Berlin*[58] and *Gedenkrede auf*

---

[56] Cf. also the characterization of Nora as "eine moderne Antigone," Schr. I, 229.
[57] Schr. I, 128.
[58] *Op. cit.*, p. 447.

Henrik Ibsen,[59] written retrospectively in 1904 and 1906. In order to estimate the tremendous effect that Ibsen had on the younger Germans, it is necessary, Brahm writes, to realize the deplorable level to which German dramatic production had sunk in the 1870's. It was shortly after the Franco-Prussian War, the time of the founding of the German Empire, and the expansion of commercial activity. In the rapidly growing metropolis of Berlin, the comfortable and flabby enjoyment of newly acquired material prosperity was reflected on the German stage. The lighter form of the operetta flourished in the *Friedrich-Wilhelmstadt Theater* which was later to become the *Deutsches Theater*. The *Wallnertheater* was then celebrating the successes of Moser's vapid farces. Dumas and Sardou ruled the repertoire of the *Residenztheater*. And even in the quasi-official *Königliches Schauspielhaus* the abiding deities were nothing more than local imitators of the French whose theatrical concoctions portrayed an artificial German drawing-room atmosphere that never existed in reality. The theatre was merely a purveyor of meretricious pleasure, a postprandial interlude for complacently-tired, upper middle-class audiences.

This torpid, hothouse atmosphere in the theatre had not the slightest inkling of the vital currents that flowed from the Russians, the French and the Scandinavians:

. . . die deutsche Bühne blieb ausserhalb all dieser Entwicklungen, ein seichtes Wässerlein, ein stiller Karpfenteich, in den der nordische Hecht die ersten Erregungen bringen sollte.[60]

Then came the *Pillars of Society* and *A Doll's House*[61] to enthuse young critics like Brahm and Schlenther; but the time for Ibsen's reception was not yet ripe:

Die Darsteller fielen durch, das Publikum fiel durch . . . auch die Berliner Kritik fiel durch vor Ibsen,[62]

and Georg Brandes assured Brahm as they left the performance of *Nora* that Ibsen would never be understood in Germany. But Brahm, in all his youthful confidence, was of a different mind. Karl Frenzel, Paul Lindau, Oscar Blumenthal—at that time the

---

[59] *Op. cit.*, p. 456.   [60] *Op. cit.*, p. 449.
[61] First Berlin performances, 1878 and 1880 respectively.
[62] Schr. I, 449.

critical arbiters of the theatre in Berlin—miserably failed to realize Ibsen's significance. When *Ghosts* was printed in its German translation, Brahm's attention, strangely enough, was first called to it by Heyse who—as we have already mentioned—spoke to Brahm in accents of horror of the "*Spitalpoesie dieser Gespenster.*"[63] The destinies of *Ghosts* on the Berlin stage we have already followed out in detail.

Ibsen's newly published works, *Ein Volksfeind* and *Wildente*, remained unstaged and Brahm turned to the written word in order to advance their cause. He became personally acquainted with Ibsen in Rome in 1885, and his resulting essay, *Henrik Ibsen*, first appeared in the *Deutsche Rundschau*, and subsequently was issued in separate format in 1887.[64] Meanwhile *Ghosts* was given during the season of 1886–87 in Augsburg, in Meiningen, and in Berlin. Brahm's review of this latter performance has already been discussed. It will be recalled that it was at this occasion that Brahm himself introduced Ibsen in person to receive the plaudits of the audience. Of this stirring personal triumph of his idol Brahm writes:

> Wir hatten das Gefühl: jetzt ist gewonnen. Jetzt sind die Dämme durchbrochen, die Konventionen und Vorurteile vor diesem Riesen aufgetan hatten; und die Hörerschaft, der sich die Gewalt des Poeten so überstark wie hier offenbart hat, wird hinausgehen in die Zeit und seiner Macht Apostel sein.[65]

In rapid succession thereafter Ibsen's plays stormed the Berlin theatre. Even the *Hoftheater* succumbed to *Die Frau vom Meere*, but the episode remained unique and isolated. Just as Frederick the Great had once shown umbrage at *Götz*, which now, ironically enough, was one of the chief mainstays in the repertoire of the Royal Theatre, so William the First, Brahm tells us, turned his favor away from the author of *Ghosts:*

> . . . man weiss, wie fremd, wie abgekehrt unser regierender Herr vor allem neuen Lebendigen in Kunst und Poesie dasteht.[66]

The Janus-headed critics could not longer ignore Ibsen's influence but nevertheless ascribed it to the masterful performance of the

---

[63] *Op. cit.*, p. 450.

[65] Schr. I, 452.

[64] *Henrik Ibsen: Ein Essay*, Berl. 1887.

[66] *Op. cit.*, p. 453.

German actors. The fact that it was Ibsen who had advanced the art of the actors and not vice versa had not yet dawned upon them, to Brahm's great indignation. Nevertheless, the feeling became general that Ibsen had opened the portals of a new art, and that it was necessary to bring together those who had profited by his example. Out of this realization grew the *Freie Bühne* and the introduction of Tolstoi, Hauptmann, Holz and Schlaf, Strindberg, Hartleben, and others to the German public. Ibsen is thus viewed by Brahm as the father of the modern German drama.

In his *Gedenkrede auf Henrik Ibsen* Brahm thus epitomizes Ibsen's influence upon the German theatre and dramatic art:

Sie (Ibsen's plays) haben ganz einfach die Bühne revolutioniert und aus dem Theater wieder das gemacht, was unsere Klassiker begonnen hatten, aus ihm zu machen: keinen Ort der blossen Unterhaltung, sondern einen Kulturfaktor, eine ungeheuere Macht über die Seelen, eine weithin tragende Leuchte geistiger und künstlerischer Vorgänge.[67]

I. *Hauptmann*

It is clear from Brahm's espousal of Ibsen's cause that the larger purpose of providing a model and an inspiration for the younger German dramatists was constantly in his mind. The social criticism and the dramatic technique of Ibsen provided the ferment out of which was to issue a revolutionized German drama. Hauptmann, consequently, appears on the scene as the first considerable fruit of Ibsen's inspiration, a concrete fulfilment of Brahm's prediction that, given wholesome models congenial to the German spirit and a free medium of theatrical expression, the German drama was bound to reassert itself.

We have already indicated in the section dealing with Brahm's relations with Fontane, how Brahm accepted *Vor Sonnenaufgang* for presentation by the *Freie Bühne* and had already sent an enthusiastic article on the play to the printers when he received the letter written on Hauptmann's behalf by Fontane. The readiness with which Brahm accepted the play was not only due to his realization of its dramatic power but also to the crying need for a

---

[67] *Op. cit.*, p. 459; cf. also Brahm's extended essay on *Ibsenforschung*, *N. Rdsch.*, 1906; Schr. II, 372.

German dramatist. Speaking of the predominance of foreign dramatists on the tentative roster of the *Freie Bühne*, Brahm sadly admits that, compared with the foreign drama, the modern German drama does not yet exist:

> Brauche ich im Ernst zu sagen, mit wie gutem Grunde eine Bühne, die der ‚stockenden Entwicklung des deutschen Dramas frische Impulse‘ zuführen will, die für eine neue Kunst eintritt und dem Alten und Abgelebten, der Schablone und Konvention Krieg ansagt— dass sie ohne den Beistand des Auslandes noch nicht leben kann? Dass sie nur das tatsächlich bestehende Verhältnis in Ziffern kennzeichnet, wenn sie dem deutschen Drama die kleinere Hälfte ihres Spielplans einräumt?[68]

An encouraging symptom of new life had already made its appearance under a Scandinavian pseudonym: *Papa Hamlet* by Bjarne P. Holmsen (Holz and Schlaf). This volume of three dramatic sketches, from the first of which comes its title, betrayed its German authorship by its accurate portrayal of German locales and customs. Brahm realized this immediately.[69] Instead of decrying *Papa Hamlet* for its pseudo-nordic pretensions, Brahm welcomes it all the more because it has been written by a German. Among the giant figures of Scandinavian literature Bjarne P. Holmsen would be dwarfed, writes Brahm; it is as a German that his poetic efforts really assume significance. Brahm contrasts the author of *Papa Hamlet* with the critics who have been crying out for a literary protectionism which would erect customs barriers against intellectual goods in order to coddle along German production. Brahm points out that Bjarne P. Holmsen also fights against foreign importations but by the vastly more effective way of creating a competitive home product. Brahm is a free-trader in spiritual goods and believes in free competition on the open world market of the intellect:

> Schutz der nationalen Arbeit! forderten die einen, literarischen Protektionismus, welcher Zollschranken aufrichtet, auch vor der geistigen Ware, die anderen; die Produktiven aber wagten es mit einer dichterischen Verkleidung.[70]

In the *Nation* of September 14, 1889, Brahm tells of a play he

[68] Schr. I, 254.   [69] *Ibid.*
[70] Schr. I, 263.

has received dedicated by the author to Bjarne P. Holmsen. It was
Gerhart Hauptmann's first play, *Vor Sonnenaufgang*. Immediately
Brahm senses the remarkable talent of the author. He does not
grope for words nor pause overlong to deliberate. His recognition
is immediate and unreserved:

Gerhart Hauptmann erscheint mir als eines der merkwürdigsten
Talente, das ich in den letzten Jahren kennen gelernt habe . . . [71]

Brahm concedes the fact that in the prevailing impoverishment of
the German drama it is not extraordinary for him to find someone
worthy of note among the younger German dramatists. Dramatic
production has been so meagre and the younger writers so full of
pretension and so deficient in performance that among these blind,
groping talents one who possessed the sight of even one eye might
be called upon to lead them. Nevertheless Hauptmann's intrinsic
genius is undeniable:

Doch was uns in Gerhart Hauptmann, einem bisher unbekannten,
aber in kürzerer oder längerer Frist vermutlich allgemein bekannten
Autor, entgegentritt, ist mehr als ein nur relatives Talent: es ist
Eigenart, klare dramatische Anschauung, ist neue Kunst, die nicht
auf Nachahmung der grossen Muster nur beruht, sondern sicher und
selbstgewiss ihre eigenen Wege geht, jugendlich irrend und über-
treibend vielleicht, aber stetig und tapfer in jedem Schritt.[72]

Brahm quotes the well-known passage from *Vor Sonnenaufgang*
in which Loth, speaking to Helene of Zola and Ibsen, says that
they are not poets but necessary evils who supply nothing positive
to the healthy imagination. To Loth these authors have a therapeutic value for those diseased in spirit. (*"Was Zola und Ibsen
bieten, ist Medizin"*).[73] Although warning his readers against the
superficial tendency to identify this opinion of one of Hauptmann's
characters with the opinions of Hauptmann himself, Brahm nevertheless points out the influence these authors have had on the play.
This influence in no way detracts from the independent genius of
Hauptmann but its trace is unmistakable. According to Brahm,
Hauptmann derived from Ibsen his naturalness of dialogue and
characterization, his richness of typifying detail, and his absten-

---

[71] *Op. cit.*, p. 255.   [72] *Op. cit.*, p. 256.
[73] In Act II. Gerhart Hauptmann, *Ausgewählte Werke*, 6 Bde. Berl. 1925; Bd. I, p. 48.

tion from superficial action or theatrical melodrama. From Zola, Hauptmann had his theme of heredity and the inexorably real portrayal of peasant life as an antidote to the idyllic bathos of the traditional German *Bauernnovelle.* Between the idealism of Loth and the cynicism of Dr. Schimmelpfennig Brahm detects a resemblance to the contrast between Ibsen's Dr. Relling and Gregers Werle.[74] Brahm is also struck by the dramatic contrast of coarse humor and relentless tragedy in Hauptmann's play. In his enthusiastic reaction to a first reading Brahm cannot sufficiently emphasize his admiration for this young and promising dramatist and is at pains to point out his originality in spite of the still visible traces of his literary antecedents:

> . . . eine so originelle Begabung, wie sie uns hier überraschand entgegengetreten ist, mag ihren Weg unbeirrt weiter schreiten, von niemandem beraten als von dem eigenen Talent.[75]

After the stormy performance of *Vor Sonnenaufgang* by the *Freie Bühne,* reviewed by Brahm in the *Nation,*[76] he champions Hauptmann with renewed zeal. This is Brahm's last review for the *Nation,* the editors of which felt impelled to append an editorial note disclaiming responsibility for the views expressed in Brahm's article.[77] In this review Brahm describes the exciting events accompanying the performance. Part of the audience expressed its reactions towards certain naturalistic excesses by shouting, applauding, hissing, and by the use of various noise-making devices. The love scene in the fourth act, however, evoked applause even from those who had come to mock. Before the performance, several of the actors had received threatening notes from anonymous senders, and during the performance the opposition used every possible means of disconcerting the players. In

---

[74] Schr. I, 257.   [75] *Op. cit.,* p. 259.
[76] 26. 10. 1899, Schr. I, 255ff.
[77] "Die Redaktion der 'Nation' bringt die Ausführungen des Herrn Dr. Brahm gern zum Ausdruck, ohne sie im vorliegenden Falle völlig zu teilen. Sie begrüsst die lebhafte Bewegung, die sich im Anschluss an die Aufführung des Hauptmannschen Dramas entwickelt hat, und wünscht dem Naturalismus jede Möglichkeit zu schaffen, seine Lebensfähigkeit vor aller Welt zu erweisen. Indem die 'Nation' dem Naturalismus gerecht zu werden sucht, gehört sie damit aber nicht zugleich zu den Parteigängern des Naturalismus. Man kann etwas als Gegengift für nützlich halten, ohne es als Nahrung zu empfehlen." *Nation,* 26. 10. 1889; Schr. I, p. 262f.

spite of all this, however, this second "Hernani triumph" went on
to a successful conclusion. Brahm is proud of the mission which
the *Freie Bühne* has fulfilled in presenting this play. This performance has aroused literary discussion, stimulated the exchange
of ideas in regard to art and the theatre, and has brought vital
conflict and animation to replace the stagnation into which letters
and the theatre had settled.[78]

The aftermath of critical indignation by the apologists of the
older tradition offers Brahm an opportunity to expose the pusillanimity of the objections which have been raised against Hauptmann's play. He considers a detailed account of the raucous and
ill-mannered strictures echoing from this critical "witches' sab-
bath," as he calls it, beneath contempt. The general undertone of
all these adverse criticisms resolves itself into a mere *argumentum
ad hominem*, according to Brahm. The epithets hurled at the
agitator, Loth, assumed this character and Hauptmann himself
to be one and the same individual. Brahm admits the weakness of
this particular character; he is a doctrinaire idealist whose stiff-
necked principles and belief in certain theories of heredity impel
him to the inhuman desertion of Helene. But no sound criticism
can rest upon a mechanical identification of Hauptmann with one
of his characters. In berating this widespread critical fallacy
Brahm also uncovers a profound analogy between this fallacy and
the subjective temper of classical idealism as over against the
objectivity of realistic art. The modern poet, whether he be Ibsen,
Tolstoi, or Hauptmann, creates no such heroes as did his predecessors, says Brahm:

Posa mag Schillers Held und idealisiertes Abbild sein, aber Loth
ist eine Gestalt mit vielen individuellen Zügen, kein Ideal und kein
Träger einer subjektiven dichterischen Tendenz.[79]

The characters of Loth and Helene are not purveyors of ideas but
distinctly independent individuals who act and live in their own
right. They are not mere figureheads for whose utterances the
author himself is personally responsible. Their ideas and actions
spring from the inner logic of their existence within the matrix
of the play itself.

[78] Schr. I, 259f.   [79] *Op. cit.*, p. 261.

In these first two essays on *Vor Sonnenaufgang* Brahm unequivocally shows his confidence in the future development of
Hauptmann's genius. Hauptmann is the living embodiment of all
that Brahm has been striving for, a German dramatist following
in the footsteps of Zola and Ibsen, and yet developing in an independent direction. Hauptmann is the first considerable justification for all of Brahm's agitation for the reform of the German
theatre. In this moment of his triumph Brahm cannot deprive
himself of the satisfaction of gloating at the discomfiture of those
critical detractors against whom he has been waging unremitting
battle:

> Aber es scheint mir nicht die Aufgabe einer lebensvollen Kritik,
> die natürlichen Mängel eines Erstlingswerkes, seine jugendlichen
> Auswüchse und Unreifheiten mit breiter Selbstbehaglichkeit zu
> zergliedern und seine eminenten Vorzüge leicht beiseite zu schieben.
> Bei mir wenigstens überwiegt, wie nach der ersten Lektüre so auch
> nach der ersten Aufführung, die helle Freude über dieses grosse, über
> Nacht uns entstandene Talent alle Bedenklichkeiten; und ich ver-
> traue: der Weg einer so mächtig und voll einsetzenden Begabung
> werde zu den höchsten Höhen der Kunst emporleiten. Und dass der
> Widerspruch der Kunstphilister den Dichter nicht um einen Schritt
> von seinem Pfade abführen wird, dessen bin ich gewiss; diese Herren
> haben stets nur für das Ewiggestrige den Sinn gehabt, nicht für das
> Werdende, und so mögen sie am Gesindetisch der Kritik denn sitzen
> bleiben, jetzt und immer.[80]

We have seen how a new theatrical structure was essential to
the development of the modern German drama. This reform however, could not remain isolated within the organization of the
theatre itself. Broader avenues of contact with the public had to
be opened up in order that the message of the theatre might be
transmitted beyond the comparatively limited range of a select
audience. Just as the existing forms of the commercial theatre
callously stifled the cries of an infant drama, so did the existing
forms of the commercial and conservative literary press prevent
it from maturing into articulation. The editorial disclaimer of
Brahm's article on *Vor Sonnenaufgang* concretely showed the
necessity for an independent periodical in harmony with the

[80] *Op. cit.*, p. 262.

aspirations of the *Freie Bühne*. The founding of the periodical *Freie Bühne für modernes Leben*,[81] with Brahm as editor, was the solution to this dilemma. Whatever other literary purposes this periodical served—and we shall discuss them presently—one thing was certain: to Brahm it meant an unrestrained freedom of expression in regard to his pet enthusiasm. From this point on we have extended analytic essays on Hauptmann's early plays as they appeared in book form and on the stage. Brahm's essays deal not only with the literary and aesthetic elements of Hauptmann's plays but also with the technical stage problems which they embody, for Brahm is now functioning in his dual capacity of stage director and literary editor.

After the tumultuous appearance of *Vor Sonnenaufgang*, speculation was rife concerning the future development of its author. Brahm tells us that this question formed the substance of his conversations with Hauptmann after he had made the young author's acquaintance.[82] Did Hauptmann intend to remain within the locale of his first play? Was he to become the Anzengruber of Silesia? Would the local-color element prevail or would the social element assume the ascendency? Brahm cites the parallel of Schiller's development to forestall any hasty prognostications. If a contemporary critic of Schiller had ventured to predict the future course of the dramatist on the strength of *Fiesco*, how could he have possibly foreseen *Kabale und Liebe*? The evolution of literary genius does not proceed along hard and set lines; there is an imponderable fluctuation that must be taken into account. These considerations are not prompted by Brahm's desire to forestall any criticism of Hauptmann's second play. Brahm, in his critical integrity, however, finds it necessary to emphasize the uncertainty of premature acclaim or condemnation.

The complete change of locale and the shift to the psychological motif in *Das Friedensfest* is to Brahm further proof of the individual trend of Hauptmann's genius and his imperviousness to external criticism.[83] There follows one of those enlightening comparisons and contrasts between Ibsen and Hauptmann that serve

[81] 29. 1. 1890 is the date of the first issue. It is now known as the *Neue Rundschau*.
[82] Schr. I, 294. [83] *Op. cit.*, p. 295.

Brahm so aptly, here as elsewhere, in characterizing Hauptmann's originality. As we have seen, Ibsen is Brahm's frame of reference for the interpretation of other dramatists. Like *Ghosts*, *Das Friedensfest* is a drama of family conflict. But Hauptmann portrays in the present what Ibsen had relegated to the past. Hauptmann actually shows us the marriage about which Ibsen merely speaks. So much for technique of exposition. Brahm also sees an intellectual kinship between the two dramas, not a purely external imitation on the part of Hauptmann but an inner correspondence of ideas which lead them from similar philosophical premises to related conclusions. What Brahm refers to here is the doctrine of heredity as involving the destruction of free will, a theme which is poetically incorporated in both dramas. Brahm evades the charge of a spineless fatalism which this view implies by referring cavillers to the scientists and philosophers who have promulgated it rather than to the poets who reflect it in their works. In his opinion the only aim of the artist is to reflect faithfully the views of modern philosophy. This, of course, is begging the question, and we shall see later how this justification *in petitio principii* was the gnawing canker at the heart of naturalist doctrine. We can also understand how such an evasion of moral and social decisiveness, such so-called naturalist "objectivity" toward the problems of existence, which made the artist a passive mirror of life, accounts in part for Hauptmann's shifting attitudes in the face of shifting temporal realities.

That a portrayal of reality at that particular moment in the history of German letters was wholesome and to some extent even revolutionary is not to be denied. And it is in this very respect that Brahm sees the significance of *Das Friedensfest*. He dwells with admiration on its realistic detail, its natural characterization, its lack of declamatory and lyrical balderdash, and at the same time its observance of the technical demands of the stage.[84] To those accustomed to the traditional book-drama Brahm shows that the superabundance of stage directions and the diacritical interpolations, which perhaps interfere at first with the reading of the dialogue, are nonetheless designed to supplant the plastic atmosphere of the stage and thus permit the reader actually to see the

[84] *Op. cit.*, p. 299.

characters as they react and move about in their environment, as well as to hear their spoken words.[85]

So far these remarks of Brahm are based on his reading of the play. His final summation expresses a dissatisfaction with the finite limits of mere criticism when faced with living works. "Works which are like life itself, how can one grasp their infinite meaning by means of words?" he writes.[86] He is unable as yet to see Hauptmann clearly in all his literary stature, at least not enough to satisfy his own curiosity, and impatiently awaits his next work.

In the space of a year and a half after the *Freie Bühne* had provided an outlet for Hauptmann's first two works the established commercial theatres were already clamoring for his plays. *Einsame Menschen* was given on the 21st of March, 1891, at the *Deutsches Theater*, the most considerable of the German theatres from the point of view of artistic pretensions. The occasion unloosens a series of *tempora mutantur* lucubrations from Brahm's pen. He refers caustically to the recently converted opponents of Hauptmann who approve of the "sublimated naturalism" ("*den gereinigten Naturalismus*") of *Einsame Menschen* so shortly after they had been outraged by the naturalistic "excesses" of *Vor Sonnenaufgang*.[87] It is an example of the same confused identification of content with form, or rather, the substitution of form by content. The critics who had objected to Hauptmann's naturalism in *Vor Sonnenaufgang* were swayed by the subject matter of the play and not by its artistic treatment. But now that the subject matter is more palatable, from their point of view, they discover that they really have no quarrel with naturalism *per se*.[88] In *Einsame Menschen*, however, Brahm sees no concession on the part of Hauptmann to his critics. There is only a free adaptation of the original naturalistic form to a new content. The technique and the form remain essentially the same. Consequently, as a work of art, this play is to be rated on an equal basis with the preceding ones. Brahm always regards naturalism as a form of artistic expression rather than the choice of an agreeable or disagreeable subject matter.[89]

At this point Brahm sums up Hauptmann's significance as being

---

[85] *Ibid.*
[86] Schr. I, p. 310.
[87] *Op. cit.*, p. 350.
[88] *Ibid.*
[89] *Ibid.*

revolutionary because of his real portrayal of life unhampered by literary and theatrical convention. This element is to Brahm the epitome of all that is valuable and new in Hauptmann and all that sets him apart from the other dramatists of his time. Hauptmann has rescued the German drama once and for all time from the *Epigonentum* of the classical period. Brahm sees in Hauptmann the continuator of Kleist, Hebbel, and Ludwig in the refashioning of the Germanic drama of character.[90]

There follows another of the unfailing comparisons and contrasts, with Ibsen as the measure of all values. Brahm disclaims any quantitative or categorical motive in comparing Hauptmann with Ibsen. He is not concerned with the question as to which of the two is the "better" dramatist, or with the problem of fitting each into some ordinal category. On the contrary, such comparisons are largely impossible owing to the discrepancy between the two dramatists in point of age, origin, career, etc. Ibsen has been closely identified with the theatre from the very beginning of his career, and in his plays there is a perceptible accommodation to what is theatrically appropriate. Hauptmann, on the other hand, is close to the soil, and comes from the realm of the plastic arts. He is a keen observer of nature and creates dramatic atmosphere and *milieu* as well as characters; whereas Ibsen's characters often seem to move about in a vacuum.[91] Brahm speaks of Hauptmann's "impressionism" in the scenes evocative of nature: the dawn in *Vor Sonnenaufgang*, the awakening of nature, the *Müggelsee*, and the susurrant wasps. Certain critics had questioned whether this sort of mood and nature painting was really dramatic, whether it did not really belong in a novel rather than in a drama.[92] Brahm shows that the same objection as to the confusion between an epic and a dramatic style had been raised against Ibsen, and with as little justification. The true creative artist can expand the boundaries of art. Only those who approach Hauptmann's plays with preconceived notions of the "laws" of art can call him an "undramatic" dramatist.[93]

The single subscription performance of *Einsame Menschen* by

[90] *Op. cit.*, p. 351.
[92] *Op. cit.*, p. 353.
[91] *Op. cit.*, p. 352.
[93] *Ibid.*

the *Freie Bühne* disclosed certain retardive elements in its third act, and on the advice of Brahm and the directors of the *Deutsches Theater*, this act was deleted from the play by Hauptmann.[94] Brahm regrets the irreverent use of the blue pencil but shows that in this case the cutting has been justified and has even increased the dramatic effectiveness of the play. We see here an example of Brahm's view of the function of the critic in his dual role as aesthetic arbiter and as a man of the theatre. The literary and the theatrical supplement each other and lead to the artistic perfection of the dramatist.

Brahm continues this article on *Einsame Menschen* with a personal observation. Hauptmann's creative works now belong to the theatre at large, thanks to the pioneer work of the *Freie Bühne*. But Brahm asks for no acclaim or praise as the "discoverer" of Hauptmann; Hauptmann was merely the logical result of the *Freie Bühne*. When *Vor Sonnenaufgang* came to Brahm's attention there was no particular credit due him for having accepted it. On the contrary, it would have been a crime to refuse it. Even Karl Frenzel, if he had been in Brahm's place, would have had to accept the play unless he wished to betray the entire purpose of the *Freie Bühne*, says Brahm.[95] It is on this diffident note that Brahm concludes, secure in the knowledge that Hauptmann has finally come into his own as a German dramatist.

Hauptmann's first essay into the field of comedy was an event significant enough to become the subject of an editorial note by Brahm, discussing the work in progress.[96] The author of *Vor Sonnenaufgang* with its tragic emphasis on the evils of alcohol was now to show the comical aspects of alcoholic indulgence in the character of a bibulous professor, *Kollege Crampton*. Brahm's polemic leanings turn his article on the performance of this play into a diatribe against its hostile critics. Once again they indulge in a formalistic play of categories to show that Hauptmann may be a poet but is not a genuine dramatist. They fail to see the plot, the action, the complication in this play, thinking no doubt of the traditional Sardou or Scribe melodrama. That life affords no such neat com-

[94] *Op. cit.*, p. 354.   [95] *Op. cit.*, p. 355.
[96] *Freie Bühne*, 3. 12. 91.

plications does not occur to these convention-bound critics.[97] Ironically, Brahm writes that in his theoretical innocence he had supposed that whoever writes something that achieves its strongest and finest effects on the stage, that attracts people to the theatre for repeated performances, and that evokes very hearty applause, must be a dramatist, and must have written a stage play.[98]

Another objection raised by detracting critics was that the success of *Kollege Crampton* has been due to the performers rather than to any intrinsic qualities of the play itself. Brahm does not wish to go to the other extreme of belittling the performance of Herr Engels who had played the leading role. What Brahm does insist upon, however, is that the excellence of the performance was due to the fact that Engels faithfully interpreted Hauptmann's intentions. Engels was able to "exceed himself" because of the potential merits already latent in the character to be portrayed. The character had already been given life by the poet, and the actor had merely to portray the part faithfully in order to make it live. Objections had also been raised against the painfully minute detail and the microscopic care in the portrayal of Professor Crampton. But Brahm replies that even if there were no external proof that Hauptmann had dashed off the play on a fortnight, an examination of the play itself would demonstrate that the main character had been conceived as a whole and had not been pieced together with painful deliberation.[99]

In defence of the static character of Crampton, who remains at the end of the play exactly as he had been at the beginning, Brahm educes the example of Molière.[100] Harpagon and Argan are presented to us as completed characters without any development during the course of the play. The center of gravity in Molière is in the characters rather than in the plot. There has been a progressive deterioration of the Spanish and the French comedy since Molière, the emphasis having shifted from character to situation as the nucleus of drama. Hauptmann has returned to the tradition of Molière, not consciously but through his instinctive genius.

[97] Schr. I, 378.
[99] *Op. cit.*, p. 379.
[98] *Ibid.*
[100] *Op. cit.*, p. 380.

And more yet: Hauptmann has gone beyond Molière by availing himself of modern modes of expression. Hauptmann's characters are no longer types but individual creations.[101]

A further criticism of critics whose judgments are superficial and quantitative and whose criteria are artificial "standards" according to which all works of art must conform or else be rejected, concludes this review of *Kollege Crampton*. *"Das kritische Beckmessertum"* Brahm calls such critics who stand over the artist with a book of rules. We shall discuss the details of Brahm's criticism of criticism in a subsequent chapter. Considering that Hauptmann has not yet passed his thirtieth year, Brahm looks forward with assurance to his further development.

Brahm's activity as a critic of the drama is now nearing its conclusion. Very soon now he is to take up the directorship of the *Deutsches Theater*. There will be no further leisure for journalistic or literary efforts except of a dilatory nature. However, the list of his reviews still includes Hauptmann's *Die Weber*, to which we shall now turn.[102]

Any discussion of *Die Weber* naturally brings with it a consideration of the problem of censorship. Brahm differs with the police authorities' interpretation of *Die Weber* as a controversial play and as a menace to the public order. His contention is that the play is a composition of artistic objectivity and does not take sides or defend a specific thesis. Whoever suppresses *Die Weber* as a *Tendenzstück* must also suppress *Wilhelm Tell* and every other play in which there is an artistic portrayal of revolution or the striving for freedom. The fact that the play can arouse profound sympathy and compassion does not alter its artistic objectivity; such stirring effects as the play may have on an aroused audience are the result of its honesty and truth and not of any political propaganda.

In regard to the play's truth of portrayal, Brahm praises its naturalistic dialogue, the pathetic inarticulateness and groping for words of these poor, oppressed creatures, their pitiful attempts at humor. These coarse and simple stammerings are more effective than any lofty phrases and declamation, Brahm feels. Certain lines in the play such as, *"A jeda Mensch hoat halt an'n Sahnsucht,"*

---

[101] *Op. cit.*, p. 381.   [102] *Op. cit.*, pp. 406ff.

and old father Baumert's cry that human beings must sometimes have a breath of air, are to Brahm symbolic of German *Volksgefühl* in its subjective longing and desire for a higher existence. Brahm also hails the new type of mass-drama in which the hero is not a single outstanding individual but an entire social stratum. He also sees rare artistic achievement in the occasional emergence of individuals from the mass, so that there is a combination of the typical and of the individual in these characters.

In support of the play's objectivity Brahm shows how antithetical characters are juxtaposed for what they really are, without partisanship or prejudice. Old Hilse is shown in his passive religious confidence in a beatific future; while the younger Luise shows her passionate impatience and scorn for those who merely pray, by inciting her husband to rebellion and by fiercely demanding bread for her children. And over against these characters, the figure of the factory-owner, Dreissiger, is honestly portrayed in his naïve self-righteousness and inflexibility, without the slightest trace of caricature. The futility of the rebellion and the wild excesses of the revolutionists also balance the picture. Since all these factors make *Die Weber* a genuine work of art in Brahm's estimation, he is confident that the police censorship will eventually relent and permit its performance.

J. *The Classics*

Before proceeding to the general theoretical principles which can be educed from Brahm's critical essays and reviews we must first justify what may superficially seem to be the glaring omission of the classics from the preceding analysis of materials. The classics have always been an abiding institution in the dramatic repertoire of the German stage; it was impossible for a professional critic like Brahm to exclude them from his reviews. And indeed, he does review performances of the plays of the Greeks, Shakespeare, Goethe and Schiller, Hebbel, Ludwig, and Kleist. Schiller and Kleist in particular were the subjects of extensive biographies, as we have seen. Nevertheless, it is a matter of record that Brahm viewed the classics mainly in the light of their significance to the modern theatre. And from that point of view it follows that his

concern is with technical problems of staging, acting, and dramaturgy for the purpose of making the classics acceptable to modern
audiences. He accepts the classics as permanent and immutable
values both culturally and aesthetically. Like his great preceptor,
Wilhelm Scherer, he carries with him an inexpungeable reverence
for Goethe as the supreme standard of values in German literature.
Brahm's first published work, his exhaustive and technical study
of the German *Ritterdrama*, derives its sole justification from the
fact that these unimportant dramas were the offspring of Goethe's
Götz von Berlichingen. Thus, Brahm viewed anything remotely
touching upon Goethe as having the value of a sacred relic.[103]

To Schiller he devoted two exhaustive volumes of such thorough-
ness and breadth of scope that the work as a whole was never
completed. Frankly overcoming his youthful repugnance to
Schiller, Brahm in this fragment created a monument of atone-
ment. Scherer, writing during the spiritually barren days after the
founding of the empire, saw in Goethe and Schiller a peak of
achievement followed only by decline. But Brahm lived through
the tumultuous days of the literary revival at the end of the
nineteenth century. He was himself instrumental in the birth of
the new literature. In the stress of a new creative immediacy the
classics were overshadowed by contemporary works. And for the
classics to have any significance at all commensurable with their
intrinsic worth, a process of reinterpretation became a necessity.
This reinterpretation, when undertaken in Brahm's sphere of
activity, the theatre, became a matter of dramaturgy, of creative
staging, of a new style of acting. Brahm was not an Olympian
philosopher-critic who engaged in the subtle dialectics of un-
ravelling modern meanings and undertones from the text of the
classics. His problem was to destroy the traditions of virtuosity,
the heavy Weimar pathos and declamation, and to erect in their
stead a modern style of rendition that would make the classics
less austere, less "dated" to modern audiences. This aim had the

---

[103] "Wenn das Äusserliche, Hohle, und Fratzenhafte so manches unter diesen
Werken nur zu oft geeignet ist, Widerwillen und Zorn in uns zu erregen, so mag es die
Betrachtung milder stimmen, dass der erste Impuls, dem die Bewegung ihren Ur-
sprung verdankte, ein Gefühl war, das uns alle beseelt: tätige Bewunderung des
Einzigen." *Op. cit.*, p. 167.

virtue of retaining the spirit of the original text insofar as it tallied with the author's intention—and nevertheless of reestablishing contact between the past and the present by formal, communicative means.

For this reason Brahm's reviews of classical performances abound with technical discussions of staging, *décor*, acting, etc. Hence we shall evaluate these reviews of the classics in the chapters dealing with the technique of the theatre. We can now turn our attention to a summary of the principles expounded in the course of Brahm's reviews of the modern drama.

THE PRINCIPLES

III. *Art and Nature*

A. *Contradictions of Naturalism*

As is immediately evident upon even the most cursory examination, "pure" naturalism is an impossibility in literary art. The time-space limitations of writing and even of consciousness (of which writing must necessarily be but a sequential record) preclude a simultaneous reproduction of the infinite continuum which is life or nature. At best, the writer who is committed to a naturalistic doctrine can only create the illusion of naturalistic portrayal by a more or less artistic selection of certain detached and finite aspects of his subject which he depicts in apparently infinitesimal detail. The very act of selection, however, as well as the subjective character of language itself, is contradictory to the theoretically unselective objectivity of "pure" naturalism. Furthermore, the personality of the writer, his conditioned orientation, the inevitably limited perspective from which he views his subject matter, and the fluctuant, temporal character of all phenomena, preclude anything but the observation and recording of impressions. It follows, therefore, that the opponents of naturalism in this sense were engaging in a battle against ghosts, against mythical enemies that existed only through the fiat of their own distortive imaginations. How then can we account for the bitterness and stubborn duration of the conflict?

The answer is that we must view naturalism primarily as a philosophic ideology expressing itself imperfectly in an artistic technique. Naturalism celebrated its short-lived glory towards the end of the 19th century as the artistic correlate of scientific determinism and materialism in philosophy. The theories of heredity and environment as the predominant molding forces of human beings, ideas and institutions were accentuated over and above the dialectically converse possibilities, which were lost sight of for the time being. When we see the reflection of this unilateral philosophy in literature, which deals with man and society, we observe a static and pessimistic state of affairs which not only annihilates free will but is also a flat negation of the idea of social progress. In other words, "pure" naturalism (determinism) in the realm of ideas and sociology would portray only what is; it could not, by very reason of its illusion of impersonal objectivity, portray what might or what ought to be.

Now literature, although nominally making theoretical concessions to this ideology (Zola, Holz), never succeeded in its practical application. Aside from the technical impossibility of absolute naturalism in literature, the constructive genius and human compassion of the greater so-called naturalists led them far beyond their theories. Zola rode the hobby-horse of naturalistic theory partly through motives of publicity and opportunism. Actually he invented more than he observed.[1] Holz indulged in a jejune game with the term naturalism. What he was really arguing for was the elimination of consciousness from the process of literary creation.[2] This gave rise to the superficial notion (still repeated in many histories of literature) that whereas Zola still included the intermediary *tempérament* in his definition of art as *"un coin de la nature,"* Holz eliminated the *tempérament* altogether, thus making art equal nature. Nothing could be more egregiously false, for Holz does not stop with the elimination of consciousness. For consciousness he would substitute the unconscious or subconscious; this of course does not eliminate the subjective personality of the writer *(tempérament)* which can express itself unconsciously as well. Thus, although luxuriantly wallowing with theoretical abandon in the turgid quagmire of naturalism, literary artists in actual practice followed other dictates.

[1] Cf. *Zola and His Time* by Matthew Josephson, N. Y., 1928, p. 243 et passim. Josephson records Zola's conversation with Flaubert: "And by Jove, I say the devil with Naturalism (!) like you; and yet I shall repeat those ideas and go on repeating them, because new things must be baptized before the public, so that they may think them new . . . " In this conection note also that Zola's "naturalistic" novels, *e.g.* Le Ventre de Paris and L'Assommoir were written before his acquaintance with Claude Bernard's essay which inspired him to write *Le Roman expérimental;* that is, the novels came first and the campaign for naturalism followed. *Ibid.* Very significantly, Zola's abandonment of the naturalistic technique (beginning with *Germinal*) was coincident with his espousal of Socialism. *Op. cit.*, p. 293.

[2] Arno Holz, *Die Kunst: Ihr Wesen und Ihre Gesetze,* Berlin, 1891, p. 60. Cf. also Holz's admission " . . . dass die Kunst in Wirklichkeit tatsächlich nie und unter keinen Umständen mit der Natur zusammenfällt." *Op. cit.*, Neue Folge, 1892.

Even in the social field literary naturalism, by selecting the lowly and the oppressed for depiction, exercised, if only by implication, a devastating criticism of the existing social order. The technique of exact observation, imperfect as we have shown it to be, when applied to the life and environment of victims of society, reveals a situation which idealistic and romantic writers can very easily attenuate by a gloss of artistic detachment and sentimentality. Naturalism, on the other hand, exposed the dirty linen of contemporary society by projecting the misery of an expanding fourth estate (naturalism did not yet depict the industrial proletariat) into the willfully-blind equanimity of the middle and upper classes.

We need not search any further for the real roots of the opposition to Zola and to the German naturalists.[3] Under the veil of aesthetics (pure art), of outraged idealism, of the "genteel" tradition, of good form, of religion, in short, of all those attributes of which a plutocratic social caste is the real essence—a fierce barrage of invective and condemnation was laid down upon the hapless naturalists.

We have seen that "pure" naturalism is impossible as a technique although it exists as an ideology. As a literary technique it is largely negated by its technical impossibility in the medium of literature. And even as a literary ideology it contradicts its putative determinism by an implicit criticism of bourgeois society through the "discovery" of the proletariat (as yet, the lower middle class). We have also seen that, in spite of the patent impossibility of a "pure" naturalism, nevertheless this type of naturalism was imputed to the so-called naturalists by their opponents, who used this imputation as a handy means of attack. So far as can be ascertained from their creative as well as from their theoretical works neither Émile Zola, nor Arno Holz, nor Gerhart Hauptmann was a "pure" naturalist in the extreme sense.[4] They

[3] Cf. Winthrop Root, *German Criticism of Zola, 1875–1893*, (Diss. Col.), N. Y., 1931.

[4] Cf. supra, notes 1 and 2. Also Brahm's contention: " . . . dass nur der enge Sinn der Gegner es war, der uns an dieses Kreuz des Zolaschen, des Arno Holzischen Naturalismus zu nageln versuchte; und es heisst Worte, die in der Hitze des Gefechts gefallen sind, parteiisch verewigen, es heisst subjektive Stimmungen des Augenblickes, wie die freundschaftliche Widmung von Hauptmanns erstem Drama an seine Anreger Holz

were nonetheless the objects of an essentially myopic criticism which might best be described as an abusive calling of names. It was an example of the familiar demagogic subterfuge of re-defining an enemy's position not as it actually is, but in general terms which must necessarily meet with universal disapproval.

These are the general principles to which Brahm's identification with naturalism can be subsumed. His theoretical opposition to "pure" naturalism is a constant factor, as it must be in the very nature of things. His support of the so-called naturalists is based on their uncompromisingly faithful portrayal of life. He recognized in the naturalists those writers who were most vitally imbued with the realistic spirit of the times. At the same time his Goethean principle of the dynamic interrelation of life and art left ample room for growth and change.

B. *Zola's Influence*

Throughout all of Brahm's more mature work there runs in consonance with the spirit of his time the problem of realism as an omnipresent *leitmotif* dominating his entire pattern of thought. Whatever minor themes may resolve themselves out of this major theme, they are constantly evocative of the same central problem. Like most of his German contemporaries, Brahm was largely dependent upon Zola for his ideas of naturalism. He began with an early condemnation of the great French naturalist, whom he knew only at second hand through the conventional views promulgated by the myopic Zola opposition as pictured above. These views naturally depicted Zola as a moral radical who was little better than a pornographer, a depraved writer reveling in filth and brutality. His works were an affront to "good taste," to accepted moral and social standards. In short he was considered a degenerate influence if not an out and out public menace. To the constricted minds of conservative German critics Zola was a mere purveyor of *Schundliteratur*, a fit subject for the censor, a writer

---

und Schlaf, parteiisch aufbauschen, wenn man mit jenen Schlagworten von der Beschränktheit des deutschen Naturalismus immer noch krebsen geht . . . ", Schr. I, 469. Cf. also Naumann's treatment of Hauptmann and of Holz. Very significantly Naumann goes to Strindberg for his exposition of naturalist theory and shows in his discussion of German "naturalists" how they exceeded the bounds of this theory. *Op. cit.*, pp. 14f. et passim.

whose works were indistinguishable from those other categories of literature for which the Germans have such a wealth of opprobrious epithets such as, *Hintertreppenromane, Kolportageromane, Schmutzliteratur*, etc.[5]

Through the pioneer efforts of Michael Georg Conrad, among others, the works of Zola were made available to larger masses of readers who were for the most part unconcerned with naturalistic theories but who read Zola either through prurient curiosity or because he had something really vital to say to them and said it unfastidiously, without mincing his words. The newer generation of writers and intellectuals also found in Zola a breadth of vision, a refreshing immediacy to contemporary life and its problems, a fearless indignation against social cant and hypocrisy, which were notoriously absent from their own literature. They embraced Zola as a prophet, and many of them imitated him externally, with the result that they appropriated many of his excesses without possessing the saving grace of his vision and genius.

The early condemnation of Zola derived largely from the false assumption (as we have shown above) that his theory of naturalism was a critical absolute, thus tending to degrade the art of literature into a mechanical portrayal of reality. Zola himself capitalized on his slogan of naturalism as a propagandistic device; his pretensions of making literature an exact science were largely an opportune measure to attract attention, arouse discussion, and to draw the fire of outraged critical solons. His latest biographers even point out evidence that he himself only half believed in the theories which he expounded.[6] However that may be, we do know that in his novels Zola transcended the confines of his theories and unconscionably left them behind for embattled aestheticians and moralists. In his creative practice as distinguished from his theories, Zola created great symbolic epics of architectonic majesty, alight with social vision, with soaring aspirations for a better society, and with an intensely passionate condemnation of the existing order. Zola outstripped his theories, as was soon recognized by all except the purblind adherents of a moribund tradition. More and more it was recognized that Zola's naturalism was subservient to a broader aim and content. And it was also be-

---

[5] Cf. Root, *op. cit.*   [6] Cf. supra, note 1.

latedly realized (even though Zola's dictum had long been there for all to observe, *viz.* that there is a temperament interposed between art and reality) that Zola's practical naturalism allowed free play to the critical imagination and to the other subjective elements in the makeup of the literary artist. The artist was no mere reproducer of reality (as if that were possible) but an unhampered technician as free to create, to invent, to combine and to juxtapose as was the non-naturalistic artist. Nor was the naturalist artist committed to a pessimistic view of life (under "pure" naturalism there can be no future perfectability if art is the mere reproduction of a present reality), for he could exercise social criticism implicitly through his selection of subjects and characters.

C. *Brahm's Three Attitudes*

In the light of the above principles three separate attitudes on the part of Brahm towards naturalism can be distinguished from his many expressions on the subject. They may be subsumed as follows: first, the stage of classical idealism in which literature is considered to be the transfigured symbol of reality, and in which the perfection of literary form is dominant; second, the stage of poetic realism in which literature adheres as closely as possible to physical and psychological reality and to the contemporary scene, but always as seen filtered through the medium of poetic genius; third, the final stage, in which literature is considered to be a fusion between realism and poetry, wherein by poetry is meant the symbolic, the interpretative, and the universalizing elements of literature. This sequence of attitudes is, of course, abstracted from a maze of varied and even contradictory statements; but it is accurate within its schematic limits. It may be seen to follow the Hegelian pattern of thesis, antithesis, synthesis; but in addition there is a constant anti-naturalistic substratum running through all three stages. At no stage do we have an adherence to the vulgar interpretation of naturalism as the mechanical and photographic reflection of reality.

1. *Classical Idealism*

Thus we see as instances of the first stage Brahm's reference to *"die wüsten Orgien des Naturalismus"*[7] in connection with a criti-

---

[7] Schlenther, *op. cit.*, p. 68.

cism of Zola whom he can scarcely have read as yet; and an exhortation to his contemporaries in a memorial essay on *Goethe und Berlin*[8]

... an den Überlieferungen jener Kunst festzuhalten, die das Poetische nicht in der platten Wiedergabe der allgemeinen Alltäglichkeit findet, sondern die in klassisch-durchgebildeter Form das erhöhte Abbild der edlen Wirklichkeit festzuhalten trachtet.

In this period Brahm also condemns the naturalistic staging of the Meininger as representing the confusion of Art with Nature. In acting technique he considers *"der poesielose Naturalismus"* as reprehensible.[9]

2. Poetic Realism

An approach to the second stage is afforded by an essay on *Pariser Theatereindrücke*,[10] in which Brahm gives his impressions of a sojourn in Paris during which he made the rounds of the theatres. As becomes evident from a reading of this essay, Emil Zola's *Le Naturalisme au Théâtre* was Brahm's guide in the criticism of the French Theatre. In this essay we come upon what seems to be an astonishing anticipation of Arno Holz' formula for art, three years before the publication of *Die Kunst, Ihr Wesen und Ihre Gesetze*. However, there is no point in trying to ferret out the priority of an idea that was common property at the time. Here we also read an attack against the venerable convention of the Parisian stage as a stifling influence in the evolution of dramatic art:

Auf Zeichen und Übereinkommen, auf einer mehr oder minder willkürlichen Formel beruht vielleicht alle Kunst der Bühne, allein diese Zeichen wechseln und suchen der Natur näher zu kommen in der Folge der Zeiten.[11]

The quotation above is representative of Brahm's second attitude toward naturalism in that it emphasizes the tendency toward realism. But this second attitude is also noted for its emphasis on the present, on the temporal scene; for it is Brahm's conviction that literature cannot exist in a timeless void but must arise out of, and be pertinent to, some temporal context at the time of its creation:

---

[8] Berlin, 1880.   [9] Schr. I, 13.   [10] *Op. cit.*, p. 172.   [11] *Ibid.*

Es fehlte das neuere Drama, das Drama unserer Zeit und unseres Jahrhunderts, und nur spät und nicht ohne den drängenden Einfluss der Kritik hat man begonnen auch diese ernsteste Pflicht einzulösen.[12]

Stärker werden wir niemals und unwiderstehlicher zur Teilnahme herangezogen, als wenn der Pulsschlag und das Empfinden unserer Zeit, Fleisch von unserem Fleisch und Bein von unserem Bein, auf der Szene lebendig wird.[13]

Now this does not mean that the historical genre is to be eschewed altogether. By no means! But it does mean that preferably only such historical situations should be chosen as offer some parallel with present conditions. Or, lacking this, the historical drama must be so shaped as to seem immediate and modern. Realism in the historical genre, as we have already noted in Brahm's critique of Wildenbruch's *Die Quitzows*, is a necessity if the historical drama is to attain significance on the contemporary stage:

Dass solches Fortschreiten für die Kunst der Gegenwärtigen nur in der Hinwendung zum Realismus bestehen kann, dass gerade das historische Drama, wenn es überall fortleben soll, lernen muss, an Stelle der traditionellen Motive von Liebe und Aufopferung die harte Macht der Realitäten in der Geschichte zu zeigen, das ist meine tiefinnere Anschauung.[14]

Another important aspect of this second attitude (and indeed the constant idea that pervades all three attitudes) is the intermediary role of the writer's imagination or "temperament" between reality and its literary counterpart. We see here that Brahm has read his Zola this time and has overcome his former prejudice based on the vulgar conception of "pure" naturalism.[15] He pays due tribute to the subjective element in all writing but shows that where this subjectivity predominates there is bound to be a preconceived imposition of the writer's views upon reality. The writer who can portray the essence of things without this subjectivity predominating (*e.g.* Shakespeare and Goethe) achieves the ideal of realism according to Brahm's definition. We see, therefore, that Brahm is far removed from the opposition's misleading imputation of "pure" naturalism. He uses the term "naturalism" according to a special definition of his own whereby naturalism is identified with the sublimated higher objectivity of a universal or classical

---

[12] *Op. cit.*, p. 82.　　　[13] *Ibid.*　　　[14] Schr. I, 268.
[15] Cf. Brahm's essay on Zola, Schr. II, 357ff.

literature. In an essay on Fontane's *Irrungen Wirrungen* Brahm makes this point clear in the course of a reference to Zola:

> Der grosse Naturalist selbst erkennt hier, dass ein einfaches Abschildern des Wirklichen weder genügen noch überhaupt glücken kann, dass stets und stets die Lebensanschauung und die Stimmung des Dichters, seine fröhlichen und herben Erfahrungen, sein schwerer oder leichter Sinn, mit einem Wort: dass sein Temperament modifizierend einwirkt auf das Bild der Welt, welches sich ihm darstellt. Das Temperament ist die Brille, die so oder so anders gefärbte, rosenrote oder schwarze Brille, durch die der Dichter die Natur anschaut; und freilich wäre der der Grösste, der ohne alle subjektive Beleuchtung die Dinge ganz unmittelbar auffasste. Es ist Shakespeares und Goethes Ruhm, solchem Ideal am nächsten gekommen zu sein. Vorwiegend ethisch gestimmte Dichter dagegen, wie Schiller und Zola, Ibsen und Fontane, lassen das "Temperament" am stärksten und im Ursprung walten; und die Frage vor jedem einzelnen Werk wird darum sein, gerade vom Standpunkt unserer gegenwärtigen realistischen Kunstanschauung aus: ob das Temperament die Natur, ob die Idee die Wirklichkeit gemeistert hat oder nicht?[16]

3. The Synthesis of Naturalism and Romanticism

The third stage of Brahm's attitude toward naturalism is conceived from the perspective gained after the *"Überwindung des Naturalismus"* as a literary movement in the narrower sense. In the course of a review of Bahr's *Zur Kritik der Moderne*[17] Brahm recalls a phrase from an early essay of his own[18] in which he had anticipated Bahr's contention that:*"Die Synthese von Naturalismus und Romantik ist die gegenwärtige Aufgabe der Literatur."* As Brahm had stated it in his own essay years before:

> In der Vereinigung des Realistischen und Phantastischen liegt der Weg, wie mir scheinen will, welchen die Dichtung der Zukunft wird beschreiten müssen, wenn sie nicht einseitig sich bescheiden will, entweder auf das spezifisch „Poetische" zu verzichten, oder auf das spezifisch Moderne.[19]

Brahm defines his position still more accurately in a review of Maeterlinck's *La Princesse maleine*,[20] in which he attacks the neoromantic and impressionistic tendency which this work of the Belgian poet exemplifies to him. Nevertheless, Brahm's criticism

---

[16] Schr. II, 261ff.
[17] *Freie Bühne*, 30. 4. 1890.
[18] *Deutsche Rundschau*, Juni, 1882.
[19] *Freie Bühne, loc. cit.*
[20] *Freie Bühne*, 1891, p. 383.

is not conceived in a narrow naturalistic frame of reference. He
states that the movement of naturalism had its justification as
representing a vital tendency of the times. But since times change,
Brahm realizes that naturalism must in turn yield its supremacy
to some other formula or tendency representing the newer, changed
state of affairs:

Auch ich halte den Naturalismus nicht für das letzte Wort der
Kunst: einmal, weil ich an kein letztes Wort der modernen Kunst
glaube, und sodann, weil in derselben fruchtbaren Einseitigkeit, in
derselben tief aus den Bedürfnissen der Zeit geschöpfte Modernität,
welche den Naturalismus sieghaft gemacht hat, auch die Bedingungen
liegen müssen zur Überwindung des Naturalismus durch ein Neues.[21]

D. *The Program of the Freie Bühne*

Perhaps the most eloquent expression of the basic idea that
underlies all three of Brahm's attitudes toward the movement of
naturalism—and the one most quoted in histories of literature—
is to be found in his editorial program in the first number of the
Freie Bühne für modernes Leben.[22] It is highly significant that a
denial of the basic idea of "pure" naturalism and an expression of
belief in the mere temporary significance of naturalism should be
included in the program of a periodical whose inception was mainly
due to the desire of supplying a journalistic organ for the naturalistic writers after the other literary journals had shown themselves
inhospitable to the whole movement. In a sense, the very founding
of this periodical, which might be superficially taken as a sign of
the triumph of naturalism, was in reality an expression of the
supersedence of naturalism. The apparent contradiction of a
naturalistic periodical disclaiming the tenets of naturalism can
only be resolved if we remember—as we have shown above—that
there never was at any time a consistent practice of naturalism
as a technique because of the inherent impossibility of this practice.

Brahm's attitudes toward the movement of naturalism in
literature can be taken, by and large, as representative of the
attitudes of many of the literary figures within, and sympathetic
to, the movement. At no time was there a categorical denial of the
intermediary role of the imagination in literary creation. At no
time was there a consistent practice of relegating literature into a

[21] *Ibid.*   [22] 29. 1. 90; Schr. I, p. 285.

mechanical portrayal of reality. What did exist was the desire to reflect in literature the temporal scene without the idealistic and sentimental distortions of the neo-romantic and neo-classical writers. Now what was this temporal scene? It was governed by the doctrines of evolution and deterministic causality in the intellectual sphere. It reflected the social discords of an industrial era. It pictured man as an impotent product of heredity and environment. It abounded with the moral frictions attendant upon the breakdown of religious and social traditions. When the naturalists spoke of truth, what they meant was that literature must reflect these temporal forces and influences. When they spoke of falsehood, what they meant was the ignoring or glossing over of this truth.

Thus, when Brahm perorates on the theme of *Wahrheit* as the guiding motto of the new art, he emphasizes that it is a truth *"auf jedem Lebenspfade";* that is, it encompasses every aspect of existence. Nor is it to be an objective, transcendental truth serenely poised above the heat of conflict; it is to be the truth as manifested to those fearless and independent spirits actually engaged in the struggle (an affirmation of the subjective character of literary creation):

> Nicht die objektive Wahrheit, die den Kämpfenden entgeht, sondern die individuelle Wahrheit, welche aus der innersten Überzeugung frei geschöpft ist und frei ausgesprochen: die Wahrheit des unabhängigen Geistes, der nichts zu beschönigen und nichts zu vertuschen hat, und der darum nur einen Gegner kennt, seinen Erbfeind und Todfeind: die Lüge in jeglicher Gestalt.[23]

Art must have an immediate correlation to reality and to contemporary existence. We have seen this principle as dominant in Brahm's acceptance of naturalism. It is not so much the doctrine of naturalism *per se*, as the fact that the movement stems from the demands of the present that attracts Brahm. This same principle is affirmed in the program of the *Freie Bühne:*

> ... die neue Kunst, die die Wirklichkeit anschaut und das gegenwärtige Dasein ... nur wer die Forderungen der gegenwärtigen Stunde im Innern frei empfindet, wird die bewegenden geistigen Mächte durchdringen, als ein moderner Mensch.[24]

[23] *Ibid.*   [24] *Ibid.*

But life and art are not bound up to some changeless absolute. There is a dynamic interrelation between the two, both of which are in a state of eternal flux. Therefore an adherence to the past must necessarily do violence to the demands of the present. The artist, as in the Goethean concept, must be involved in a continuous process of growth. The emphasis must be on the continuous present and future rather than on a stultifying past:

Dem Werdenden gilt unser Streben, und aufmerksamer richtet sich der Blick auf das, was kommen will, als auf jenes ewig Gestrige, dass sich vermisst, in Konventionen und Satzungen unendliche Möglichkeiten der Menschheit, einmal für immer festzuhalten.[25]

There is a recognition of the present significance of naturalism, but like all literary creeds, it too is transitory and can have only historical significance. (This in the very midst of the triumph of naturalism!) Therefore the editor of this periodical accepts the naturalist writers, but leaves the way open to some further and as yet unpredictable development of the future; for the ceaseless evolution of human culture cannot be bound to any hard and set formula:

Die moderne Kunst, wo sie ihre lebensvollsten Triebe ansetzt, hat auf dem Boden des Naturalismus Wurzel geschlagen. Sie hat, einem tiefinnern Zuge dieser Zeit gehorchend, sich auf die Erkenntnis der natürlichen Daseinsmächte gerichtet und zeigt uns mit rücksichtslosem Wahrheitstriebe die Welt wie sie ist. Dem Naturalismus Freund, wollen wir eine gute Strecke Weges mit ihm schreiten, allein es soll uns nicht erstaunen, wenn im Verlaufe der Wanderschaft, an einem Punkt, den wir heute noch nicht überschauen, die Strasse plötzlich sich biegt und überraschende neue Blicke in Kunst und Leben sich auftun. Denn an keine Formel, auch an die jüngste nicht, ist die unendliche Entwicklung menschlicher Kultur gebunden; und in dieser Zuversicht, im Glauben an das ewig Werdende . . . etc., etc.[26]

E. *Brahm's Aesthetic Credo*

It would be appropriate to append to these observations on Brahm's attitudes toward the movement of naturalism an account of his positive philosophy of aesthetics. His main ideas on the subject have already been stated, particularly in the above-

[25] *Op. cit.*, p. 286.   [26] *Op. cit.*, p. 287.

rendered excerpts from the program of the *Freie Bühne für modernes Leben*. What this program reveals, however, is an oblique statement of his philosophy only insofar as he is obliged to clarify his position in regard to the movement of naturalism. It is a negative expression of his aesthetic credo in contrast with the unilateral, naturalistic frame of reference which was the dominant concern of the moment. But there are more abstract and more universal aspects of aesthetics in regard to which every literary movement finds it imperative to take some definite stand. What is meant here are such problems as are posed by the dual categories of art and nature, art and ethics, content and form, etc. The shifting degrees of emphasis upon one or the other of these dual references afford a key to the social and temporal characterization of many aesthetic philosophies.

Otto Brahm has given us a definitive statement of his aesthetic creed at the conclusion of his brochure on Henrik Ibsen.[27] This "*ästhetisches Glaubensbekenntnis*," as he calls it, was so apt and perfect an expression of his philosophy of art, that he quotes it verbatim in a subsequent review.[28] He pays homage to Goethe and Schiller as his spiritual godfathers in aesthetics. In conformity with the Weimar tradition, he emphasizes the importance of form. And any content is conceivably suitable provided its inner essence has been molded into artistic form. Not the content itself but its manner of treatment is the salient factor in art.[29] This dominant principle resolves for Brahm all apparent contradictions between the ideal aesthetics of Weimar and the contemporary realistic art of Ibsen. In both of these periods the constant principle of a disinterested art is dominant; only the content has changed with the change of the times.

In regard to nature and art, Brahm accepts the notion of an irreconcilable dualism between these two concepts. But the demands of Brahm's era and the evolution of art itself point to an increasing approach to nature or realism. In regard to the ethical

[27] Berlin, 1887.   [28] *Ibsens Gespenster in Berlin*, Schr. I, 106f.
[29] Cf. Goethe's classical expression of this: "Es kommt nicht darauf an, was für Gegenstände der Künstler bearbeitet, sondern vielmehr, in welchen Gegenständen er nach seiner Natur das innere Leben erkennt und welche er wieder nach allen Wirkungen ihres Lebens hinstellen kann." Letter to Fr. Müller, 1781.

purpose of art, Brahm also adheres to the Weimar principle that great art will inevitably exert a moral influence but that this influence is subservient to the work of art itself. In other words, to posit *a priori* ethical standards for art is destructive of the creative principle.[30] We shall see in the following chapter how these principles are observed in Brahm's theories of criticism. The intellectual constellation of the man is a consistent and organic unity manifesting itself automatically both in the sphere of art and of criticism. The following is Brahm's *"ästhetisches Glaubensbekenntnis"*:

In der ganzen weiten Welt, bei den Menschen und den Dingen, sehe ich nichts, unbedingt nichts, was einer künstlerischen Behandlung nicht könnte unterzogen werden: offen und frei liegt Alles da, nur zuzugreifen hat der Dichter, von keinem Schlagbaum der Theorie gehemmt. Nicht das Was entscheidet, sondern allein das Wie in der Dichtung; und hier freilich liegen die schwierigsten Probleme verborgen und jeder einzelne Fall gibt, nicht dem Nachahmer, aber auf eigenen Wegen furchtlos Wandelnden, neue Rätsel auf. Die ästhetischen Gesetzgeber unserer Nation haben über diese Fragen, prinzipiell gesehen, nicht anders gedacht; und immer wieder hat Schiller seinem Humboldt, hat Goethe es Eckermann gegenüber ausgesprochen, wie die Beherrschung des Stoffes durch die Form oberstes Gesetz der Poesie sei. ‚Unsere deutschen Aesthetiker,' sagte Goethe, ‚reden zwar viel von poetischen und unpoetischen Gegenständen und sie mögen auch in gewisser Hinsicht nicht ganz Unrecht haben. *Allein im Grunde bleibt kein realer Gegenstand unpoetisch,* sobald der Dichter ihn gehörig zu gebrauchen weiss.' Und wenn solcher theoretischen Anschauung die künstlerische Praxis Goethes und Schillers nicht völlig entsprechen will, wenn die idealistische Dichtung der Weimar Zeit und die realistische eines Ibsen einander entgegenzulaufen scheinen, so irrt uns dies nicht. Anders ist die Forderung unserer Tage an den Poeten, anders das Bedürfnis jener gewesenen Zeit.[31]

[30] Cf. Goethe's letter to Zelter: "Natur und Kunst sind zu gross, um auf Zwecke auszugehen." 29. Jan. 1830; and also the oft-quoted words from *Dichtung und Wahrheit:* "Ein gutes Kunstwerk kann und wird zwar moralische Folgen haben, aber moralische Zwecke vom Künstler fordern, heisst ihm sein Handwerk verderben." 3. Teil, 12. Buch.

[31] Schr. I, 106f.

IV. *The Critical Process*

In the application of scientific method to the thought process itself lies the hope for a truly objective estimation of values and of experience, which is the essence of criticism. For very obviously, if our habits of thought and the verbalisms by means of which thoughts are manifested are distorted, then the reality which they are intended to reflect will also appear distorted. In the field of literary criticism a conscious self-criticism of the critic is all the more required if he is not to be a mere impressionistic conversationalist haphazardly judging, epithetizing, giving unrestrained vent to his accidental whims, crotchets, and vague afflatus. The true critic, as distinguished from the oracular pontificator of arbitrary and fortuitous judgments, is constantly under the impulsion of self-examination. He is constantly on the lookout for new orientations, for flexibility of approach, for acid tests not only in regard to the object under consideration but especially in regard to his personal criteria of judgment. If we may adapt Ibsen's dictum on creative literary composition as the author's passing judgment on himself,[1] then creative criticism may similarly be conceived, in part, as the critic's engaging in a process of self-judgment.[2]

Furthermore, there is not only a technical aspect to dramatic criticism in which the critic examines the play in terms of its formal and contentual elements, but there is also a subjective aspect in which the critic expresses his personal reactions to the play. Undoubtedly a closer examination will reveal a linkage between the technical and the subjective aspects of criticism. Nevertheless, the critic who emphasizes one of these aspects to the neglect of the other is substituting a part for the whole; for the

[1] Cf. Ibsen's verses:
> *"Leben, das heisst bekriegen*
> *In Hirn und Herz die Gewalten;*
> *Und dichten: über sich selber*
> *Den Gerichtstag halten."*

Quoted by Brahm in *Henrik Ibsen*, Berlin, 1887, p. 68.

[2] Cf. Lessing's emphasis on self-criticism: "Nur dass sich nicht jeder kleine Kritikaster für das Publikum halte, und derjenige, dessen Erwartungen getäuscht werden, auch ein wenig mit sich selbst zu Rate gehe, von welcher Art seine Erwartungen gewesen." *Hamburgische Dramaturgie*, Ankündigung.

complete process of criticism, if it is to do justice to the total relationship of the critic and the object criticized, should include both aspects.[3]

These theoretical remarks derive their pertinence from the necessity of classifying the technical processes and devices in Brahm's dramatic criticism. Brahm's critical writings constantly remind us of the fact that he gave a good deal of thought to the mechanics and dynamics of his vocation. Organically interwoven with the main body of his work there runs a prominent thread of analysis and theoretical discussion in regard to criticism as such. Over and over again he launches into some excursus in justification of his method or into a polemical analysis of the critical errors of some colleague. Thus, the very content of our subject matter makes it incumbent upon us to enter into an examination of what Brahm considers to be the *function* of dramatic criticism.

Evidently, before we can speak of a *function* or *purpose* of criticism, we must be clear about the more elementary fact as to what Brahm considered criticism to be; or more accurately, what he considered it *ought* to be. This leads us into an examination of the nature of the critical process. Once we have determined Brahm's stand in regard to the process of criticism, there will naturally be brought into relief his scarification of the fallacies and false orientations which represent its converse; that is, what criticism *ought not* to be. Having defined Brahm's view of the process of criticism both as such and conversely, we can then properly examine what he considers to be the function of criticism, for the one will naturally follow from and be dependent upon the other.

We must bear in mind that our separate discussion of the "process" as distinguished from the "function" of criticism is a logical convenience which derives its justification from the difference in emphasis placed by Brahm on these two aspects of criticism. The above order of discussion is not intended to give rise to the impression that a conception of the function of criticism can only be formulated upon a conception of the critical process; that is, that the former is merely the logical conclusion of the latter.

---

[3] I am indebted for the clarification of these ideas to I. A. Richards, *Principles of Literary Criticism*, N. Y. and London, 1924, 1934.[5]

From what we know of the multiple interactions among the psychological, the logical, and the real, we can also conceive that a conception of the function of criticism in turn may determine the conception of its process. To suggest this dialectic possibility within the limits of logical presentation shall be a corollary aim of the subsequent argument.

We must also predicate these general considerations upon the temporal scene in the theatre that confronted Brahm, since very obviously we cannot consider our critic merely from the general and timeless perspective which the above considerations would seem to imply. Throughout we shall try not only to quote representative statements by Brahm covering the schema outlined above but shall also couple them to a running commentary which will elucidate their proper relationship to the conditioning influences to which he was subjected. We shall also attempt to distinguish between the material reality which confronted him in the theatre and his ideal demands for criticism to prepare the way for a theatre of the future.

A. *Scherer and Empirical Criticism*

We have already seen the complete domination of Scherer's influence on Otto Brahm's modes of thought. We need not be surprised therefore if we find in Scherer's principles of criticism the germs of Brahm's ideas on the subject. The debt is openly acknowledged by Brahm in a review of an interesting and little-known brochure entitled *Poetik*,[4] posthumously published and composed of Scherer's notes arranged by some of his pupils and supplemented by their lecture notes. Brahm's summary of the essential contents and of the point of view embodied in this work affords us a precise statement as to what he considered to be the nature of criticism.[5]

We hear typical echoes of the period of natural science and evolution in the formulation that criticism must not approach its task with metaphysical preconceptions but must derive its essence from the facts of experience. It must rest on a flexible, empirical basis. It must eschew extraneous imperatives and superimposed

[4] Berlin, 1888.   [5] Schr. II, 296ff.

prescriptions in favor of direct observation and evaluation in terms of the subject itself. The principles of art, furthermore, are to be empirically derived from a scientific historical study of art in the past and in the several epochs of culture, seen from the perspective of evolution and change rather than from that of immutable categories. Criticism must learn from the natural sciences, from statistics, from political economy, and from anthropology. And insofar as it endeavors to borrow from ethics and from psychology, it does not borrow from the old, metaphysical systems that go by these names but from their modern, empirical counterparts.[6] In short, criticism since Herder and Darwin is no longer a subject for metaphysical speculation; the critic must approach his task like the student of natural science; his concern is not so much with traditional philosophy and aesthetics as with an aesthetics built upon historical evolution and natural science.[7] It follows that the emphasis in criticism is to be placed upon understanding rather than judging.

B. The "Naturalistic" Critic

There is a close analogy between this conception of the nature of criticism and naturalistic theory in general. Just as the naturalistic artist endeavors (in theory, of course) to portray reality as it actually is, without the imposition of subjective interpretations of that reality, so the naturalistic critic endeavors to contemplate the work of art as it actually is, without the intrusion of subjectivity; furthermore, he educes his criteria from that very work of art itself. Goethe's distinction between destructive and creative criticism seems to find an echo here. "What has the author proposed to do? Is his proposal reasonable and understandable? How far has he succeeded in carrying it out?"[8] These were Goethe's desiderata for a creative criticism. But to measure the work of art against extraneous standards, Goethe called "destructive criti-

---

[6] *Ibid.*   [7] Schr. II, 305.

[8] "Es gibt eine zerstörende Kritik und eine produktive. Jene ist sehr leicht; denn man darf sich nur irgendeinen Massstab, irgendein Musterbild, so borniert sie auch seien, in Gedanken aufstellen, sodann aber kühnlich versichern: vorliegendes Kunstwerk passe nicht dazu, tauge deswegen nichts . . . , so befreit man sich von aller Dankbarkeit gegen den Künstler. Die produktive Kritik ist um ein gutes Teil schwerer; sie fragt: Was hat sich der Autor vorgesetzt? ist dieser Vorsatz vernünftig und verständig? und inwiefern ist es gelungen, ihn auszuführen?" Über Manzonis *Carmagnola*, 1820.

cism." We thus see the wideness of Otto Brahm's conception of the "naturalistic" critic, since it could include Lessing's[9] and Goethe's position as well as that of the nineteenth century literary naturalists, two positions that in most cases represent extremes.

Brahm makes this credo of the naturalistic critic clear in a review of Hauptmann's *Einsame Menschen:*

... ich versuche zunächst nur, was eine grosse poetische Natur will, zu begreifen von eben dieser Natur aus—wie es sich ziemt für den naturalistischen Kritiker.[9a]

C. *The "Laws" of Art*

How sharply this empirical and evolutionary formulation of the nature of criticism must clash with the preceptual, authoritarian tradition becomes clear from Brahm's strictures against those who presume to set up eternal "laws" of art. He is bitterly opposed to what he calls the Hegelian vice of mastering the world of phenomena merely by conceptual means.[10] Since concepts are only mental formulations of things and not the things themselves, a system based upon concepts cannot jibe with reality. The static rigidity of such procedure leads to the positing of *a priori* imperatives, of standards and of models, of hidebound laws which tend to restrict the infinite sphere of art. The very phrase: *"the laws of art"* becomes a hideous bugbear to Brahm:

Wo sind sie, die Gesetze der Kunst, auf die du dich berufst, worin gründet ihre Gültigkeit für uns, die wir nicht ästhetische Gesetz' und Rechte wie eine ewige Krankheit fortschleppen, sondern aus eigenen Augen sehen und nach der Norm unserer Zeit nur urteilen wollen? Nicht in einer von aussen an die Dinge herantretenden, überalterten Weisheit der philosophischen Kategorien, nur in der Erfahrung, in der Einsicht: wie Kunst ward und sich entwickelt von Anfang der menschlichen Kultur her, durch alle Völker und Zeiten, kann solche Norm gefunden werden; *und nicht was Kunst soll, nur was Kunst will und ist—so lautet die Frage.*[11]

The laying of these *"ästhetische Gespenster"* and the undermining of

---

[9] "Der wahre Kunstrichter folgert keine Regeln aus seinem Geschmacke, sondern hat seinen Geschmack nach den Regeln gebildet, welche die Natur der Sache erfordert." *Hamburgische Dramaturgie,* 19. Stück.

[9a] Schr. I, 353f.

[10] " . . . die Welt der Erscheinungen zu meistern aus Begriffen." Schr. II, 306.

[11] Schr. II, 307.

the stultifying influence of this *"ästhetische Hegelei"* are a major premise in Scherer's and also in Brahm's approach to criticism.[12]

D. *The Ethical Fallacy*

This fundamental position of Brahm is most clearly emphasized in his objection to the ethical tendency of the prevalent criticism of his time. Ibsen and Hauptmann, as we have seen, were at first attacked on ethical grounds. Brahm considers this sort of identification of ethics and aesthetics as a jejune fallacy comparable to the teleological philosophy of old. Like Goethe, he considers the aesthetic function of art as the supreme factor to be posited in any logical criticism of that art:[13]

Und so gut wie die Philosophie, die die Weltordnung auf Zweckmässige Wirkungen stellt, heute überwunden ist, so gut wird es den Gottsched und Gellert überlassen bleiben, von dem Zweck der Poesie zu reden und moralische Wirkungen zu suchen, wo nur ästhetische gelten.[13a]

E. *Polemics*

The cardinal principles of Scherer's *Poetik*, expanded and qualified by his own experiences in dramatic criticism, present to Brahm a broad and inclusive frame of reference in the light of which he evaluates not only his own critical procedures but those of his journalistic colleagues. In his polemical asides he gives us a negative expression of his view of the nature of criticism. Thus, in following his delineation of what criticism *should not* be, we can imply its positive side as well. Also, because of the fact that his reviews appeared in a weekly publication (that is, after the notices of the daily press) Brahm had an ample field in which to exercise a retrospective criticism of critics.

The program of the *Freie Bühne*, in addition to its positive challenge to aspiring writers, also contains a declaration of war against superannuated criticism:

. . . die abgelebte Kritik, die mit angelernter Buchstabenweisheit dem Werdenden sich entgegenstemmt—sie sind es, denen unser Kampfruf gilt.[14]

---

[12] *Ibid.*   [13] Cf. supra, note 30, Chapter III.   [13a] Schr. II, 309f.
[14] Schr. I, 286.

There is a long tradition of critical ineptitude in German letters, and Brahm constantly compares his errant colleagues with the representatives of this tradition. He recalls Gottsched's inanities with regard to Shakespeare[15] and compares the contemporary condemnation of Ibsen and Hauptmann to the glaring errors of judgment in the *Vossische Zeitung* with regard to young Schiller.[16] The mere summary of his choice of epithets is an eloquent testimonial to a degree of feeling in the matter of critical pusillanimity which lent wings to his vocabulary of invective. For those who approach art with rules and standards he coins the term: *"das kritische Beckmessertum"*;[17] for those critics who lavish irrelevant and condescending advice upon young dramatists there is the term: *"das kritische Poloniustum"*;[18] the indignant moralists are dubbed the *"ästhetische Polizei"*;[19] those who judge from the perspective of a questionably eternal and absolute system of values are referred to as *"jene ästhetisch Superklugen"*[20] and *"die kritischen Alleswisser"*;[21] a hapless reviewer is referred to as: *"der im Irrgarten der Poesie herumwandelnde Kavalier, der in der Vossischen Zeitung über die Modernen leitartikelt."*[22] Repeatedly his ironic scorn is directed against *"die publizistischen Vertreter des Alten"*; against *"diejenigen, deren Beruf es scheint, ästhetische Begriffsverwirrung zu stiften"*; against *"sonderbare Schwärmer, so sich Kritiker heissen."*[23] And he raises a recurrent lament at *"der beschämend niedrige Stand unserer öffentlichen Kritik."*[24]

F. *Poetry and "Tendenz"*

Similar to the coupling of aesthetics with ethics Brahm views the critical confusion of art with *Tendenz* or propaganda. The opinion that a play cannot be a good play merely because it advocates a point of view is an egregious error propagated by those who happen to be opposed to that particular point of view. Instead of examining the play for its aesthetic points, it is merely the *Tendenz* factor which is taken into consideration, a substitution of a part for the

---

[15] Schr. I, 254.
[16] Schr. I, 114.
[17] Schr. I, 381.
[18] Schr. I, 235, 346, 382.
[19] Schr. I, 410.
[20] Schr. I, 339.
[21] Schr. I, 323, 345.
[22] Schr. I, 379f.
[23] Schr. I, 378.
[24] Schr. I, 142.

whole. A play is a good play not because its message happens to be one with which the critic agrees or disagrees but because it realizes certain dramatic values. Thus, in discussing the objections of the critical fraternity to Max Kretzer's play: *Bürgerlicher Tod*, Brahm finds their damning of its *Tendenz* as a point ill-taken. For it is precisely in the ineffectiveness of its *Tendenz* that Brahm sees the weakness of the play. In other words, *Tendenz* as such is not necessarily a damning element in a play; the question is: has that *Tendenz* been effectively translated into dramatic terms?[25] Brahm defines the problem very succinctly:

> Der ästhetischen Betrachtung Sache ist es nicht, über die Tendenz, welche ein Dichter in seinem Werk entfaltet hat, zu Gericht zu sitzen; ihre Sympathien und Antipathien zu der Fragestellung selbst beiseite schiebend, hat sie vielmehr zuerst und zuletzt nur zu entscheiden, wie viel von dem Gewollten künstlerisch verwirklicht ist durch Gestalten und Geschehen.[26]

The problem of *Tendenz* in art always emerges with particular urgency and bitterness in a great deal of criticism of the social drama. Brahm's point of view emphasizes the self-effacement of the critic insofar as his personal likes and dislikes are concerned in the judgment of a play. Criticism from this restricted and subjective coign of vantage will necessarily be superficial and unjust: " . . . *denn die Frage in aller Kunst ist nicht: sympathisch oder unsympathisch? sondern allein diese: lebendig oder tot?*"[27]

G. *The Autobiographical Fallacy*

Another one of Brahm's pet antipathies is what we may call "the autobiographical fallacy." We have seen Brahm himself bringing down on his head the wrath of old Gottfried Keller for this mechanical identification of the views expounded by some character, with the author's personal views. To consider this sort of procedure a fallacy does not at all imply the correctness of its other extreme, that the dramatist is to be considered as entirely dissociated from his characters. This would lead to a denial of the factor of personal experience which permeates most great art, and

---

[25] " . . . nicht auf das Was des Stoffes, auf das Wie der poetischen Anschauung kommt es an . . . ", Schr. I, 275.

[26] Schr. I, 216.   [27] Schr. I, 268.

therefore dramatic art as well. Often we can indeed recognize the personality of a dramatist expressed with apparent directness in the words of some character, especially if we find a whole series of correspondences and resemblances between author and character. But the character is also involved in a dramatic situation in which he reacts to other characters according to the logic of that situation. And in this sense we can speak of an objectivity or detachment of the author in regard to the character. Now, if the author has done justice to all the characters, then he has imparted to each some of the essence of his own personality. It is therefore too general and irrelevant, in this sense, to single out any one character without further ado and set this character up as the embodiment of the author's ideas. If we look for the expression of an author's views in a play, we must consider the import of the play as a whole. Stated differently, if the characters are fully-rounded human beings, then they will express both the author's and their own sentiments, engage in both commendable and reprehensible actions, and we shall thus find traces of the author's personality in all his characters; but just as all characters partake of the author's personality, so no single character in himself can be a complete counterpart of the author.

Speaking of the identification of Dr. Relling in *The Wild Duck* with Ibsen, Brahm writes:

Da sich Irrungen dieser Art stets und stets wiederholen, so muss auch immer von neuem wieder festgestellt werden, dass die Objektivität des Dramas, wie sie Ibsen anstrebt, solche Gleichsetzung nicht zulässt. Welchem Verständigen wird es einfallen, etwa aus einer Shakespeareschen Figur, auch wenn der Dichter sie mit seiner Sympathie begleitet, Tendenzen des Autors ohne weiteres abzuziehen. Auch Ibsen besitzt in seinen besten Werken diese Shakespearesche Allseitigkeit, welche ihn, um ein Wort Otto Ludwigs aufzunehmen, nicht mit der Parteilichkeit eines Advokaten für seine Person plädieren, sondern ihn in der strengen Sachlichkeit des Richters über sie Urteilen lässt. . . . Nicht der eine oder der andere spricht Ibsens Tendenz aus, sondern in beiden miteinander ist ein Teil des Rechten, . . . [28]

Another objection to the autobiographical fallacy is that it shifts the emphasis from the play as a work of art to the author

[28] Schr. I, 161.

and his relation to the play. But the cardinal thing is the play itself: whether it incorporates living characters; whether it realizes dramatic values; whether its form is organically related to its content; etc. The fact that the author may be projecting his personality across the foot-lights, or that he is in any way engaged in an act of self-revelation through the medium of a single character becomes important only according to the degree of effectiveness with which this self-revelation is organically and unobtrusively accomplished. Thus, all criteria deriving from a mechanical, subjective identification of the author with some single character are largely invalid because of the objectivity of characters involved in a dramatic complex with other characters, because of the shifting of emphasis from the play itself to the author, and finally because the unwary critic, when indulging this fallacy, tends to lapse into a mere *argumentum ad hominem;* as for example in the instance which Brahm quotes of Karl Frenzel, the authoritarian arbiter of Berlin dramatic criticism, who, together with Paul Lindau and Oscar Blumenthal, completely failed to realize the significance of Ibsen:

Aber auch die Berliner Kritik fiel durch vor Ibsen, jetzt und öfter. Karl Frenzel, Paul Lindau, Oscar Blumenthal, alle Zierden unseres kritischen Barreaus versagten. „Nora verlangt, dass Helmer ihre Schuld auf sich nimmt," schrieb Frenzel, „würde es vielleicht Ibsen tun?" Dieses wundervolle Argumentum ad hominem, in der „Deutschen Rundschau" aufgelesen, verdiente wohl als klassischer Unverstand weiterzuleben.[29]

It was particularly in the hostile reception to Hauptmann's *Vor Sonnenaufgang* that a critical *Hexensabbat*[30] raised its raucous wail in an orgy of moralistic indignation and personal invective. Critics believed they were assailing the poet himself by calumniating the central character of the play, Alfred Loth. He was denounced as a doctrinarian agitator, a mere puppet whose strings were being pulled by the author. Hauptmann was identified with this character and with his views on heredity and alcoholism. Both the hero of the play and Hauptmann were interchangeably dubbed fools. Brahm's rejoinder was that this character as well as the

[29] Schr. I, 450f.   [30] Schr. I, 260.

others in the play are clearly-conceived individuals who live in their own right and who are not mere vehicles of ideas for which the author is to be held responsible.[31] Brahm also shows that the modern dramatist, whether he be Ibsen, Tolstoi, or Hauptmann, knows of no hero in the sense of the older drama:

Posa mag Schillers Held und idealisiertes Abbild sein, aber Loth ist eine Gestalt mit vielen individuellen Zügen, kein Ideal und kein Träger einer subjektiven dichterischen Tendenz.[32]

Once again Brahm emphasizes that there can be no genuine conception of art in those who bring their own material sympathies and antipathies to the work of literature and make the author personally responsible for every judgment and every point of view expressed by his characters.[33] In *Vor Sonnenaufgang* a peasant woman, Madame Krause, delivers herself of a literary pronunciamento in exceedingly unadorned language.[34] To be consistent, the critics who mechanically establish autobiographical parallels between the author and his characters should place the responsibility for Madame Krause's choice bit of aesthetic criticism directly upon Hauptmann and assert that those words represent his own views on literature.[35] This *reductio ad absurdum*, effected with caustic irony by Brahm, relegates into its proper perspective what we have chosen to call "the autobiographical fallacy."

H. *Poetische Platzverteilung*

One of the common expedients of a type of criticism which asseverates rather than distinguishes is the passing of ordinal judgments. It is true that in the field of art and literature certain works and certain men stand out above others. The extremes of genius and mediocrity provide us with two points between which all works and authors theoretically belong in some more or less exact linear order. But we perceive at once that with the possible exception of wide extremes of excellence and bathos, where the

---

[31] Schr. I, 261.   [32] *Ibid.*
[33] Schr. I, 262.
[34] "Oaber da Schillerich oaber a Gethemoan, a sune tumm'n Scheisskarle, die de nischt kinn'n als lieja:" Act I, p. 38.
[35] Schr. I, 262.

difference is so obvious as to pass for axiomatic without further proof, we must resort to qualitative distinctions, based chiefly on aesthetic considerations, before we have the right to prefer one work to another, or to adjudge one author superior to another. Purely ordinal judgments, however, avoid this necessary critical process; they postulate exactly that which is to be proven. *A* is arbitrarily considered superior to *B; C* is classified with *A*, and therefore *C* is also superior to *B*. Or work *A* of an author is summarily pronounced superior to his work *B*, and consequently, work *B* is insignificant and a failure. Similarly, an author's works are measured according to his previous works but never on their own intrinsic merits. The escape from criticism in such puerile, algebraic juxtapositions is glaringly obvious. And yet how widespread Brahm found this intellectually indolent habit of approaching with mechanical and quantitative design the dynamic and qualitative essence of a work of art and of an artistic personality.

This fallacy is related to the preceding ones in its assumption of exactly that which is to be proven. Like the ethical fallacy, it springs from a subconscious maze of personal prejudice and uncritical arbitrariness. It places the critic in the irresponsible and unassailable role of an absolutist delivering himself of august decrees which are often as irrelevant as they are banal, and which reveal more about the intellectual myopia of the critic than about the object of his supposed criticism. Indeed, the ordinal fallacy often coincides with the ethical fallacy; as for example, when one work of art is praised as being "good," "moral," or "satisfactory" (whatever that may mean), whereas another is condemned as "bad," "immoral," or "unsatisfactory." Here there is an ordinal series of ethical judgments according to which works are mechanically arranged along a line extending from point "good" to point "bad." As Brahm points out to the detractors of Ibsen's *Ghosts* and *An Enemy of the People:*

Die Allgemeinheit dieser Ausdrücke beweist nur, dass man mit gewissen Abstrakten Anforderungen auch an das originelle Kunstwerk herantritt, anstatt erst aus ihm selber die Normen des Urteils unmittelbar abzuziehen. Es scheint mir nicht, dass die Bezeichnung „unbefriedigend" überhaupt ein künstlerisches Urteil einschliesse. . .[36]

[36] Schr. I, 129.

In discussing Hauptmann's *Einsame Menschen* Brahm draws a comparison between Ibsen and Hauptmann. He shows the influence and the inspiration which Ibsen provided for Hauptmann. But in this sensitive appreciation Brahm also maintains his spirit of self-criticism in delimiting the significance of this comparison by including a contrast as well. Not only resemblances but differences are dwelt upon, and the effort is to understand and appreciate each of the dramatists in his own right rather than to prefer one to the other or to apply an ordinal or quantitative rating to each; for as Brahm remarks:

> Es kann mir nicht in den Sinn kommen, hier Ibsen und Hauptmann gegeneinander abschätzen zu wollen. Abgesehen davon, dass mir alle poetische Platzverteilung roh erscheint, die da spricht: Du kommst auf Nr. 2, du aber bist der Primus omnium . . . [37]

Brahm's exposure of what we have been calling "the ordinal fallacy" is nowhere more clearly and sensitively expressed than in his criticism of Ibsen. Brahm followed the career of the Scandinavian dramatist in Germany from *Ghosts* right through to *When We Dead Awaken*. He is intimately acquainted with all of Ibsen's plays in the order of their creation. He has a synoptic view of all the coincidences of character, action, motif, development, dramatic technique and form throughout the whole sequence of plays. The plays do not exist merely as distinct and separate entities for Brahm. Each one is inextricably linked and interwoven with the whole matrix of Ibsen's achievement. The temptation for ordinal judgments, therefore, is nowhere greater than in regard to Ibsen. How acutely Brahm was aware of this and how shrewdly he was able to circumvent this temptation is revealed in his introduction to Ibsen's *Pillars of Society*. Brahm not only defines the nature of the ordinal fallacy but also exposes its flagrant irrelevancy in criticism:

> Dem deutschen Kunsturteil ist es geläufig, Zensuren zu erteilen: recht gut, gut, genügend. Man straft ab, man unterscheidet Dichter ersten, zweiten, dritten Ranges, und unablässig spielt man die einzelnen Künstler, die einzelnen Werke gegeneinander aus. Die berühmte Zweifelsfrage: wer ist grösser, Schiller oder Goethe? ist nur

[37] Schr. I, 351.

in Deutschland denkbar; aber wie wir froh sein sollten, nach Goethes
Wort, zwei solche Kerle zu haben wie Schiller und ihn, so sollten wir
auch den Lebenden gegenüber bedeutender Schöpfungen froh sein
und nicht beständig fragen, welche von ihnen denn nun Nummer eins
verdiene. Wir sollten, wenn wir etwa vor Ibsens Dichtungen stehen,
nicht das *Puppenheim* gegen die *Wildente* und die *Wildente* gegen die
Frau vom Meere abschätzen, sondern unbefangen ein jedes für sich
in seinen Vorzügen und Eigenheiten zu erfassen streben; wir sollten
weder die Knospe auf Kosten der Blume erheben noch umgekehrt
der reichen Frucht vorwerfen, dass ihr die frühlingshaften Reize der
Jugend doch mangeln. Und wenn wir dann vom ästhetischen An-
schauen zum historischen Begreifen übergehen, so werden wir noch
deutlicher erkennen, wie hier Notwendigkeiten der Entwicklung
vorliegen, denen mit einem bloss abstrakten, lässlichen Kunsturteil
nicht beizukommen ist.[38]

I. *Dramatic or Undramatic?*

In addition to these general fallacies which Brahm exposes and
which might apply to all aesthetic criticism, there are specialized
problems which are peculiar to criticism of the drama, taking their
formulation and scope from the very nature of dramatic structure.
In the criticism inimical to his *protégés* Brahm was often obliged
to answer the charge that a play was poor because it was essentially narrative (*episch*) rather than dramatic (*dramatisch*). The
distinction is an exceedingly nice one and has long been a favorite
topic for theorists of the drama. The crux of the problem lies in
the broader question as to the accuracy of demarcation between
literary types in general.

1. *Literary Types and Styles*

It is true that we constantly refer to such types as prose, poetry,
and drama, and to the subtler stylistic distinctions such as narrative, descriptive, expository, and dramatic. But just as in nature
there is no particular flower that fully represents the *genus* flower,
so in the field of literature there is no particular style that fully
represents its type.[39] This, however, does not invalidate the use
of these literary types in criticism any more than reference to any

---

[38] Schr. I, 239f.
[39] The point is made by Emil Ermatinger in his discussion of dramatic types: *Die
Kunstform des Dramas*, Leipzig, 1931, p. 14.

general species is invalid because no single one of its living examples is the species itself. Logical categories and abstractions are indispensable to thought and are useful in proportion to the degree in which we remain aware of their conceptual, rather than real, character. Thus, there is very rarely, if ever, a pure narrative type or a pure dramatic type. The types very frequently, if not always, overlap.

Criticism, in classifying works according to literary types (this classification is assumed, for instance, when a play is called "undramatic"), or in adjudging defective a work that is not purely the type it nominally claims to be, must proceed warily if it is not to cancel itself out by disregarding the overlapping nature of literary types in general. Perhaps the solution of this difficulty is best effected if a sharper distinction is made between "types" and "styles." Types of literature are objective categories representing ideal entities; whereas styles are subjective, psychological, and vary with the particular author. Types almost always overlap each other but styles may be conceived of as consistently the same throughout varying types. For example, a dramatic style may occur not only in a drama but also in a narrative work, or in a poem. Style may be considered the reflection of the author's psychological make-up.[40] And as such it carries over into whatever type of literature he may be writing. There are among literary artists examples whose style of expression is almost exclusively dramatic no matter what type of literature they may be writing. Naturally, their best and most copious work is confined to the type which most generally corresponds to their style. Shakespeare, Lessing, Schiller, Kleist, Hebbel, are writers whose style is preeminently dramatic even in those of their works which are not dramas.[41]

2. *Fluctuant Criteria*

Another point to be taken into account is the shifting conception through the ages of what constitutes the "dramatic" type. The long, exalted soliloquies of classical drama appear more suited to a narrative or descriptive type from the point of view of the

[40] *Ibid.*   [41] *Op. cit.*, p. 18.

short, staccato dialogue of the realistic drama. With a few illustrious exceptions, the drama in verse has been generally deemed
unsuitable by the modern realistic dramatist. On the other hand,
a naturalistic dramatist may incorporate into his play long passages in which, as in real life, some character describes a state of
soul or indulges in a rambling, incoherent soliloquy verbally re-
producing his stream of consciousness. It follows then, that far
from being bound by hard and set rules, dramatic style or its absence cannot be unerringly recognized by an atomic examination
of the details of a play. Indeed, the question of dramatic style rests
upon such fluctuant criteria that it must be considered of periph-
eral significance as a guide in the judgment of a play. What
remains central is the dramatic effect of the play as a whole. The
dramatist of genius can expand the presumed categories of his art.

How irrelevant is it to condemn a play which shows characters
in dramatic conflict and which arouses emotional participation on
the part of its audience, merely by isolating certain of its stylistic
aspects and arbitrarily dubbing them "undramatic?" And how
doubly irrelevant is it to praise a play which has no dramatic effect
as a whole, by pointing out its nominally "dramatic" style?

What problems do these considerations present to the critic?
Most certainly, as Brahm shows, no critic is justified in calling a
dramatist "undramatic" on a superficial basis of literary "types."
It is only the general "style" and all the subtle complexities which
style involves that can serve as a valid basis for such a criticism:

Ob Hauptmanns feiner Impressionismus „eigentlich" dramatisch
ist? Das Problematische in seiner Kunst . . . liegt hier; und für die
oberflächliche Betrachtung scheint es bereits entschieden, dass dergleichen modischer Unfug allenfalls wohl der Novelle ziemt, doch
nicht der Tragödie. Von einem „Wust" der Einzelzüge spricht eben
so derb wie unzutreffend Herr Neumann-Hofer; und sein kritischer
Verstand, der sich das erste Mal in besagtem Wust noch verlor, steht
nun betroffen still vor seiner „belanglosen Fadheit." Ich würde zwar
nicht so hanebüchenen Urteilen, aber vielleicht den feiner geformten
trauen, erinnerte ich mich nicht gar zu gut, wie der gleiche Vorwurf
auch Henrik Ibsen entgegenscholl, vor wenigen Jahren noch: diese
„Nora" ist wohl ein Roman, aber niemals ein Drama, so wies etwa
Friedrich Spielhagen nach, so scharfsinnig wie elegant. Spielhagen
der Ibsen über dramatische Wirkungen aufklärt—heute lächelt man

darüber; und so wird man vielleicht auch Hauptmanns inneres
Drängen auf eine Erneuerung dramatischer Formen noch anders
werten lernen . . . die Frage kann hier nur sein, ob die „Grenzen"
des Dramatischen, die Hauptmann zu überschreiten scheint, so scharf
gehütet sind, wie die einen versichern, oder ob ein Kühner Eroberer
sie weitern kann, wie wir anderen es hoffen.[42]

3. *Dramatic Style*

Before quoting further representative passages which reveal
Brahm's insight into these problems of literary types and styles,
a more positive review of his conception of dramatic style is in
order. He draws a sharp distinction between internal and external
dramatic action.[43] Mere external action is to Brahm a vulgar and
literal travesty on genuine dramatic structure. He refers to it
pejoratively as *"das sogenannte 'eigentliche' Dramatische."*[44] He also
expresses himself scathingly, as we have seen, concerning critics
who demand a literal plot or complication leading to a neat
dénouement in the manner of the French *pièce bien faite* school. This
sort of artificial plot is a dead, schematic constriction of living
themes and characters which tumbles down like a house of cards
in the face of a realistic portrayal of life:

. . . Und doch gibt es immer noch Leute, sonderbare Schwärmer, so
sich Kritiker heissen, welche von einem modernen Drama vor allem
„Handlung" fordern, einen sichtbaren Knoten, eine fesselnde Ver-
wicklung: ob das moderne Leben dergleichen bietet, gilt ihnen einerlei,
genug, dass die Forderung in der heiligen Konvention begründet ist,
und dass sie engagiert sind, sie aufrecht zu erhalten. Darum stehen
sie achselzuckend, warnend mit erhobenem Finger vor Hauptmanns
neuer Komödie; der Erfolg freilich ist da, und sie müssen ihn be-
scheinigen—aber ein „Bühnenstück" hat Hauptmann dennoch nicht
geschaffen; ein Dichter ist er ja wohl, aber kein eigentlicher Dramatiker. Schade nur, dass man uns nicht auch anvertraut, woran man
denn, an welchem objektiven Kriterium, den „eigentlichen" Dramatiker wohl erkennt; ich hatte mir immer gedacht, in meiner theoretischen Unschuld: wer ein Ding schreibt, das von der Bühne herab die
stärksten und die feinsten Wirkungen tut, das die Leute ins Theater
lockt zu manchen Wiederholungen und den herzlichsten Beifall ent-
fesselt—wer das schreibt, müsse wohl ein Dramatiker sein und ein
„Bühnenstück" geschaffen haben.[45]

---

[42] Schr. I, 352f. [43] Schr. I, 257.
[44] *Ibid.* [45] Schr. I, 378.

From the comparison of Ibsen with the tradition of Greek tragedy, which we have already discussed, Brahm deduces the dramatic value of concentration of action. Elsewhere he praises the eschewal of purely incidental dramatic retardation. He insists on the vital "objectivity" or inner logic of character and of situation. He also praises the development of characters and of situations by indirection, *i.e.* by dialogue and action. Thus, he admires in Hauptmann's *Friedensfest* the apparent aimlessness of its development whereby in the course of conversation and action the fate of an entire family is portrayed in minute detail:

> ... kein Wort fällt, das ausdrücklich zur Aufklärung des Lesers gesprochen würde, keine breiten Erzählungen geschehen, die den Gang des Dramas willkürlich hemmten; sondern aus höchst gegenständlichen Gesprächen macht sich uns die Lage dieser Menschen anschaulich ... [46]

Another desideratum of dramatic style, which Brahm finds supplied by Hauptmann, is its dynamic and plastic essence. In the true dramatist, all thought and conflict are translated into living forms:

> Wenn der Musiker in Tönen denkt, so denkt der echte Dramatiker, so denkt Hauptmann in Gestalten: alles setzt sich ihm in Rede und Erscheinung um, und in jedem Augenblicke, deutlich bis ins kleinste, mit Geste und Miene, sieht er seine Menschen vor sich stehen.[47]

4. *Tragisch—Komisch*

Similar arbitrary classifications of dramatic types occur in the literal distinction often made between the tragic and the comic. This over-simplification of a complex subject is exposed in two aspects in Brahm's criticism of critics. On the one hand a sharp and inflexible distinction is made between the tragic and the comic, with no allowance for a fusion or overlapping of the two. And on the other hand a certain theme is arbitrarily linked with either the tragic or the comic type, and the treatment of this theme in the type with which it is not linked is considered inadmissable because it creates a discrepancy between content and form.

Brahm merely applies the test of reality in attacking the critics

---

[46] Schr. I, 297.   [47] Schr. I, 299.

who propound this tragic-comic confusion. Does life afford us any
such sharp division between the tragic and the comic? Since it
does not, then art, which is the reflection of life, should not create
this false distinction. The problem emerges in the critical miscomprehension of Ibsen's *Hedda Gabler*, which incorporates tragi-
comical motifs. To Brahm, dramatic effect is heightened by such
motifs because they bring the tragedy into more poignant relief.
His realistic point of view is illustrated in the following passage:

. . . aber was wäre denn poetisch deutlich genug, dass die kritischen
Alleswisser es nicht verdunkelten? Da erscheint es als ein völliges
Vergreifen etwa, dass „eine verbummelte Nacht" das Drama wendet:
das sei ein „Possenmotiv," nichts weiter. Du lieber Gott, als ob das
Leben extra für die Herren Dramatiker und Kritiker in zwei Teile
verfiele: einen tragischen und einen komischen; und als ob nicht die
Verknüpfung grade der verschiedenen „Motive" Heddas Pein ver-
stärkte: „Ach das Lächerliche und das Gemeine," so klagt sie selbst,
„es legt sich wie ein Fluch auf alles, was ich nur anrühre." Das sind,
mit Verlaub, Gottschedische Weisheiten, die die Herren so selbst-
bewusst zu Markte tragen; und in der Tat hat die gute Madame
Gottsched ja vor Shakespeares Genie einst ähnlich Gescheites geredet:
Desdemonas Schnupftuch erschien ihr so possenhaft-unmöglich, wie
nur Herrn Neumann-Hofer der angeblich „schnappstrinkende" Löv-
borg, der sein bestes vertan hat in einer Nacht.[48]

Brahm applies the same test of reality in a review of Hebbel's
Gyges. Because the theme has been treated before in a comic vein,
it has been associated with the comedy type. Since Hebbel had
made his play a tragedy, critics spoke of the discrepancy between
content and form. Brahm shows that there is no sharp distinction
between tragedy and comedy, and that the genius of the author
may interpret reality either as one or the other or as both. But
more important yet, he shows the inevitability and the fitness of
Hebbel's translation of the fable into the tragic rather than the
comic as issuing out of a Germanic rather than a Latin attitude
towards sexual *mores:*

Ein Missverhältnis von Stoff und Form hat man in dieser Entwicklung gefunden und hat gemeint, ein „Komödienmotiv" sei hier gewaltsam ins Tragische gewendet worden. Nun glaube ich einmal, dass
die Kunst, gleichwie die Natur, diese doppelte Buchführung von

[48] Schr. I, 323.

Komödien- und Tragödienmotiv gar nicht kennt, mit welcher eine verzopfte Ästhetik sich so gross tut; das Leben in den meisten Fällen ist tragi-komisch, und welche Seite der Dichter fassen will, ist einzig Frage seines Temperaments. Und oft schon erschien dem nüchternen Beurteiler niedrig-komisch, was ein Poet im Zusammenhang der Dinge tragisch genannt hat.[49]

Brahm, as we see, makes short shrift of these problems and confusions without going into the profounder implications of the nature of tragedy and of comedy. But the aesthetics of tragedy and the relation of tragedy to comedy are complex subjects, an analysis of which is imperative before one can properly approach the problems raised by these summary distinctions between the tragic and the comic. However, at this point we have confined ourselves to the simpler approach to these problems, as Brahm has done in disposing of them effectively and in short order by applying the test of reality. The subtler and more intricate phases of a theory of tragedy do not figure in Brahm's journalistic criticism of the drama.

5. Complexity of the Problem

If we measure the problem of the dramatic over against the undramatic as revealed in Brahm's more representative passages on the subject, we see that the fundamental question is whether there can be any hard and set rules for the distinction of literary types. To Brahm the problem further simplifies itself to the old bugbear about the "laws" of art. Because Goethe and Schiller once wrote dramas from which certain rules of dramatic art may be deduced, critics tend to consider these rules final and unchangeable. These rules are general and eternal and permit of no individual differences, according to authoritarian critics. But Brahm points out that rules are irrelevant in the fact of forward-looking, creative genius. To be guided wholly by the past is to forego the present.[50] Brahm views the criticism which is based on the mechanical distinction between types of literature, such as *episch-dramatisch* and *tragisch-komisch*, as a superficial confusion which attempts to set up aesthetic laws incompatible with an empirical reality. The boundaries of the narrative and the

[49] Schr. I, 397.   [50] Schr. I, 346.

dramatic types are shifting lines which are constantly altered by literary modes and by the fiat of genius. Not to take this into consideration is to revert to mere arbitrary pronouncements rather than to enter into analytic criticism. An illuminating discussion by Brahm of this problem follows. In spite of its length, its quotation is justified because it is revelatory of Brahm's polemical satire which can elucidate principles at the same time that it devastates the propounders of errors:

Die Frage nach den Gesetzen von Novelle und Drama ist wieder einmal ästhetische Tagesfrage. Gerhart Hauptmanns „Einsame Menschen,“ die so viel Anregung gegeben, haben bei grauen und bei grünen Theoretikern die Frage in Fluss gebracht, wie sich Erzählung und Drama gegen einander abgrenzen. Vielmehr nicht die Frage: die kritischen Alleswisser, die durch kein Kunstereignis aus ihrem seligmachenden Selbstvertrauen aufzuscheuchen sind, haben die Formel auch diesmal, fertig für alle Zeiten, in der Tasche; und indem sie auch vor der Schöpfung des Genies kein anderes Bedürfnis haben, als ihre eigene kluge Vorzüglichkeit zu erweisen, schreiben sie geruhig die Worte nieder: „Ein Dramatiker ist Gerhart Hauptmann nicht.“ Sie nehmen nicht wahr, wie die ganze dramatische Bewegung der Moderne, seit Ibsen her, jene unersteiglich hohe Mauer abtragen will, die Epik und Dramatik von einander schied; wie sie zwar nicht die Bretterwelt unter die Bedingungen des Buches stellen, aber doch sie befreien will von den spanischen Stiefeln willkürlicher Sonderregeln. Alledem zum Trotz bleibt es dabei: Ibsen ist „eigentlich“ ein Novellist, Hauptmann ist ein Novellist; und merkwürdig ist nur das eine, das diese schrullenhaften, übrigens nicht unbegabten Männer eifrig fortfahren, Dramen zu schreiben, nichts als Dramen, nicht achtend alle bessere Zurede der Frenzel und solcher, die es werden wollen.[51]

[51] Schr. I, 345.

V. *The Function of Criticism*

Up to this point we have discussed Brahm's conception of the nature of the critical process. This conception has emerged not only positively, in his theoretical ideal of the "naturalistic critic," but also negatively, in his polemical arraignment of critical fallacies, over-simplifications, and of the raising of problems extraneous to aesthetic criticism. The detailed analysis of Brahm's critical acumen in concrete action can now serve us admirably as a departure for the discussion of what Brahm conceived to be the *purpose* or *function* of criticism. For once we subject the German theatre, both in its traditional and contemporary aspects, to the tests of his critical process, there will naturally be revealed shortcomings, defects, deleterious and retrograde features, the diagnosis and correction of which coincidentally provide criticism with its tasks and problems. If we compare the critical process with a diagnostic method applied to the ailing theatre, then the interpretation of symptoms which this diagnosis affords will determine the therapeutic method; in other words, it will give us an insight into the function of criticism.

A. *The Ideal Theatre*

Otto Brahm's ideal demands for the German theatre may at first seem to us rather austere and exacting. He seems to think of the theatre as rightfully belonging in a rarefied, Olympian sphere. We read his description of the German stage at the peak of its contemporary development, *i.e.* the triumph of Ibsen, and come across such phrases as: *"die grosse Kulturmacht"*—*"die Führerin im Geistesleben"*—*"Gebieterin über die Seelen"*—*"die Tempel aller Kunstformen"*[1]—*"kein Ort der blossen Unterhaltung, sondern ein Kulturfaktor, eine ungeheuere Macht über die Seelen, eine weithin tragende Leuchte geistiger und künstlerischer Vorgänge."*[2] We recall his designation of the theatre as the most invaluable vehicle for literary agitation.[3] And superficially it may seem that Brahm ignores the many other aspects of a living theatre: its gratification of the pleasure principle, its molding of a group-consciousness, its

[1] Schr. I, 146.　　　[2] Schr. I, 459.　　　[3] Schr. I, 273f.

effect on morals and manners, etc. Yet upon closer examination we find that Brahm does not altogether ignore these other aspects.[4] Nevertheless, with him it is a question of emphasis. And when we examine the factors which govern this emphasis, then we realize its complete justification, its necessity, and perhaps even its inevitability.

Otto Brahm's overwhelming emphasis on the intellectual and the literary aspects in his ideal conception of the stage, considered moreover as an aesthetic and cultural institution, derives historically from a like tradition among the great German dramatists and men of the theatre. Lessing, Goethe, Schiller, and Hebbel, although vividly aware through personal experience of the discrepant dualism between drama and theatre, nevertheless had an exalted conception of the theatre and of its possibilities. To Lessing the theatre had among other functions that of *Geschmacksbildung*.[5] To Goethe the theatre was primarily *"eine Lehranstalt zur Kunst mit Heiterkeit."*[6] To Schiller it was *"eine moralische Anstalt"* and *"eine Schule der praktischen Weisheit."*[7] And Hebbel considered the theatre the indispensable means of expression of the drama, which, in his opinion, was the pinnacle of all the arts.[8] Hence, Otto Brahm's high conception of the theatre follows the tradition of these illustrious forebears.

B. *Criticism as Rationalization*

Brahm's intellectualism derives more particularly from the influence of his spiritual environment which was steeped in the Hamburg-Berlin rationalistic tradition. His preoccupation with literature derives from the educational influence of Scherer, who imparted to his pupil, along with his highly rationalized method of philological research, a profound reverence for the classics of German literature and an inexpungeable ideal of the high seriousness of literary endeavor. So formed and so conditioned, Brahm approached the field of dramatic criticism.

[4] Schr. I, 459.
[5] Cf. *Hamburgische Dramaturgie*, Ankündigung, et passim.
[6] Annalen, 1794.
[7] *Über die Schaubühne als moralische Anstalt*, 1785.
[8] *Das deutsche Theater*, 1859.

Now, what was the condition of literature, *i.e.* the drama, when Brahm appeared on the critical scene? The stage was stodgily plodding along on an anemic diet of considerably diluted neo-classicism (Wildenbruch, Wilbrandt), of the hollow mechanics of Sardou, Augier, and Scribe and their German emulators, and of a moribund declamatory tradition in the acting and staging of the German classics. Since the death of Hebbel no drama worthy of the tradition of German classicism had been produced. Naturally, this decline of the drama also had a decisive influence in leading Brahm to emphasize the literary aspect of the stage. His pervasive intellectualism together with his one-sided literary predilection furnished the strength and unity of purpose leading to Brahm's notable achievements. On the other hand, intellectualism and literature also govern his limitations.

Corresponding to the essentially intellectual process of criticism, which seeks for the reasons underlying an aesthetic effect, the first and foremost function of criticism is to rationalize and to classify; and this in turn leads to the necessity for making distinctions. "*Kritisieren heisst unterscheiden*" wrote Brahm at the outset of his career.[9] His subsequent writings constantly revert to this axiom. He finds it necessary to distinguish the sheep from the goats, genius from mere talent, drama from melodrama, living characters from dangling puppets, the essence of a play from its accidental effects, the effect of the printed version of a play from the effect produced by the performance, the achievement of the dramatist as distinguished from that of the actor, etc. etc.[10] We have seen in the preceding chapter his exposure of false and superficial distinctions. But he does not categorically deny the necessity for such distinctions. He merely insists that they be real rather than apparent, that they be based upon an organic conception of all the subtle and intricate factors involved rather than upon a haphazard selection of this or the other incidental factor.

C. *The Criticism of Criticism*

In order to obviate the drawing of such fortuitous distinctions it is essential for criticism to exercise its analytic function upon

---

[9] Schr. I, 68.   [10] *Ibid.* and *op. cit.*, I, 302 et passim.

itself. Thus, another basic function of criticism is what has often been called "the criticism of criticism." How often and how aptly Brahm employs this function we have seen in his polemics against critics and their foibles, and in his self-criticism, whereby he analyzes and justifies his own critical procedures.

D. *The Catalytic Function*

Dramatic criticism also has a catalytic function. It stirs up fruitful discussion by means of the dissemination of ideas and the positing of tasks, problems, and projects for the theatre. Like Lessing, Brahm also regards this catalytic function very highly and feels that if his criticism has accomplished nothing more than the propagation of *fermenta cognitionis*, it will have justified itself. We see this function exemplified in Brahm's view of the theatre as a means of literary propaganda. But criticism can only act indirectly in this function because the ultimate effect is produced by the theatre itself.

. . . nicht das heisseste kritische Bemühen, nicht der glänzendst geschriebene Essay kann wirken, was ein echter Erfolg der Szene wirkt.[11]

Nevertheless, criticism, in preparing the way for literary propaganda on the stage, is fulfilling a similar task. In discussing retrospectively the *Freie Bühne's* presentation of *Vor Sonnenaufgang,* Brahm remarks:

. . . hätte die Freie Bühne auch weiter kein Verdienst, als dass sie durch die Ankündigung dieses Stückes literarische Diskussionen geweckt, Anregungen aller Art gegeben und an Stelle der Stagnation den Kampf und die Bewegung gebracht hat, so dürfte sie schon ihres Wirkens froh sein, . . . [12]

A more direct influence of dramatic criticism in its catalytic function is represented by the ideals and projects which it sets up for the future progress of the theatre. Brahm repeatedly agitates for realism both in the drama and on the stage. He points to Ibsen as a model to be followed. He urges the performance of Ibsen cycles and, as we have seen, even suggests complete casts for some

[11] Schr. I, 273.　　　　[12] Schr. I, 260.

of the plays long before any German producer has summoned up the hardihood to stage them.[13] He champions Naturalism in the drama because he sees in it a wholesome, if somewhat transitory, influence. He sees the limitations of the commercial theatre and is active in the fight against censorship by setting up a *Freie Bühne*.[14] The crying need to awaken the German theatre out of its torpor and stagnation is to free it from its atrophied convention and formality by bringing it into contact with vital and contemporary currents.

The theatre, however, must not cut itself off completely from the past. On the contrary, it must take the great classics which have been handed down to it and reinterpret them so that they will live again for contemporary audiences. The reinterpretation of the classics by means of a revolutionized staging and acting is one of the greatest tasks which Brahm's criticism poses for the German theatre. Thus, in speaking of Schiller's intentions with regard to the presentation of *Don Carlos*, Brahm shows the inanity of using a literal and uncut version of the text for the stage:

Wir wollen nicht einem Buchstabenglauben huldigen, der zur Erstarrung führt, sondern unsere Klassiker mit lebendiger Verehrung, aus dem Empfinden unserer Zeit heraus, umfassen: das ist die wahre Pietät.[15]

He repeats this necessity for reinterpretation with increasing emphasis. This is a technical problem, however, for the actor, the director, and the dramaturgist.[16] Consequently, we shall return to the details of these problems in our discussion of the technique of the theatre.

E. *The Social Function*

Thus far we have mentioned the intellectual and rationalizing functions of criticism and their supplementary implications. These are logical aspects of criticism considered purely as a technical process. But criticism also has moral and social functions which are organically connected with its technical processes. Criticism of the theatre, just like the theatre itself (and like all art that is not willfully dissevered from life) has an umbilical connection with

---

[13] Schr. I, 73.
[15] Schr. I, 53.
[14] Schr. I, 273.
[16] Schr. I, 87ff.

the public, in other words, a social and moral responsibility. It is this social function which concerns us here. Let us examine its manifestations in Brahm's criticism.

Perhaps the most elementary social function of the critic is to act as an interpretative intermediary between the work of art and the public. Because of his presumably superior powers of aesthetic judgment due to training, practice, and certain native talents which he may bring to his vocation, he is more or less fitted to point out the merits and demerits of a play. The critic's intermediation is particularly important in explaining novel, problematical, or revolutionary art, the meaning and effect of which may be vague and puzzling to a naïve audience. The critic's influence naturally extends beyond the immediate audience of a play; he commands a broader public to which he has access by reason of his journalistic medium. A social responsibility is thus imposed upon the critic by the very nature of this intermediary function.

The importance of this elementary fact can scarcely be over-emphasized in Brahm's opinion. The failure of many critics to appreciate the novel significance of Hauptmann can be ascribed to their dereliction with regard to this basic responsibility, according to Brahm. Instead of seeking to understand and to interpret Hauptmann's plays for the benefit of the public, they vulgarize and oversimplify their task by mechanical, plus-or-minus judgments. Brahm points out the need for honesty and integrity in the critic's fulfilment of his intermediary role. To him, the critic is first and foremost *"ein ehrlicher Makler."*[17] Discussing the critical detractors of Hauptmann's *Kollege Crampton*, Brahm says:

Ich habe versucht, einige der Einwände, welche man gegen Hauptmanns Stück erhoben hat, zu widerlegen, nicht, weil ich glaubte, dass es gegen jeden Einwand gefeit sei, sondern weil die am Hergebrachten haftende Art unserer deutschen Kritik, die noch immer nicht lernen will, künstlerischer Besonderheit verstehend nachzugehen, den Widerspruch notwendig heraufrufen muss. Man glaubt, ein Kritiker sei ein Mann, welcher feststellt: dies ist lobenswert und das ist tadelnswert; und denen in den Zeitungen sprechen die im Publikum so grobe

[17] Schr. I, 382.

Kritik vor und nach. Das kritische Beckmessertum, das mit den Tabulaturen in der Hand den Kunsttempel bewacht und zornig warnt:

Singet dem Volk auf Markt und Gassen
Hier wird nach den Regeln nur eingelassen!

und das kritische Poloniustum, das zwar die schlotterichte Königin gut findet, aber vor jeder Feinheit stöhnt: „Das ist zu lang"—sie gehen brüllend um und suchen, wen sie verschlingen; aber dass ein Kritiker auch derjenige ist, welcher die Intentionen eigenartiger Kunst den Hörern nur aufzuschliessen sucht als ein ehrlicher Makler —davon haben die Herren noch nichts gehört.[18]

In carrying out his interpretative and intermediary functions, the critic necessarily exercises an educational influence. The critic as a pedagogue can influence not only the public but also all those who engage professionally in the art of the theatre: the dramatist, the actor, the director, etc. We have already mentioned Brahm's efforts to recruit and educate the Berlin public so that they might become *ibsenreif.* His admonitions to dramatists can also be viewed in the light of an educational function. In a warning against the superficial facility of Sudermann, Brahm expands the effect of his remarks by pointing out the way which a dramatist of integrity would follow if he wished to avoid the pitfall of easy success through an unconscionable catering to sensationalism and the mere surface gratification of his audience:

Zwei Wege stehen also dem jungen Dramatiker für seine zukünftige Produktion offen: er kann in jener dem Publikum genehmen Mischung von altem und neuem Stil, von Konvention und Natur, von präparierten, geistreichen Problemen und bescheidener Wahrheit fortfahren; oder er kann sich entschlossener auf die Seite des Realismus stellen, und allen überlieferten Motiven des „Feuilletonromanes" resolut entsagen. Wohin ihn Temperament und Geschmack nun treiben werden, bleibt abzuwarten; ein beliebter Theaterschriftsteller kann er auf dem einen Wege werden, dessen Stücke bei der Bettelarmut unserer Produktion allen Bühnen willkommen sein müssen; auf dem anderen Pfade kann er die poetische Entwicklung an seinem Teile fördern und eine literarische Bedeutung gewinnen, über den Kreis der theatralischen Vergnügungen hinaus.[19]

The pointlessness of producing great drama without actors sufficiently intelligent and skilled to interpret it was forced on

[18] Schr. I, 381f.   [19] Schr. I, 282f.

Brahm's attention through the miserable rendition of realistic plays by actors schooled in the traditions of declamation and virtuosity. More and more the realization of the organic interdependence of dramatist, actor, and public grew upon Brahm. The educational function of criticism, if it was to be effective all along the line, would also have to be exerted on the actor. Brahm's efforts in this direction will be detailed in our discussion of the art of acting in the chapter on the technique of the theatre.

Brahm's conception of the national mission of the stage is also social in its implications. In the political sphere as well, Brahm's quarrels with the censors of *Die Weber*, his condemnation of Wilhelm, The First, his realization of the class basis of the commercial theatre, and his efforts to bring the theatre to the people (he gave his full support to the *Volksbühne*), all testify to his sense of social responsibility.[20]

F. *Theory and Practice*

An ultimate function of dramatic criticism is one in which it supersedes itself, so to speak, by translating its theory into action. Brahm's criticism sets up a dual qualification for the critic. On the one hand he must exercise the literary and aesthetic aspects of his vocation; but on the other, he must also master the technique of the theatre. In order to attain this mastery, he must have intimate, first hand contact with the stage, must actually participate in its technical functioning. Only through this direct participation can he derive the insights which practical experience affords. By actively engaging in the work of the theatre, he subjects his criteria to the acid tests of practical reality. The critic's lofty and detached theorizing remains sterile unless it is brought to grips with concrete practice. Hence, the higher validity of all dramatic criticism is the graduation of its ideals, standards, and aesthetic demands into the sphere of the living theatre.

Now it may be argued that the inevitable specialization into which we are all forced because of the multiple complexity of social and intellectual life, limits the possibility of the critic's being anything else but a critic. But Brahm does not make a virtue out

[20] Cf. Brahm's essay: *Wiener und Berliner Volksbühne*, Schr. I, p. 429ff.

of a necessity. There seems to be a steady drift towards the stage in all of his theoretical work. His advice, suggestions, his negative criticisms, all bear at least the implication, if not the literal assertion, that had he been in a position of authority on the stage, he would have done otherwise. It was, therefore, no accident that he was elected to direct the *Freie Bühne*. His directorship was the natural consequence of his dramatic criticism. And as the director of the *Freie Bühne*, while at the same time the editor of its periodical of the same name, he was enabled to write critical reviews from the inside, so to speak. He reviewed the plays which he himself had chosen and staged, so that we see them not merely as detached entities but within the context of their practical staging problems.

This is the organic unity of criticism and dramaturgy which forms the ultimate degree of Brahm's activity as a critic. It is a last, brilliant interval in which his critical powers realize themselves to the full before the theatre claims him wholly. The translation of word into deed, the call to which is implicit in all of Brahm's virile, restive criticism, is here effected. And the last function of dramatic criticism for Brahm is its merging with stage practice.

VI. *History and Organization of the Theatre*

A. *Berliner Hoftheater*

Although Brahm's senior colleague, Fontane, reviewed the performances in the *Berliner Hoftheater* for the *Vossische Zeitung*, there are indirect references to this theatre's decline in Brahm's reviews of the commercial theatre. This reference becomes evident first, in the fact that Brahm condemns almost everything that this theatre stands for; and second, in the fact that he accords an enthusiastic welcome to the establishment of new theatres which compensate for the deficiencies of the *Hoftheater*.

After a brief period of intermittent success under Iffland and under Tieck, the Prussian *Hoftheater* rapidly declined until by the 70's and 80's it had become an official shell of tradition remote from any semblance of art or even of outstanding national significance. Its directors were state officials (Botho von Hülsen was an army officer before becoming *Intendant* of the *Hoftheater*), and its repertoire was limited by royal idiosyncrasy to the classics, the hollow iambic-tragedies of the Schiller epigons, and, as a grudging concession to contemporaneity, the shoddy farces of Benedix or the stodgy, sentimental melodrama of Charlotte Birch-Pfeiffer.[1] Wildenbruch was obliged to struggle for more than a decade before bringing himself to the favorable attention of the comatose directorship of the *Hoftheater*. The theatre stagnated in this *"schlafsüchtige Epoche,"* to use Bab's expression.[2] Except for Meiningen and Bayreuth, royalty had largely exhausted its role as a patron of the theatrical arts in Germany, and the future development of the theatre was to proceed along commercial (*Unternehmerbetrieb*) and social (*Gesellschaftsbetrieb*) lines.[3]

B. *Adolf-Ernst Theater*

Among the first of the Berlin theatres that Brahm greets is the *Adolf-Ernst Theater* (*Viktoriatheater*), particularly for Herr Ernst's

---

[1] Cf. Julius Bab, *Das Theater der Gegenwart*, Leipzig, 1928, p. 12.
[2] *Ibid.*
[3] Schr. I, 431; The sociological development of the German theatre, from *Hoftheater, Geschäftstheater,* to *Volkstheater*, is traced by Julius Bab: *Das Theater im Lichte der Soziologie*, Leipzig, 1931; cf. particularly p. 174–182.

courage and insight in giving Wildenbruch's *Karolinger* a hearing
Brahm remarks that the long struggle Wildenbruch has had in
establishing contact with the living theatre throws a bad light on
the directorship of German theatres. He exhorts the support of
those to whom the theatre means more than just entertainment:

... wer immer noch Sinn hat für eine edlere Bühnenkunst und in
dem Theater mehr sucht als eine blosse Vergnügungsanstalt, ist
schuldig, die Bestrebungen des Herrn Ernst nach Kräften zu unter-
stützen.[4]

To Brahm the *Adolf-Ernst Theater* in its origins was a manifestation of social reform in the theatre. It was an attempt to establish
a popular theatre, a theatre of the masses.[5] Laudable as this attempt was, Brahm nevertheless points out its dangers. The masses
can be educated; these simple workers and tradesmen in their
naïve receptivity are indeed to be preferred to the jaded, effete
aristocracy and upper middle classes. But only a fearless and enter-
prising director of artistic probity can be successful here.[6] Such a
director the *Adolf-Ernst Theater* lacked; it soon degenerated into
an amusement machine:

Prompt schneidet diese tüchtige Futtermachine, wenn auch nicht
geräuschlos, unserem grossen Publikum sein Quantum an Unter-
haltungsbedürfnis zu, jahraus, jahrein: in der Flucht der Erscheinungen, unter seltsam wechselnden Titeln, bleibt sie bestehen, die Adolf-
Ernst-Posse mit dem grossen Verkleidungsquodlibet in der Mitte,
mit dem aufmarschierenden Jungfrauen, dem behäbigen Allerwelts-
onkel und all den anderen, auf beliebige Darsteller fest zugeschnit-
tenen Typen.[7]

This process of suiting the character types to the actors is the
opposite of Brahm's basic conception of theatrical art. Only a
mechanical, stereotyped result can ensue:

Bewundernd steht man vor diesem sicher fungierenden, herrlichen
Automaten: man werfe oben Goethes „Iphigenie" hinein—und mit
tödlicher Sicherheit kommt unten dennoch nichts anderes heraus als
die Adolf-Ernst-Normalposse.[8]

[4] Schr. I, 5.
[5] "Den anschwellenden breiten Massen genug zu tun, welche Theaterhungrig
beiseite standen . . . ", Schr. I, 432.
[6] " . . . nur ein völlig kunstsicherer Leiter, so ein volksfreundlicher 'Volksfeind,'
welcher zielbewusst 'experimentiert' . . . ", Schr. I, 433.
[7] Schr. I, 435.   [8] *Ibid.*

C. *Wallnertheater*

The *Wallnertheater*, at first an artistically significant haven for the *Berliner Lokalposse* and a commercial enterprise from which much was to be expected in contrast to the *Hoftheater*, also declined rapidly, in Brahm's estimation. The *genre* which had flourished during the heyday of this theatre declined with it. The *Lokalposse* and the *politische Posse*, which had developed parallel with the transition of Berlin into a metropolis, with its tangible city types, its vital conflicts, its rapport between urban satire and a receptive public, had subsided into vacuous and repetitious posturings. Political references were sedulously avoided because of a conservative fear of conflicting opinions. The courage of opposition was needed:

Auch Aristophanes war ein Reaktionär, und er tat dem Sokrates bitter Unrecht an, als er ihn unter die Sophisten setzte; allein der erste Possendichter ist er doch darum geblieben und auch das liberale Athen hat ihn müssen gelten lassen.[9]

An important factor in the decline of the *Wallnertheater*, according to Brahm, was the rise of the *Soloposse*[10] with all the excesses of virtuosity it brought in its wake. For all the genius and versatility of a great comic actor, the emphasis fell upon meretricious externalities conceived solely for their momentary effect on the audience. The theatre became an end in itself, divorced from life. Regretfully, but nonetheless firmly, Brahm charges the directors of the *Wallnertheater* with a lack of artistic vision:

Aber der rechte künstlerische Ehrgeiz—es muss endlich einmal ausgesprochen werden—scheint den Leitern des Wallnertheaters mehr und mehr abhanden zu kommen.[11]

D. *The Meininger in Berlin*

Brahm's critical threnody on the organization of the Berlin theatre assumes a more sprightly note during the Berlin performances of the Meiningen Court Players.[12] Since the first visit of the Meininger to Berlin,[13] their astounding mass effects had led to a

---

[9] Schr. I, 5.   [10] Schr. I, 93.   [11] Schr. I, 7.

[12] April, 1882. For a complete account of the history, aims, and organization of the Meiningen Court Players written by one of the troupe, cf. Max Grube, *Geschichte der Meininger*, Stuttgart, 1926.   [13] 1874.

partisan distortion of their true significance. *Meiningertum* had become a loose epithet to designate meticulous exactitude in staging, the magnification of the theatrical arts to the detriment of the dramatic word. But Brahm, as we know, abhors such vague generalizations and mechanically extremist views. The Meininger are to him no model of either absolutely good or absolutely bad theatrical art. Their significance is chiefly relative and transitional. In contrast to the apathy of the Berlin stage, the Meininger assumed prodigious magnitude; their stature was correspondingly dwarfed in Vienna where Dingelstedt had anticipated their technique.[14] Thus the influence of the Meininger is relative. As an absolute principle of technique *Meiningertum* is reprehensible, but as a catalytic influence it is salutory:

Von dem Augenblicke an, wo man das Meiningertum als kanonisches Vorbild hinstellt, ist es zu bekämpfen; will man es als ein blosses Ferment gelten lassen, so ist es uns willkommen.[15]

Although caustic in regard to their historicism and their archaeological precision of *décor*, which resulted in an unrelieved naturalistic technique of staging, Brahm is more intensely interested in those positive virtues of the Meininger the lack of which he has been deploring in the Berlin theatre. He comments on the success of their mass scenes in which dynamic ensemble effects are achieved.[16] This principle of ensemble playing, of a homogeneous company of the various artists engaged in a theatrical production, all co-operating towards a total and unified effect, is one of Brahm's most important ideals in the organization of the theatre. For all their one-sided success in mass-scenes (primarily a triumph of the director manipulating his drilled supernumeraries), and their failure in more intimate effects requiring the masterful genius of an individual actor, the totality of the Meininger's artistic organization exerts a profound and lasting influence on Brahm, just as it later does on Antoine[17] and Stanislawsky.[18] The organizational

---

[14] "Ein Meininger vor den Meiningern," Schr. I, 11.

[15] *Ibid.*   [16] Schr. I, 12.

[17] Cf. André Antoine, *Mes Souvenirs sur le Théâtre libre,* Paris, 1921; particularly Antoine's letter to Sarcey on the Meininger, July 23, 1888.

[18] For Stanislawski's observations on Chronegk and the Meininger cf. *My Life in Art,* Boston, 1924, pp. 196–201 and p. 229.

nucleus of the art theatre comes into modern being with the Meininger, and Brahm adopts this idea in his critical demands for the organization of the Berlin theatre.

E. *Deutsches Theater*

Undoubtedly the most significant event during Brahm's early career as a dramatic critic was the founding of the *Deutsches Theater* in Berlin.[19] Brahm is carried away by the momentousness of the occasion. Here was an opportunity to put an end to the stultifying monopoly of the *Hoftheater*. Although at this time a mere onlooker in his capacity as a representative of the press, he senses the almost unlimited cultural possibilities of the new theatre, and on the eve of its opening performance he pens a list of ideal demands to arouse the directors to a vivid realization of their tasks and responsibilities.[20]

1. *Geschmacksbildung*

The political growth of Germany after 1870 still lacked its cultural counterpart, and in order to develop this, a process of aesthetic education (Brahm speakes of Schiller's *"äesthetische Erziehung des Menschen"*) was necessary. This process of aesthetic education or *Geschmacksbildung* as Brahm calls it, is of national import to him, as it was to Lessing and Goethe:

An der nationalen Mission der Bühne, trotz all der kleinlichen Misere, die der Tag uns bringt, müssen auch wir heute festhalten.[21]

Thus the function of the new theatre, as Brahm envisions it, is to develop the national consciousness along cultural and aesthetic lines.[22] All other possible and presumable functions of the theatre are subservient to that of aesthetic education, a notion that may seem rather esoteric when viewed as an unqualified extreme. For note that Schiller's idea of the stage exercising its primary function through the refinement of manners here becomes the refinement of "good taste" or the "aesthetic sense." But the inner insepara-

---

[19] 1883.   [20] Schr. I, 30ff.   [21] Schr. I, 33.

[22] Cf. Brahm's praise of the contemporary patriotic significance of Kleist's *Prinz von Homburg* and his condemnation of Carl Caro's *Am Herzogshof* because it is a timeless and placeless tragedy far from the center of Germany's national development. Schr. I, 86.

bility of ethics from aesthetics provides the stage with both these functions. Consequently, we must explain Brahm's unilateral emphasis on the aesthetic as a compensatory gesture against the cultural ebb of Germany at this time. Taking issue with young Schiller's dictum, Brahm writes:

> Die Bühnenkunst, wie alle Kunst, hat keine anderen unmittelbaren Zwecke als ästhetische; die Schaubühne ist keine Anstalt der Moral, sondern eine Anstalt der Geschmacksbildung.[23]

This function of *Geschmacksbildung* is the decisive bond between the theatre and the public, since it is in essence a social function.[24] But there is no question of dictatorial pre-emption on the part of the theatre. The aesthetic education must be a reciprocal process.[25] The theatre must learn from its public; it must draw upon vital sources from all the degrees of its social and temporal milieu. Then it must assimilate this influence and transfigure it through the medium of art. In turn, the public is molded by this artistic trans-figuration of itself:

> Im künstlerischen Sinne soll der Schauspieler den Ton angeben; im sozialen Sinne soll er ihn vom Publikum empfangen. Er soll, will er moderne Gestalten verkörpern, sie im Stile unserer Gesellschaft verkörpern. Er soll achtsam und bildsam dem tausendstimmigen Echo lauschen, das ihm zurückkommt und dessen wert sich erhöht, je mannigfältiger es aus allen Schichten der Grossstadt, hoch und niedrig, vornehm und arm im Geiste, sich zusammensetzt.[26]

Brahm's ideal demand in regard to the repertory of the *Deutsches Theater* is that it establish contact with contemporary life. The eternal classics are a vital integer in the educative process, but no living theatre can derive permanent sustenance from the treasures of the past alone. Fresh blood, untapped vitality, the breath of contemporary life must infuse the arteries of a living theatre:

> Alle die Mächte, die in dem Handeln und in dem Bewusstsein der Zeit wirksam sind, haben auch auf der Bühne ihr Recht der Existenz; und niemals wird uns der Dichter tiefer ins Herz treffen, als wenn wir uns selbst in seinem Werke wiederfinden, unsere Gedanken, unser Empfinden, Bein von unserm Bein und Fleisch von unserm Fleisch.[27]

---

[23] Schr. I, 33.   [24] Schr. I, 34.
[25] "Eine Wechselwirkung zwischen Szene und Parterre," *Ibid.*
[26] Schr. I, 35.   [27] *Ibid.*

2. National Mission

Brahm also points out the ideal advantage of the *Deutsches Theater* because of its situation in a great urban center. Grillparzer and Raimund are scarcely thinkable except in reference to Vienna; Shakespeare and Molière are inseparably associated with London and Paris; Kleist remained unknown because of his isolation from such a theatrical center. And in general the comedy of manners flourishes in the compact society of a metropolis which is the center of a nation. Such are the unexampled advantages which Berlin offers to the theatre and the dramatist. This urban center, furthermore, is the focus of Germany's national development and Brahm feels that the national spirit can best be creatively expressed only within such a focus:

Denn nur, wo die deutsche Geschichte gemacht wird, kann auch das deutsche Drama erstehen.[28]

A further advantage lies in the splendid *esprit de corps* of the German acting profession powerfully united in the *Deutsche Bühnengenossenschaft*.[29] Brahm expects a great deal of self-effacement and spirited co-operation from the actors of the *Deutsches Theater* who have shown in the past that they are capable of rising to peaks of achievement under the spur of an ideal.[30]

A word of praise for the daring enterprise of the Director and a declaration of war against mediocrity and self-seeking close Brahm's greeting and exhortation to the *Deutsches Theater*. His subsequent reviews show how jealously he defended each of his demands as they were respectively fulfilled or disregarded in the opening seasons of the *Deutsches Theater*.

3. Ensemble

During the first two seasons of the *Deutsches Theater* there follows a series of exemplary performances, outstanding among which were the classics. *Kabale und Liebe, Minna von Barnhelm Iphigenie, Don Carlos, Romeo und Julia, Wilhelm Tell,*—the brilliant succession of stage triumphs is greeted with acclaim by

---

[28] Schr. I, 86.
[29] Founded in 1871.
[30] Schr. I, 37.

Brahm. He takes issue only with minor matters: the deficiencies of some player, an error in casting, poor taste in a setting, a neglected detail of dramaturgic interpretation, etc. By and large, however, he praises if not always the achievement, at least the high purpose, of the *Deutsches Theater*. He comments on the various members of the ensemble, not always in a laudatory vein, but approvingly on the whole. Kainz's Don Carlos, Barnay's Orestes, Sommerstorff's Posa, Frl. Haverland's Iphigenie are unforgettably beautiful renditions of single roles; whereas Haase's Hofmarschall Kalb, Frl. Ramazetta's Luise, and Frl. Sandrock's Minna are examples of the respective excesses or deficiencies of empty virtuosity or inexperience. But the total effect of this ensemble's performances was vivifying (*"Es war Zug in der Szene"*); there was continuity (*"Alles griff gut gefugt ineinander"*); there was dynamic atmosphere (*"alles war Leben und Stimmung und Vorwärtsstreben"*). The dynamic unity of the ensemble scenes was a joy to Brahm:

> Kein einzelner mit seinem Einzelspiel ward hier bemerkt, sondern nur das Ineinanderspiel aller; niemand wirkte in der Isolierung, sondern alle traten in Beziehung zu allen: und das Resultat war doch kein ,,lebendes Bild,'' sondern eine mannigfach bewegte Gruppe in stets wechselnden Beleuchtungen.[31]

4. Direction—Settings—Repertory

In the same approving tone Brahm comments on the harmony of the settings with the atmosphere of the play, the masterful coping with problems of interpretation, the almost magical evocation of the spirit of a play, the good and bad performances of the actors, (Kainz's Don Carlos, as contrasted to Haase's Grossinquisitor), and the high artistic plane of the repertoire.[32] At the end of the first season Brahm congratulates the directors of the *Deutsches Theater* on their brilliant, if occasionally checkered, achievement. He condones the routine classical repertoire as an expedient designed to assure success to a new enterprise:

> An Schatten, sieht man, fehlt es nicht; aber das Licht überstrahlte ihn siegreich, und mit freudiger Sicherheit können die Leiter des Deutschen Theaters in die Zukunft sehen. Sie werden ihre Bühne um

[31] Schr. I, 39.   [32] Schr. I, 40ff.

so fester begründen, je entschiedener sie sich in diesem ersten Jahre
dem Ausserordentlichen, dem Experiment fern halten; wer wird auch
in Kriegszeiten neue Gewehre einführen wollen?[33]

The second year of the *Deutsches Theater* introduces a more
querulous if not outright critical note in Brahm's reviews. The
incipient enterprise has been encouraged, has been coddled into
lusty infancy. At least a modicum of its bright promise should be
redeemed, felt Brahm. An otherwise estimable performance of
Wilhelm Tell is thrown off balance by the excessive *Meiningertum*
of its mass scenes:

. . . mit Drängen und Stossen und Meiningischen Schreien ist nichts
getan. Meiningertum aber machte sich leider überall geltend, und
das gesprochene Wort musste oft unter den vordringlichen Künsten
der Machinisten leiden; dieses Heulen des Windes, dieses Tosen der
Wellen verschlang sogleich die erste Szene . . . Mir ist aber ein
Schillerischer Vers wichtiger als Viktoriatheaterkünste, und wenn
Kainz spricht, so mögen die Steine schweigen![34]

The intimacy of Tell's great monologue is disturbed by realistic
music from the wedding procession off-stage. To Brahm these
faults are examples of a false sense of style (*Stillosigkeit*) on the
part of the stage director.

Brahm is also disturbed at the lack of imagination and enterprise on the part of the directors with regard to repertory. The
contrast in this respect with the first season is unpleasantly acute.
The center of gravity in the repertory has shifted from the classics
to the comedies and farces of the Moser type. "Where are the
promised novelties of *Götz*, *Hamlet*, and *Fiesko?*" Brahm queries.
Heyse and Wildenbruch are also clamoring for attention. Kleist
and Grillparzer, indeed the entire drama of the nineteenth century,
do not yet exist for the *Deutsches Theater*, Brahm complains.[35]

Brahm continues to remind the directors of the *Deutsches
Theater* of their responsibility. He suggests to them the perform-
ance of Ibsen's *Ghosts*[36] with Kainz as Oswald, Frl. Haverland as
Mrs. Alving, Frl. Sorma as Regina, and Herr Förster as Pastor
Manders (*"Hier wäre . . . eine Aufgabe für das Deutsche Theater"*).

[33] Schr. I, 55. [34] Schr. I, 69.
[35] Schr. I, 71f.
[36] Vossische Zeitung, 2. 2. 1884; Schr. I, 73.

But of course, as we have seen, Ibsen is as yet *persona non grata* in Germany.

Estimating the total achievement of the *Deutsches Theater* at the end of its second season, Brahm places its technical contribution far above its contribution to contemporary drama.[37] The revivals of Lessing, Goethe, Schiller, and Shakespeare have attained a new level of theatrical technique and have brought back to the theatre many who had hitherto neglected it. But this could not exhaust the possibilities of an exemplary theatre of national significance. What was lacking was the modern drama. The task which this gap in the repertory placed upon the theatre was the formation of an audience (in co-operation with the critic who had already anticipated the problem), educated to appreciate contemporary production:

> Es fehlte das neuere Drama, das Drama unserer Zeit und unseres Jahrhunderts, und nur spät und nicht ohne den drängenden Einfluss der Kritik hat man begonnen, auch diese ernsteste Pflicht einzulösen. Dass leichte Erfolge hier nicht zu erringen sind, und dass eine Strömung in unserem Publikum dem Geforderten entgegenläuft, erklärt das zögernde Verfahren; aber es ist die schöne Aufgabe des Bühnenleiters, nicht nur die Kunst seiner Darsteller, sondern auch den Geschmack seines Publikums mit planvoller Vorsicht zu führen und zu bilden.[38]

Brahm's high regard for the *Deutsches Theater* has been amply evidenced by the exacting tasks which he has set for it. He sees its mission primarily as a national and cultural one. The *Deutsches Theater* is ideally situated in Germany's center of national development. Its artistic ideals exert an exemplary influence. It develops an organic ensemble technique among its actors. It molds and educates its public. It successfully copes with dramaturgic problems in the revival of the classics; yet it also relieves the austerity of its repertory with comedy and farce. Unfortunately, its one glaring blindspot is the absence of the modern drama. But the monopoly of the *Hoftheater* has been definitely abrogated. The anachronistic theatre of feudal aristocracy has given way to the commercial theatre.

[37] " . . . seine grössten Verdienste liegen in der mit allen höheren Kunstmitteln bewirkten Inszenesetzung." Schr. I, 82.   [38] *Ibid.*

For more than a decade (1883–1894) Brahm follows the work of the *Deutsches Theater* with jealous pride. Towards the end of this period, shortly before he is to take over the theatre himself, he writes retrospectively:

> Es sind jetzt neun Jahre vergangen, seit das Deutsche Theater mit Werken von Schiller, Goethe, Lessing eröffnet wurde: ein einschneidendes Ereignis für das Berliner Bühnenleben, das dem Monopol des Hoftheaters mit einem Schlage ein Ende bereitete und jene reichere Entwicklung klassischer und moderner Schauspielkunst einleitete, deren Zeugen wir seit dem Herbst 1883 gewesen sind.[39]

The cultural mile-stones which Brahm pauses to describe in the history of the German theatre are *Antigone, Macbeth, Clavigo, Götz, Die Räuber,* and *Fausts Tod.* Berlin's aesthetic education proceeds apace and Brahm plays an important part as one of its cultural solons. His demands and suggestions exert a definite influence and are carried out within the limits of practicality. In 1894, when L'Arronge turned over the *Deutsches Theater* to Otto Brahm, not the least among the considerations which prompted him was the fact that Brahm had been the theatre's most honest and unflinching critic, and at the same time its most warmly appreciative friend.[40] There is no doubt but that a great measure of the *Deutsches Theater's* celebrity and high achievement must have been due to Brahm's critical support and acclaim. His own directorial tenure of the *Deutsches Theater* (1894–1904) witnessed the fulfilment of his hitherto neglected critical demand, and the modern German drama came into its own on the German stage.[41]

F. *Lessingtheater—Berliner Theater*

Berlin's growth into a metropolis of millions led to a natural increase of the theatrical public. The greater number of people

[39] Schr. I, 438.

[40] "Die vorrückenden Jahre haben ihren Mahnzettel auch bei mir abgegeben, ich überlasse darum mein Theater einer jungen Kraft und vielleicht neuen Zielen, jedenfalls aber—und das war das Entscheidende für mich bei der Wahl meines Nachfolgers—solchen Zielen, die durch ernste künstlerische und literarische Erwägungen bestimmt sein werden." From Adolf L'Arronge's *Abschiedsrede* (6.30.1894) quoted by Brahm, Schr. I, 474f.

[41] For an exemplary treatment of Otto Brahm's tenure of the Deutsches Theater, cf. Herbert Henze, *Otto Brahm und das 'Deutsche Theater' in Berlin,* (Diss.) Erlangen, 1930.

visiting the theatre and the correspondingly greater variety of classes and interests which they represented developed a need for more theatres. This social necessity joined to the greater money-making possibilities in a sphere of free competition led to an expansion of the commercial theatre in Berlin. The German penchant for technical organization expressed itself in the founding of several new theatres, among which the *Lessingtheater* and the *Berliner Theater* (both opened in 1888) were the most prominent.

1. *The Commercial Theatre*

Brahm, of course, is not interested particularly in the financial success of these theatres. His main concern is with the art of the theatre, and he wonders whether such a struggle for commercial existence may not have an injurious effect on art.[42] He has no doubt that there will be enough of an audience. Neither will there be a dearth of actors. But once again, as in the case of the *Deutsches Theater*, the salient problem is that of repertory ("*Die Frage der Repertoirebildung*"). Hence it is precisely in this respect that Brahm welcomes the multiplication of theatres in Berlin; for the poverty of German dramatic production, already keenly felt in a single prominent theatre, must soon become more glaringly evident in several prominent theatres. This will lead to freer possibilities for striving dramatists and stage artists, so that, even if the theatrical entrepreneurs should lose on their ventures, literature and the theatre could only benefit.[43]

2. *Evils of the Actor-Director System*

Aside from the commercial organization of these two theatres, it is interesting to note that their technical directors were prominent actors: in the *Lessingtheater*, Herr Possart, in the *Berliner Theater*, Herr Barnay. As elsewhere, Brahm sees the vices of individualistic virtuosity in such a state of affairs. Placing the leading actor in a directorial position leads to distortions of theatrical symmetry. Repertory, settings, styles of acting, dramaturgy, in fact the whole complex of the theatre will tend to be used merely as a foil to set off the virtuoso. Thus, at the opening of the *Lessingtheater* Brahm

[42] Schr. I, 191.   [43] Schr. I, 192.

is mystified at the choice of *Nathan der Weise* unless it be that Herr Possart had wished to introduce himself to the public in a dominating role.[44] The desire for individualistic effects also destroys the total effect, and Brahm finds the ensembles of the *Lessingtheater* very rough and unfinished. However, his final judgment is charitable. In spite of the failure of the opening performance Brahm sees no need for fatal auguries, for he feels that the future of this theatre will depend on the modern drama rather than on the classics.[45]

Although the *Berliner Theater* staged at its opening a successful performance of Schiller's *Demetrius*, Brahm in the course of his otherwise laudatory review points out the weaknesses to which an actor-director may be susceptible. The director's hand is too obtrusive; technical externalities obscure the spirit of the play instead of organically contributing to its emergence:

... so ist der Punkt erreicht, an welchem die Absicht des Dichters entstellt wird von vordrängender Regiekunst; und es wird die Aufgabe der neuen Bühne sein, hier Zwecke und Mittel sicherer abzuwägen und jede Überladenheit, jedes allzu deutliche Illustrieren sinnfälliger Vorgänge auf Kosten des Wortes klug zu vermeiden.[46]

Whereas Herr Possart of the *Lessingtheater* redeems himself in Brahm's eyes by presenting Ibsen (even if imperfectly), Herr Barnay continues to indulge in directorial supererogation. Barnay's sins are manifold: in one instance he interpolates lines without any artistic justification, while in another he omits stage directions expressly given by the dramatist (in Schiller's *Braut von Messina*):

Wenn man manchen anderen szenischen Effekt aus dem Text nur mühselig rechtfertigen kann, weshalb gerade den vom Dichter geforderten versagen?[47]

Barnay has also invented characters and has inserted them into the play; he has given an inordinate amount of prominence to unwarranted lighting effects (*Beleuchtungsexzessen*). The vulgar presumption of an indiscriminate virtuosity in directing raises Brahm to a high pitch of indignation:

[44] Schr. I, 190.   [45] *Ibid.*
[46] Schr. I, 194.   [47] Schr. I, 205.

. . . fort doch mit so überflüssigen Künsten, mit dem Virtuosenstückchen der Regie, die um nichts besser sind als die Virtuosenstückchen
der Schauspielkunst.[48]

Brahm's scarification of Barnay and the tendency he represents
reaches an ultimate in caustic irony at the thirtieth (sic!) jubilee
of Barnay's stage career.[49] Brahm describes each stage of the pro-
ceedings with satiric detail: the banquets, the pompous speech-
making, the ridiculously serious press-notices, and in contrast, the
shoddy, meretricious performances of Barnay revelling in a
narcissistic orgy of self-glorification at the *Berliner Theater*. Brahm
re-christens the house the *"Barnaytheater."* Barnay is the incarna-
tion of artistic intemperance and bad taste:

> Sein Verstand ist ein Bühnenverstand, der über die pappenen
> Wände nicht hinausblickt; alle seine Anordnungen sind theatralisch,
> und von dem modernen Streben nach diskreter Wahrheit weiss kein
> Berliner Theater weniger als das ,,Berliner Theater.'' Nur im Grellen
> Bunten, Lärmenden werden Effekte gesucht und gefunden: elek-
> trisches Licht, schreiende Farben, überladene Kostüme und Mas-
> sengetümmel—,,das ist deine Welt, das heisst eine Welt.''[50]

Brahm shows how this plethora of external effects, dictatorially
introduced (*"das Walten der Regie"*) for their own sakes, leads to
a distortion and falsification of the dramatist's intentions.[51]

It is evident from the above that in Brahm's estimation a vital
principle to be observed in the organization of the theatre is the
avoidance of the virtuoso type of actor-director. Brahm sees the
self-centered director as a natural enemy of what is to him the
highly co-operative and collective organization of the theatre.

G. *The Freie Bühne*

So much has been written about the founding of the *Freie
Bühne*, important enough an event to be discussed in histories of
literature as well as in histories of the theatre, that it would be
best in this treatment to confine ourselves to a brief summary of
its genesis and the principles it embodied, seen particularly from

---

[48] *Ibid.*   [49] 1890, Schr. I, 303ff.   [50] Schr. I, 305.
[51] " . . . wie eine unruhige, effekthaschende Schauspielerphantasie den klaren Sinn
der Dichtung entstellt und verfälscht." Schr. I, 307.

Otto Brahm's perspective.[52] We shall discuss the history and organization of the *Freie Bühne* as reflected in Brahm's essays on the subject and as co-ordinated into the broader scheme of this chapter.

1. *Sociological Analysis*

From the sociological point of view the *Freie Bühne* can be viewed as an anomalous development of the bourgeois commercial theatre necessitated on the one hand by its clashing with the same feudal-nationalistic set-up which it had once bested when the *Deutsches Theater* had broken the monopoly of the *Hoftheater* (this time it takes the form of *Zensur* and *"literarische Schutzzollpolitik"*), and on the other hand by the self-contradictory essence of a commercial art theatre where in the long run the demand for profits takes precedence over the demands of art.[53] The aims and organization of the *Freie Bühne* fit admirably into this analysis: first of all there is the setting up of a private corporation with a president and a board of directors (*aktive Mitglieder*) and an indefinite number of share-holders (*passive Mitglieder*) for the purpose of evading public laws of censorship. The closed organization, the special performances (generally held on a Sunday to avoid competition with the commercial theatre and to permit the volunteer aid of professional actors and technicians), and the artistically élite audience also facilitated the presentation of the foreign naturalistic dramatists hitherto excluded for the most part from the public commercial theatres either because of censorship or because of the nationalistic literary protectionism. Freedom from the yoke of profits was obtained through volunteer contributions (or at least low rates) in the matter of theatres, settings, the services of actors, directors, and technicians, etc.

The *Freie Bühne* was thus at most an ideal manifestation of the

[52] More or less objective accounts can be consulted in Schlenther's prospectus of the Freie Bühne: *Wozu der Lärm? Genesis der Freien Bühne*, Berlin, 1889 (history and organization); in Bab's *Das Theater der Gegenwart*, Leipzig, 1928 (theatrico-cultural significance); and in Soergel's *Dichtung und Dichter der Zeit*, Leipzig, 20. Aufl. 1928, (literary-historical significance).

[53] Bab omits the *Freie Bühne* in the transition from *Geschäftstheater* to *Volkstheater*. The implication is that the *Freie Bühne* represents no difference in kind from the *Geschäftstheater*, but only in degree. *Op. cit.*, pp. 174–182.

bourgeois commercial theatre endeavoring to free itself from its sterile and contradictory impasse. But it was a commercial theatre nonetheless. Its personnel was enlisted from the commercial theatres; it was able to exist because it offered no competition. On the contrary, its dramatic "finds" were not retained but were handed over to the exploitation of the commercial theatre. The financial returns accruing from the public's acceptance of Ibsen and Hauptmann amply compensated the bourgeois commercial theatre for its "disinterested" gesture on behalf of "art" as exemplified in its co-operation with the *Freie Bühne*.

2. *Ibsen—Antoine*

This sociological analysis is to be rounded out by the literary history of the *Freie Bühne* as interpreted by Brahm. The godfather of the *Freie Bühne*, according to Brahm, was Ibsen. He it was who fomented the *"Revolutionierung des Menschengeistes"*[54] which led to the most significant development of the modern stage. The symbol of this revolution was *Ghosts;* the embodiment of this symbol was its performance in the Berlin *Residenztheater*.[55] Ibsen's fearless iconoclasm induced profound repercussions in the German theatre. His vital dramatic power seemed the augury of a new era on the stage. But the police forbade any further performances, thus giving the *Freie Bühne* its first impetus. At this historic performance the future animating spirits of the *Freie Bühne* were present, among them Gerhart Hauptmann. Who were these men who, on the 15th of April, 1889, founded the *Verein Freie Bühne?* Brahm's own account follows:

Ein paar junge Leute, die sich jeden Tag im Cafe Schiller versammelten, um einen bescheidenen Marmortisch; und der grösste deutsche Dramatiker sah unserem erregten Plänemachen lächelnd zu. Antoines Théâtre libre war das Vorbild gewesen für Harden, Theodore Wolff und mich, die wir den Gedanken einer Berliner Freien Bühne, jeder an seinem Teil, zu verwirklichen strebten. Schlenther, Die Brüder Hart, zuletzt Fritz Mauthner gesellten sich uns bei, und zwei Männer der Praxis, S. Fischer und Paul Jonas, walteten als Schatzmeister und als Rechtverweser. Aber auch für den Humor war gesorgt in unserem kritischen Kreis, als unser Senior lieferte ihn in reichlichen

---

[54] Schr. I, 462.   [55] January, 1887.

Dosen Julius Stetenheim; und als das Berliner „Théâtre libre" gleich nach der Geburt an einen kritischen Wendepunkt geriet, rief der Vater Wippchens aus: Wollen wir denn das Theater lieber nicht aufmachen? Allein dieser Wendepunkt ward glücklich überschritten—nur dass leider dabei zwei Männer aus unserem Boot sprangen, Harden und Wolff—und nach Vorschlag von Heinrich Hart übertrug man das Präsidium des Vereins mir.[56]

Antoine's *Théâtre libre* was only a contributing cause to the founding of the *Freie Bühne*. The prime causes were the same social and intellectual currents in the theatre and in literature leading to the rise of the free theatre movement all over Europe and the United States.[57] We have described the particular situation in Germany leading up to the founding of the *Freie Bühne*. Monarchic censorship and the contradiction of profits and art meant the choking off of vital dramatic currents, a state of affairs expressed most vividly in the fact of the German stage's inaccessibility to Ibsen. The *Freie Bühne* was the mechanism devised by the commercial theatre to obviate this impasse. Such were the real causes which brought the *Freie Bühne* into being. We may therefore take Otto Brahm's eulogy of Antoine upon the Frenchman's visit to Berlin[58] *cum grano salis* and attribute Brahm's superlatives to the amenities of a festive atmosphere:

Und wenn sich eifrige Historiker zuweilen gefragt haben, wo denn der Ursprung unserer Freien Bühne liege, und wenn sie da und dort gesucht und doch den rechten nicht gefunden haben—hier, meine Damen und Herren, hier sitzt der Rechte vor ihnen in seiner ganzen Jugendfrische der Jahre. Seinem Beispiele nur sind wir gefolgt, als wir auch bei uns eine Freie Bühne aufschlugen.[59]

In the autumn of 1889 the *Freie Bühne* presented *Ghosts*, which was still under the ban of censorship,[60] and the work of an unknown author, entitled *Vor Sonnenaufgang*.[61] It would be doing violence to the memory of this epoch-making occasion not to recount it in the words of Brahm, who was its real animating spirit more than any other single individual.

[56] Schr. I, 467.
[57] For a history of the free theatre movement cf. Anna Irene Miller, *The Independent Theatre in Europe*, N. Y., 1931.
[58] 1893.   [59] Schr. I, 441.
[60] September, 29.   [61] October, 20.

Schon vor der Aufführung war der Streit um dieses Werk entbrannt,
die Schauspieler wurden in aufgeregten Briefen, natürlich anonymen,
vor dem drohenden Theaterskandal gewarnt, und tatsächlich schien
an mehr als einer Stelle die Möglichkeit, zu Ende zu spielen, auf-
gehoben. Auf einem Schlachtfeld glaubt man zu stehen, sagte mir als
ich auf die Bühne kam, der Darsteller des Hoffmann, Gustav Kadel-
burg: man hört die Kugeln pfeifen, nur leider, man kann nicht
zurückschiessen! Und Hauptmann, aus dem nämlichen Eindruck
heraus, schrieb mir in das neu erschienene Buch vom ,,Sonnenauf-
gang": ,,Zur Erinnerung an die Schlacht im Lessingtheater."[62]

3. The Freie Bühne and Naturalism

In this retrospective study of the *Freie Bühne* (written twenty
years later, in 1909) Brahm does not deny the identification of the
Freie Bühne with the movement of naturalism in literature. Indeed, he still believes in naturalism as a vital and permanent
phase of letters. But, as we have seen in the chapter on naturalism,
it is his own broad concept of the term to which he adheres and
which he defends. He traces the origin of the term as regards the
theatre back to Zola's demand for *"le naturalisme au théâtre"* and
its salutary fulfilment in France. But, he tells us, the word had
scarcely crossed the Rhine to deliver its full impact when its connotation was broadened so that only the most arrant and hidebound theoreticians still clung to the original formula. Brahm
recalls his personal endorsement of the imminent synthesis of
naturalism and romanticism, suggested by Hermann Bahr as
far back as 1890.[63] And he also refers to the passage in the mani-
festo of the *Freie Bühne* in which he had expressed the likelihood
of the supersedence of naturalism. Far from attributing weakness
to a doctrine thus apparently disowned and revised almost at the
same time that it was being championed, Brahm takes this as
additional evidence of its vital flexibility. For the movement of
naturalism shows its vitality by broadening and also deepening
its pioneering, and therefore extreme, connotation:

[62] Schr. I, 467.
[63] The passage Brahm refers to is "Die Synthese von Naturalismus und Romantik
ist die gegenwärtige Aufgabe der Literatur." Hermann Bahr, *Zur Kritik der Moderne*,
Wien, 1890.

Nicht laut genug können wir es ausrufen, dass nur der enge Sinn der Gegner es war, der uns an dieses Kreuz des Zolaschen, des Arno Holzischen Naturalismus zu nageln versuchte; und es heisst Worte, die in der Hitze des Gefechts gefallen sind, parteiisch verewigen, es heisst subjektive Stimmungen des Augenblicks, wie die freundschaftliche Widmung von Hauptmanns erstem Drama an seine Anreger Holz und Schlaf, parteiisch aufbauschen, wenn man mit jenen Schlagworten von der Beschränktheit des deutschen Naturalismus immer noch krebsen geht, nachdem die Freie-Bühnen-Bewegung längst historisch geworden ist und ihren Platz unter den Evolutionen des Geistes schlicht behauptet.[64]

Another disclaimer of the *Freie Bühne's* identification with the original narrow connotation of naturalism is supported by the revolution in repertory which its success brought about. The mere recountal of names is sufficient to show the absurdity of their wholesale classification as "consistent naturalists": Ibsen, Anzengruber, Ebner-Eschenbach, Tolstoi, Hauptmann, Strindberg, Zola, Holz and Schlaf, Becque, Hartleben, Rosmer, Hirschfeld, Hofmannsthal, Hardt, and others. Other dramatists who coasted into attention in the wake of the *Freie Bühne* were Sudermann, Fulda, and even Wildenbruch with his *Haubenlerche*.

In addition to its social significance, its literary influence, and its revolutionary effect on the repertory of the German theatre, the *Freie Bühne* movement also induced profound changes in the art of acting. These shall be discussed in detail in the chapter dealing with that subject.

H. *Principles of Theatre Organization*

Summarizing the principles either stated or implied by Brahm in his discussion of the history and organization of the German theatre, we find first of all that the theatre, at least in its ideal manifestations, has a national, *i.e.* a social mission. The history of the modern German theatre can thus be viewed as the history of the conflict between this social ideal and its material opposition emerging under various guises: commercialism (*Unternehmerbetrieb*), bigoted nationalism ("*literarische Schutzzollpolitik*"), vul-

---

[64] Schr. I, 469.

garity and sensationalism (*Effekthascherei*), the star system (*Prinzipalwirtschaft*), etc. The history of the German theatre in the light of this conflict is succinctly stated by Brahm:

> Und wer verkennt auf die Dauer, dass . . . soziale Verschiebungen auf das innerste des Theaterwesens reflektieren? So lange unsere deutsche Bühne in einer geordneten Folge der Entwicklung steht, das heisst also, seit gut einem Jahrhundert, hat auch die Frage: Unternehmerbetrieb oder Gesellschaftsbetrieb? nicht stillgestanden; viele kräftige Worte sind gewechselt worden, viel Tinte ward verschrieben im 18. Jahrhundert, um das Schädliche der „Prinzipalschaft," den Segen der „Nationaltheater" zu erweisen; und doch hat auf eine Zeit der Vorherrschaft subventionierter Theater unser Jahrhundert ein volles Vordringen des kapitalistischen Bühnenbetriebes gebracht, eine freie Konkurrenz, deren Vorteile und Nachteile gegeneinander abzuwägen nicht leicht ist.[65]

How does Brahm envisage the solution of these conflicts and problems? In other words, how is the social mission of the theatre to be accomplished? Brahm's first and foremost solution is to institute a process of aesthetic education (*Geschmacksbildung*) not only of the public but of all departments of the theatre. But in order for this educative process to be at all possible, the theatre must be re-organized on the basis of art (*"Was erzieht?"*) rather than of commercialism (*"Was zieht?"*); its major relevance must be to society (*Volkstheater*) rather than to profits (*Geschäftstheater*). Such a theatre must necessarily be headed by a director of the theatre's art rather than of its budget.[66]

The same artistic and social ideals must prevail in the organizational details and in the technical methods of the theatre. For one thing, the virtuose director must subordinate himself to the word of the dramatist (*"Überwuchern der Regie"*); for another, the unconscionable individualism of the star system (*Starwirtschaft*) must yield to the socially co-operative, collective ensemble. (*"Das Kunstprinzip eines durchgebildeten Ensembles."*)[67] And indeed, the entire theatre must be conceived as a dynamic and organic whole. The drama, the theatre, and the audience should engage in a reciprocal

---

[65] Schr. I, 431.

[66] " . . . den unabhangigen artistischen Leiter, dem ein geschäftsführender Beamter untergeordnet, nicht beigeordnet werden müsse . . . ", Schr. I, 430.

[67] Schr. I, 168.

communion and interchange (*"Wechselwirkung zwischen Szene und Parterre"*). The art of the theatre is not an eclectic potpourri but an organic fusion of allied arts, a *Gesamtkunstwerk*, somewhat in Wagner's sense.[68]

In the drama as contributory to the history and organization of the theatre, Brahm saw a two-fold significance. A national theatre will necessarily derive inspiration from the national cultural tradition. Hence, in the aesthetic process of *Geschmacksbildung* the theatre must not merely go back to the classics but must bring the classics forward into the contemporary atmosphere (*"lebendige Verehrung der Klassiker"*). And what provides this contemporary atmosphere? Quite obviously, contemporary social and intellectual life as reflected particularly in the modern drama. Thus the modern drama (at that time naturalism and impressionism) and the modern interpretative technique of the theatre provide a frame of reference for the judgment and interpretation of the classics. We can understand now the enormous importance which Brahm attributed to the movement of naturalism as affecting the art of the theatre. To him, the new art of reality was an Antaeus-like symbol infusing the drama with new vitality by bringing it into contact with the earth.

[68] Cf. Brahm's discussion of naturalism and impressionism in painting and in the art of the theatre (Schr. I, 427); and conversely, the mechanical borrowing from the plastic and musical arts in the Weimar style (Schr. I, 423) for Brahm's view of the theatre as the collective product of allied arts.

VII. *Dramaturgy and Technique*

The art of the theatre as conceived by Brahm has both ideal and practical aspects; there is the drama as a work of art the fullest expression of which is provided by the complex of personnel, technique, and allied arts which constitutes the theatre. There is no question of priority in these two aspects since they are reciprocally interconditioned and interdependent. If, in Brahm's criticism, we find a predominance of the ideal, it is merely an emphasis necessitated by temporal conditions. According to whether these conditions change or abide we have a dialectic shift of emphasis so that in some instances the importance of the drama predominates and the technicians of the theatre are urged to subordinate themselves to the intentions of the dramatist (*"Überwuchern der Regie"*);[1] and in other instances it is the theatre that is viewed as the fount of salvation and the technicians are exhorted to supplement the deficiencies of the dramatist (". . . *wird doch die volle Erkenntnis des einen, was not tut, bei dem verständigen Schauspieler finden, nicht bei dem grössten unserer Dichter"*).[2]

The contradiction here is apparent rather than real, for Brahm deplores the plight of dramatists out of contact with the practical theatre (Kleist, Grillparzer)[3] just as much as he inveighs against directors whose imagination does not go beyond the theatre (". . . *Bühnenverstand, der über die pappenen Wände nicht hinaus blickt;* . . . ").[4] On the contrary, the union of drama and theatre is one of Brahm's most urgent critical desiderata. The dramatist facilitates this union by accommodating his work to the demands of the stage and even by actually participating in the role of adviser during the staging of his play.[5] The theatre in turn must function as the effective yet unobtrusive medium of expression for the drama. In essence, the effecting of this union between

---

[1] Schr. I, 306; cf. Brahm's reference to a "vordrängende Regiekunst", Schr. I, 194.

[2] Schr. I, 422.

[3] Schr. I, 84.

[4] Schr. I, 305.

[5] Brahm lauds Ibsen and Hauptmann for their practical sense of the theatre. Schr. I, 299 et passim.

drama and theatre into a *Gesamtkunstwerk*[6] is what Brahm considers to be a peculiarly Germanic conception of the art of the theatre.[7]

The details of how this art is to be exercised provide the main theme of this chapter which will give an account of Brahm's principles underlying the theatrical interpretation of the drama (*Dramaturgie*), and the embodiment of the spirit of this interpretation in the theatrical arts (*Schauspielkunst*). In the previous chapter the discussion revolved about the *Direktor* (Eng. manager) as the business and executive head of the external organization of the theater. In this chapter we shall be mainly concerned with the *Regisseur* (Eng. director) whose functions extend to: (a) *dramaturgical problems*, *i.e.* the interpretation and consequent translation of the drama into terms of the theatre, and (b) *problems of technique*, *i.e.* those involved in the actual mounting (*Inszenierung*) of the play: stage direction (*Regie*), setting (*Dekoration, bezw. Bühneneinrichtung, -ausstattung*), etc.[8]

Although the director's art is intimately bound up with the art of acting, and the same principles of style govern both to a large extent, the traditional departmentalization of the theatre and the subject matter of Brahm's criticism prompt a separate treatment of the actor and his art. This may involve an apparent repetition, yet it will be noted that the discussion proceeds on a different plane and in a different context.

We may well begin with a summary of Brahm's dramaturgical criticism as embodied in his reviews of a few selected, representative plays which, because of their very problematical nature, have been subject to differing interpretations in the history of the German theatre. In defining his stand toward traditional interpretations and toward the one being reviewed, Brahm reveals his own dramaturgical principles. This procedure has the additional advantage of permitting the final summary of Brahm's principles to emerge in the form of an inductive conclusion.

[6] Schr. I, 183.

[7] Cf. Brahm's comparison of the French and German theatres, *Pariser Theatereindrücke*, Schr. I, 183.

[8] For an outline of the comparatively new field of "Theaterwissenschaft" and its divisions cf. Hans Knudsen, *Das Studium der Theaterwissenschaft in Deutschland*, Charlottenburg, 1926.

A. Dramaturgic Method: *Götz von Berlichingen*

Conceived with *Sturm und Drang* abandon under the recently canonized influence of Shakespeare, with a sovereign disregard for the dramatic unities and the conditions of the theatre, Goethe's *Götz* has remained a recurrent problem for the director. Goethe himself at various stages of his development repeatedly tried to adapt his original dramatized *Historie* for the stage, but the constant revisions and adaptations show how little he was satisfied with the results.

Given this preliminary data, how does Brahm define the dramaturgical problem? He first subjects the material at hand to a sharp scrutiny in order to obtain the facts relevant to his problem. He examines the various versions of the play in terms of their dramatic virtues and defects. Goethe's own theories and experiences in the writing and revising of his play are an invaluable aid in the delineation of the problem. Brahm summarizes these considerations as follows:[9] *Götz* was composed under the theoretical impression which Goethe derived from Shakespeare's chronicle plays, that the unity of character was the only unity necessary in the drama. But, as even Aristotle had shown, action does not become a unity merely because it revolves about one (character).[10] The unity of action and interest are an inescapable law of dramatic effect. Whereas Goethe had originally believed with Herder that not the event but the creator of the event was the decisive factor in drama, he later realized the importance of a compact plot in the sense of the classical Greek or French drama. But Goethe did not carry out this realization, which would have entailed a fundamental and organic revision of the entire play. He did make a concession to the unity of action, however, in giving the play during two evenings by separating the Weislingen from the Berlichingen theme.

These facts stated, the problem shapes itself more clearly. Very obviously, this permeating, organic change which eluded Goethe cannot be undertaken by anyone else since it would entail the

---

[9] Schr. I, 146.

[10] Cf. S. H. Butcher's translation of *The Poetics* in his *Aristotle's Theory of Poetry and Fine Art*, London, 1911[4], p. 33, VIII. "Unity of plot does not, as some persons think, consist in the unity of the hero."

writing of a new play. But the helter-skelter shifting of scenes can easily be simplified and rearranged by a skillful dramaturgist.

Another aspect of the problem now presents itself. Which of the Goethean versions is to be used? Brahm further defines the problem: the fresh and genuine tone of the earlier *Götz* should somehow be joined with the compact stage form of the later versions. Thus, the style of the original *Götz* should form the basis for a modern stage version, the more so since its realistic power is more akin to the contemporary spirit than the formalized re-touching with which the aging poet subdued the surging vitality of his original conception.[11] The brief, fleeting, and quickly interrupted scenes of the older version can be dispensed with because they would merely confuse the audience by their transient effect and because they are incompatible with stage facilities. Short, ephemeral sketches of situation and momentary dramatic flashes which merely characterize rather than serve to further the action should also be eliminated. This, in brief, is Brahm's dramaturgical interpretation for the revision of this play.

Now how does this analysis stand in relation to the actual staging of *Götz* in the *Deutsches Theater*, which Brahm is reviewing? Unfortunately, the director of the *Deutsches Theater* has evaded, or what is worse, has even failed to grasp the entire problem because he has used almost verbatim the text of Goethe's stage version. And the results are evident. True, the performance is far from being a failure, but it has not made the most of its possibilities. The lack of directorial imagination bolstered by a sound historical and theoretical knowledge of the play and its dramaturgical implications has vitiated a play of vital historical conflicts and poetic power into a run-of-the-mill *Ritterdrama*.

What general principles does Brahm make use of in the foregoing analysis? First, the *Regisseur* must form an intimate conception of the play and its broader meaning. Second, he must endeavor to translate the play into the medium of the stage. This transmutation will present certain problems both of a technical and of a theoretical nature. All relevant facts appertaining to the precise definition of these problems and pointing towards their solution must be drawn into consideration. This will entail a

[11] Schr. I, 147.

knowledge of the history of dramatic literature, of the biography
of the author, of dramatic theory in general, of the stage history
of the play, and of stage technique. All this factual information
supplemented by the insight of the director and his sensitivity
to the modern spirit is the only sound basis for coping with
dramaturgical problems.[12]

B. Evocation of Mood: *Die Räuber*

The staging of Schiller's *Die Räuber* in the *Deutsches Theater*,
similarly to that of *Götz*, offers Brahm an opportunity for a preliminary theoretical analysis against which he contrasts the actual
achievement. Once more there are two versions presenting a problem of choice. And once again there is Schiller's original text
breathing the atmosphere of its time, and the stage version (*Mann-
heimer Fassung*) which Brahm considers inferior to the first in
that it fails to evoke this atmosphere. Under pressure of circumstances and on the insistence of Dalberg, the Mannheim director,
Schiller was obliged to conceal the dangerous contemporaneity of
the play by changing the time and the locale. Furthermore, as a
concession to the vulgar, moralistic taste, the conclusion was altered from the infinitely more subtle tragedy of conscience (the
suicide of Franz) to the purely external catastrophe of his death
at the hands of the robbers in the same tower into which he had
cast his father.

Brahm regrets the traditional inertia to which the director of
the *Deutsches Theater* has succumbed in using the Mannheim text
with its dramatically inferior conclusion:

> Gerade das Deutsche Theater sollte hier sich das Verdienst ge-
> winnen: vorbildliche, für die ganze deutsche Bühne massgebende
> Texte festzustellen, welche mit genauer Übersicht über das gesamte
> Material und mit dem freien Urteil literarischer Bildung das Beste
> unseres Besitzstandes zusammenzufassen, zu voller Wirkung.[13]

In Brahm's review of this play we see once more his principle of
creative dramaturgy based on an examination of all relevant material and a subsequent reconstruction aided by the literary imagination of the director. Another important principle of dramaturgy
emerges in the demand for the re-creation of the spirit or atmos-

[12] *Ibid.*   [13] Schr. I, 198.

phere of the time in which the action of a drama unfolds. We shall see presently the importance Brahm attributes to the evocation of the atmosphere of the times as part of the creation of a more general mood contributing towards a play's unity of effect.

C. Dynamic Continuity: *Don Carlos*

Of a more complex problematical nature than the preceding plays, Schiller's *Don Carlos*, as staged in the *Deutsches Theater*, offers Brahm a further opportunity for applying the same dramaturgic theories and for introducing several important new principles.[14] The problems of *Don Carlos* exist on a multiple scale; there are organic inconsistencies in the ideology and characterization of the drama; and there is a technical disregard for the conditions of the stage (*e.g.* the length of the play, among other factors). Furthermore, the dramatic and the technical problems cross each other at several points, creating additional complexity. Schiller explicitly stated that the play was unsuited for the stage.[15] Yet, the important principle which Brahm deduces from Schiller's statement is that the dramatist himself cannot be accepted as an absolute authority on this point:

Aber „Carlos," sagt uns der Dichter, ist kein Theaterstück. Niemand wird diesen Ausspruch unterschreiben, diejenigen am wenigsten, welche die gewaltige und theatralische Wirkung der Tragödie eben erst empfunden haben. Nur das entnehmen wir Schillers Zeugnis, dass er in gewissen Stadien der Aufführung die Rücksicht auf die Bühne gering geachtet hat und dass die Bühne darum ihre Rechte hier geltend machen darf.[16]

There follows an analysis of the play's evolution in Schiller's mind in order that the inner contradictions of the completed play may be recognized and understood for purposes of dramaturgic revision. Schiller began to write the play for the stage, as is attested to by his letters to Dalberg. In these letters he denies the political implications of the play and desires merely to paint a royal family portrait.[17] In enumerating his characters he does not mention Posa, a significant omission. How this character

---

[14] Schr. I, 50.
[15] *"Carlos* ist kein Theaterstück"; quoted by Brahm, *Ibid.*
[16] Schr. I, 51.   [17] Letter to Dalberg, 7. Juni 1784.

gradually took shape in Schiller's mind is shown in his preliminary outline of the play in which Posa is a subordinate figure.[18]
Removed from the atmosphere of the theatre and under the influence of Körner, Schiller abandoned himself to the ideas of internationalism (*Weltbürgertum*) and intellectual liberty (*Gedanken-
freiheit*) which he so magnificently incorporated in the Marquis
von Posa. As can well be understood, the unity of the play was
affected by this shift to a political idea, but its powerful dramatic
tension still remained; and when Schiller completed his play, he
recognized its theatrical qualities. Nevertheless, he proceeded to
write a prose version of the play for the stage.

Again the problem of choice presents itself. And again Brahm
decides that it would be advisable to borrow elements of both
versions. The prime basis should be the original, poetic version
because Schiller's use of prose was merely a concession to a time
when verse had not yet established itself on the stage.[19] However,
the deletions which Schiller made in his stage version should be
adopted. There is no violence perpetrated on the play if the modern dramaturgist follows what Schiller himself has done.

It is in this respect that Brahm sees the chief shortcoming of
the *Deutsches Theater's* staging of the play. The original, uncut
poetic version of the play has been used, necessitating two evenings
for the performance of the play. This in itself is no insuperable
fault; witness the *Wallenstein* and *Nibelungen* trilogies. But the
components of these cycles have been conceived as rounded, independent units aside from their interconnection, whereas Schiller's
Don Carlos is an inseparable whole and was never meant to be
played piecemeal:

Besonders am zweiten Abend empfand man die Schwierigkeit, da
wieder einsetzen zu sollen, wo zwanzig Stunden vorher abgebrochen

[18] In the preliminary outlines of the play (Bauerbacher Entwurf, 1783, and the
"Thalia" Fragmente, ca. 1786) the Marquis von Posa is referred to merely as the
"Kammerjunker des Prinzen."

[19] The problem of using verse in writing for a public accustomed to prose is attested
to by Goethe's comments on the fate of his *Die Mitschuldigen* when deprived of its
metrical form: "Dass dieses Stück einiges theatralisches Verdienst habe, lässt sich auch
daraus abnehmen, dass es zu einer Zeit, wo es den deutschen Schauspielern noch vor
Rhythmen und Reimen bangte, erschienen, in Prosa übersetzt aufs Theater gebracht
worden, wo es sich freilich nicht erhalten könnte, weil ihm ein Hauptbestandteil, das
Silbenmass, und der Reim, abging." *Über das deutsche Theater,* 1812 ca.

worden war; statt wie sonst durch eine Exposition eingeführt zu werden, rasch oder zögernd, stürmisch oder langsam, sollte man mit der fertigen Stimmung ins Haus kommen. Das ist ein Ding der Unmöglichkeit, und wer es uns zumutet, verkennt, was ein Theaterstück ist.[20]

Summarizing the new principles, we find that although the dramaturgic method should include the theatrical intentions of the dramatist, these are not to be accepted as canonical but must be tested empirically against the dramatic and theoretical values inherent in the play itself. This is a statement, in the special context of dramaturgy, of the truism that the creative artist is often an unreliable commentator on the theoretical and ideological implications of his own work. In addition, Brahm makes another contribution to his theme of unity by showing the importance of dynamic continuity in achieving a unified dramatic effect.

D. Criticism of Laube: *Demetrius*

Schiller's fragment *Demetrius* runs an elusive course through the history of the German stage, from Goethe, who contemplated its completion,[21] to Hebbel, who adopted the theme for a play of his own. Aside from its missing conclusion, the play offers difficulties of staging because of its mass scenes. Worse yet, the conventional text prevalent on the German stage at this time had been arranged and concluded by Laube, whose routine versification is in appalling contrast to the lofty cadence of Schiller's poetry. As Martersteig says,[22] Laube's version dominated the German stage until naturalism made away with it. Brahm's criticism of this version thus has an added literary-historical interest.

Brahm does not waste too much indignation on the woeful ineptitude of Laube's verse. He finds it quite natural that Laube should have fallen behind Schiller in this respect. But the unforgivable sin is Laube's complete distortion of the nuclear spirit of Schiller's conception.

Der Demetrius Schillers, wie so viele seiner Helden, wie Karl Moor,

---

[20] Schr. I, 51.

[21] Cf. Robert Arnold, *Das Deutsche Drama*, München, 1925, p. 473.

[22] *Das deutsche Theater im neunzehnten Jahrhundert*, Leipzig, 2. Aufl., 1924, p. 419.

Fiesko, Wallenstein, ist ein kühner Verbrecher; Laube hat das Verbrechen begangen, ihn tugendhaft zu machen.[23]

Quoting from Schiller's own notes on the play, Brahm shows that it was Schiller's intention to make the climax of his play the entry of the false pretender as Czar into Moscow fully aware that he is not the true Czar. Thus, at the height of his fortune, Demetrius was to discover that he had been the victim of deceit. Nevertheless, impelled by circumstances and by his own imperious will, he was to carry on by force and against his own conscience what he had begun in good faith. Schiller speaks of the powerful humanity of character developed by Demetrius as he passes through these vicissitudes of fortune and tragic adversity to his death. When the pretender learns that he is not the real Demetrius, he is suffused with a spirit of tyrannical revulsion; there should be nothing tender or sentimental in him, according to Schiller; his must be a wild, unrestrained nature, proud, strong, and independent.[24] Brahm tells us what Laube has made of this imperious, elemental character:

> Ein Tugendbold ist er und bleibt er, ein unreifer Primaner, der mit einem Kodex auswendig gelernter Redensarten von Recht und idealem Streben der andringenden Fülle der Erlebnisse gegenübersteht, und der um sein Leben und Herrschen nicht kämpft, nein, der seinen Tod wehmütig erbittet . . . dieses kahle, leblose Ideal, dieses Kuckucksei von einem deutschen Tugendjüngling . . . etc., etc.[25]

Laube also destroyed a scene which in Schiller's opinion ranked with the greatest of all tragic situations, the meeting of the mothers of the real and the false Demetrius. Schiller's Demetrius at this point is already aware of his deceit, whereas Laube takes this awareness from him and has him plead for recognition with an untroubled conscience. In addition, whereas Schiller's Demetrius comports himself with the dignity of a prince and statesman, Laube's hero is a ranting, sentimental enthusiast in whom even the vestige of statesmanship is lacking. Schiller's political vision is lost on Laube, Brahm maintains.

The use of the Laube version in the *Berliner Theater* by Herr

---

[23] Schr. I, 195.   [24] *Ibid.*
[25] *Ibid.*

Barnay consequently does violence to the inner spirit and conception of Schiller's play. And in yet another respect is violence done to Schiller: the technique of staging has dominated the poetic word. When in the Polish assembly Sapieha attempted to speak the most famous lines of the play: *"Was ist die Mehrheit? Mehrheit ist der Unsinn,"*[26] he was drowned out by the clamor of the supernumeraries. The basic fault of technique which Brahm sees here is of central importance in his system of dramaturgy and technique:

... so ist der Punkt erreicht, an welchem die Absicht des Dichters entstellt wird von vordrängender Regiekunst; und es wird die Aufgabe der neuen Bühne sein, hier Zweck und Mittel sicherer abzuwägen und jede Überladenheit, jedes allzu deutliche Illustrieren sinnfälliger Vorgänge auf Kosten des Wortes klug zu vermeiden.[27]

The artistic failure of Barnay's staging of *Demetrius* is thus shown as deriving from a total disregard of the dramaturgical problem (the verbatim use of Laube's distorted version) and from a magnification of stage technique to the point at which it overshadows the poetic word. The positive principle of dramaturgy which emerge from Brahm's review of this performance is that all dramaturgical adaptation must be conceived in the spirit of the drama itself. The dramaturgist is not to usurp the author's function, *i.e.* to write a totally new play, but merely to act as an unobtrusive intermediary between the drama and the stage. To accomplish this fully, he must grasp the essential meaning of a play and make his technical alterations, his completions and deletions, entirely within the spirit of this meaning. The dramaturgist's function is essentially one of adaptation from one medium to another, and his creative urge must be disciplined within the confines of the author's intentions.

On the technical side, the director has a similar function which is also subordinate to the poetic word. He must avoid overemphasis in technique because he is not sufficient unto himself, because he is the servant of the dramatist and not *vice versa*. There are too great a number of aspects in which the director can assert his creative individuality for him to attempt to dominate, and

---

[26] Act I, line 462.   [27] Schr. I, 194.

therefore to minimize, the words of the author. Brahm's dramaturgical orientation, as seen from these remarks, is much more
literary than theatrical.

E. Stage or Closet Drama?: *Faust II*

The second part of Goethe's *Faust* with its veiled meanings, its
symbolic characters, its prolix speeches surcharged with thought,
its interior and exterior scenes shifting from the Gothic epoch to
Greek classicism, ranging through time and space, provides a well
nigh insurmountable problem for the artists and technicians of
the stage. Indeed, as eminent an authority as Volkelt,[28] in drawing
a distinction between the drama of imagination (*Phantasiedrama*)
and the stage drama (*Bühnendrama*), maintains that a stage
presentation of the second part of *Faust*, even assuming its theoretical perfection, is a misuse of medium and can only redound
to the disadvantage of the poem. Be that as it may, the history
of the German theatre chronicles a long series of directorial failures in the attempt to remold and adapt the poem for the stage.[29]
Unfortunately, Brahm has not left us an extended and definitive
treatment of the problem so that we are obliged to educe his ideas
on the subject from a review of *Fausts Tod* as presented in the
Deutsches Theater.[30]

The version which L'Arronge offered is fragmentary, consisting
of scenes from the first and the fourth act, and practically the
entire fifth act, from which the title is derived. Brahm admires
the arrangement for its bold spirit of experimentation but does
not think that it can be of exemplary influence if for no other
reason than the omission of the Helena scenes. The question which
Brahm raises is: are the Helena scenes inextricably connected with
the whole so that their deletion does violence to the organic meaning and structure of the play? This fundamental question has
apparently not occurred to the dramaturgist. The justification for
the omission of Helena seems to have been that she is an allegorical
abstraction, representing the marriage of Greek classicism to the

---

[28] *Aesthetik des Tragischen*, München, 1917, 3. Aufl., p. 75.
[29] Cf. *Faust auf dem deutschen Theater*, Georg Witkowsky, in "Bühne und Welt,"
1924.
[30] Schr. I, 246ff.

Gothic spirit (*"Vermählung des Griechentums mit dem Germanentum"*), and thus does not belong in the theatre which should portray living individuals in the concrete and the particular. In refutation of this, Brahm shows that Helena is not a figure in an allegory but a particular symbol. He supports this contention on the authority of Goethe himself, of Goethe scholars, and of the play itself as realized in actual stage practice.

Brahm recalls that Goethe regarded the Helena scenes as of centripetal and symbolic importance, and quotes Goethe's definition of symbolism:

Das ist die wahre Symbolik, wo das Besondere das Allgemeine repräsentiert, nicht als Traum und Schatten, sondern als lebendig augenblickliche Offenbarung des Unerforschlichen.[31]

There follows an excerpt from Scherer on the difference between allegory and symbol, the former superficial and of limited interpretation, the latter profound and inexhaustible in its possible meanings. Goethe's words:

. . . dass es dem bekannten magischen Gesellen geglückt, die eigentliche Helena persönlich aus dem Orkus ins Leben heraufzuführen,[32]

settle the argument for Brahm. The same misplacement of emphasis occurs when in Lessing's *Minna von Barnhelm*, it is not the marriage of Minna and Tellheim but "actually" the marriage of Saxony and Prussia that is referred to. Brahm insists that in *Faust II* as well as in *Minna von Barnhelm* it is not so much the symbolic implications behind the characters but the characters themselves that are of dramatic significance:

Hier wie dort sind es die Personen, nicht die hinter ihnen stehenden symbolischen Beziehungen, welche das poetisch Bestimmende sind.[33]

The argument is confirmed in the history of actual stage practice. Devrient, Wilbrandt, and Dingelstedt all found the Helena act theatrically effective and arranged their stage versions of *Faust* with this act in a pivotal position. Indeed, to Brahm the definitive solution of the problem in staging the whole of *Faust* has been most nearly approximated by Dingelstedt's three-fold

[31] Schr. I, 249. [32] Schr. I, 248.
[33] Schr. I, 249.

division. And in accordance with Dingelstedt, Brahm suggests the following dramaturgical scheme:

... der erste Abend brächte dann die Faustszenen und Gretchen im Glück (bis „Begreife nicht, was er an mir findt"), der zweite Abend Gretchen im Elend und die beiden ersten Akte des zweiten Teiles bis zum Schluss der klassischen Walpurgisnacht, der dritte Abend höbe mit Helenas Erscheinen machtvoll an.[34]

Brahm's realization that his suggestion belongs in the realm of the ideal impels him to appreciate the practical considerations underlying L'Arronge's staging. From the point of view of stage technique he finds a good deal to praise. L'Arronge has achieved a happy medium between modern realistic technique and the stylized, declamatory tradition of the Weimar school. And in doing this he has created an original style (*"eine Mischung von Natürlichkeit und rhythmisch beseeltem Schwung"*),[35] not only in directing the actors but also in the settings which express the same fusion of the two traditions (*"diskret bei aller Pracht"*).[36] There is a concordance with the modern spirit in the general tone of L'Arronge's staging in its attempt to express the most understandable elements of a play which is so generally considered cryptic. And perhaps even the excision of Helena from L'Arronge's version is also a responsive throb to the pulse of the times:

... und vielleicht liegt diesem Spiel noch der tiefere Sinn zu Grunde, dass eine auf Realität und Kraft der Tat dringende Zeit die klassische Schönheit, Helena benannt, glaubt entbehren zu können: wenn man das Griechentum aus der Schule weist, warum nicht aus dem Theater?[37]

The same fundamental principles which have already been operative in the previous dramaturgical analyses also emerge here: the necessity for an organic interpretation based on all relevant material, the creation of an individual style of technique in the spirit of this interpretation, response to the modern spirit, etc. The new light which this analysis throws on Brahm's dramaturgical ideas reveals the subtlety and complexity of procedure resulting from a rigorous application of these ideas: literary and

[34] Schr. I, 250.
[36] *Ibid.*
[35] Schr. I, 247.
[37] Schr. I, 250.

aesthetic analysis, biographical research, the application of experience culled from the history of the stage, etc.

F. Unity of Style and Casting: *Maria Stuart*

The fact that the *Deutsches Theater* had broken the artistic monopoly of the *Hoftheater* did not mean the complete extinction of the latter. With Graf Hochberg and Herr Anno installed as the successors of Hülsen, a new era began in the *Hoftheater*. Concessions were made to modern technique; the ideas of the *Meininger* and the *Deutsches Theater* were borrowed and adapted in a series of classical performances. But the result remained eclectic since there was no harmonious fusion of the various styles and techniques. The adaptations were largely mechanical or external and were not coordinated with the individual atmosphere of each new play. The acting ensemble was also a disintegrated collection of artists of varying temperaments working at cross purposes. Brahm shows that whereas in the *Deutsches Theater* the staging had attained its fullest effect when coupled with a high level of interpretative acting, and whereas the *Meininger* had been able to project the individual tone and style of a drama beyond the external form of its stage appearance, the *Hoftheater* had accomplished neither. Nor was the fault, according to Brahm, entirely that of the heterogeneous troupe of actors:

Nun kann man freilich schauspielerische Genies nicht aus dem Nichts erschaffen, man kann (wenn man nicht zufällig Moses ist) nicht Wasser schlagen aus dem Felsen und nicht künstlerische Funken aus Herrn Ludwig und Frau v. Hochenburger-Jürgens; wohl aber könnte auch bei mittelmässigen Kräften Einheitlichkeit des Stiles erzielt werden und ein tieferes Eindringen in die tiefere Intention der Dichtung.[38]

Thus we see that in Brahm's estimation the actors are not nearly as responsible for the failure of a play as the director who has not utilized them to their best advantage by coordinating their efforts to some central and unified design of his own which he has educed from the play. Brahm quotes a letter by Schiller concerning *Maria Stuart*[39] in which the poet lauds the excellence of a company of

[38] Schr. I, 168.   [39] To Körner, 1800.

actors not because they have any outstanding talents but because of their harmonious effect as a group:

Das Kunstprinzip eines durchgebildeten Ensembles, das hier bereits ausgesprochen ist, haben wir in unseren Tagen immer lebhafter hervortreten sehen.[40]

But the *Hoftheater* has failed miserably in this respect. The inchoate congeries of styles ranged from traditional, routine acting *("dem hergebrachten Schauspielhausstil")* through unimaginative naturalism *("der poesielose Naturalismus")* to pseudo-realism *("der nachgemachte Realismus")*.[41] The pitch and tempo varied from raucous bawling, through a precipitous flow of diction alternating with slow, natural speech, down to garrulous patter. This bewildering multiplicity of styles shows the absence of incisive direction governed by some central purpose. The factor contributing most decisively to this chaos is the failure of the director to understand the characters of the play and to cast the parts accordingly.

The problem of casting, a central function of the director, has been erroneously conceived, particularly in the case of the title role. Brahm shows how stage tradition and the failure of the dramatist to create fully the character he has conceived both contribute towards a distorting and obscuring of the dramatist's original intention. It is here that a creative director can step in and by departing from stage tradition, restore the play's original conception. How Schiller conceived his Maria can be learned from a letter written while he was working on the play.[42] Schiller did not intend Maria to arouse a tender mood. He conceived her dramatic effect to be inherent in her evocation of a general feeling of emotion rather than a personal and individual sympathy. She neither feels nor evokes tenderness; it is her fate to experience and arouse violent emotions. The failure of the *Hoftheater's* director in casting a gentle and tender actress whose emotional register was confined to girlish and lyrical overtones, is thus glaringly apparent.

The dramaturgist too has contributed to the general confusion

[40] Schr. I, 169.   [41] *Ibid.*
[42] To Goethe, 26. April, 1799.

by adhering to an uncut version of the play, thus prolonging the performance to an unconscionable length. Brahm quotes Schiller as an authority advising the cutting of his plays for the stage, and shows that far from performing an act of piety towards the author in keeping literally every line of his play, the dramaturgist has done him a disservice by producing a wearying and boring effect. Brahm concludes his remarks with an appeal to the dramaturgist and the director, who should either be one and the same person or who should function in harmony if they are separate individuals. The dramaturgist should be a vital functionary in the theatre and not a "fifth wheel on the cart of Thespis":

Das Schauspielhaus, sagt man, hat in seinem Dienst einen Dramaturgen; wir wünschen lebhaft, dass dieser bei den weiteren klassischen Darstellungen seines Amtes walte und mit den Mitteln literarischer Bildung und geistiger Anregung den Männern der Bühnenpraxis zu Hilfe komme. Denn wenn diese Aufführungen nichts weiter als neue Versatzstücke und neue Kleider bringen sollen, so ist die schöne Zeit, die man mit ihnen hinbringt, für die Kunst in der Tat verschwendet.[43]

A brief summation of the principles expressed by Brahm in his review of *Maria Stuart* includes that of unity of style both in dramaturgy and technique. This is to be achieved by the director's understanding the characters of the play and by his casting the actors in roles suitable to their temperaments and styles. The director can thus unite the variously constituted actors into an harmonious ensemble and shape them within the frame of his central design. The scenic artists and the dramaturgist must also coordinate themselves into the central design of the director. Individual excellence in any of these departments of the theatre, when achieved separately, is largely wasted, since the full effect of the theatre can only be produced by a concerted and organic effort. .

G. Individual "Tone": *Prinz Friedrich von Homburg*

Thus far the examples from which we have derived Brahm's dramaturgical principles have been largely couched in a negative vein. Applying his own apothegm on criticism, we might say that he has been showing the reverse side of his enthusiasm. Yet the

[43] Schr. I, 171.

haphazard organization of the commercial theatre and its bowing before practical circumstances has not received his condemnation nearly as much as the frequent critical incompetence of its aesthetic arbiters. The pressure of reality may sometimes bear its own condonement, but artistic mediocrity, slothful imagination, a supine yielding to the inertia of tradition, Brahm cannot leave uncensured. And this is as it should be. Nevertheless, it is with a distinct feeling of pleasure that we read his unstinted praise of a performance of Kleist's patriotic drama in the *Deutsches Theater*. Characteristically, his laudatory remarks are terse and concentrated. We repeat them at this point because they express his general philosophy of dramaturgy, if it can be called that, more positively than at any other time. To Brahm, the powerful appeal of this performance is a tribute to the art of both the poet and his interpreter:

Die höchste Aufgabe der schauspielerischen Inszenierung war hier so glücklich gelöst wie selten; die Aufgabe, den Geist einer Dichtung zu empfinden und in die Darstellung hinauszutreiben, den individuellen Ton und die Stimmung, die dieses Werk, keines sonst, geboren hat.[44]

We have already discussed Brahm's idea of the evocation of a play's atmosphere. Here this principle is further defined. Each play has a unique spiritual aura that belongs to itself alone. This individual "tone" or mood of a play must be sensed by the dramaturgist and projected into his arrangement of its stage text. This same individual mood must also be caught and projected by the director. *Kabale und Liebe* breathes an air different from that of *Egmont*, and *Egmont* in turn is couched in a poetic mood different from that in *Prinz Friedrich von Homburg*. To divine the intangible yet pervasive aura of a play and stamp it with an indelible mood that concretizes this aura for the audience is the subtle task of the theatrical artist:

Wer die Schöpfung eines Dichters zum Bühnenleben erheben will, muss fähig sein, solche stimmunggebenden Grundtöne zu vernehmen und sie durch die Vermittlung seiner Darsteller nachklingen zu machen im Hörer.[45]

[44] Schr. I, 83.   [45] Schr. I, 84.

H. Classicism and Change: Sophocles' *Antigone*

In the preceding analyses we have repeatedly encountered the term "style" used by Brahm to characterize the technique employed by the director, the actor, or the scenic artist. It has also served to designate the general spirit or atmosphere of a particular drama. Style varies with individual artists and with different plays, but its most salient meaning in Otto Brahm's use of the word is bound up with temporal change. Thus, style has for him a peculiarly historical connotation, and differences in style become accentuated in proportion as they are representative of some well-defined artistic epoch. He speaks of the "Weimar style" and the "Hamburg style" as historical points of reference corresponding roughly to a "classical" style and a "realistic" style respectively. The latter, of course, is the historical style he deemed most consonant with the modern spirit.

Now, when a so-called "classical" play is to be staged, as for example Sophocles' *Antigone*, the question arises: what is the relationship between the style of the play and the style of the technique which is to project this play? In other words, should there be a classical style of technique in the staging of a classical play, or is it possible or preferable to project it by realistic means? The question is a perennial one in the history of the theatre, and Brahm's answer to it affords us an additional insight into his philosophy of interpretation.

That there should be an organic relationship between the style of a play and the technique of its staging can be assumed from Brahm's ideas as already analyzed. However, we shall see presently that this relationship is not mechanically conceived, since it has inner implications. Brahm shows that a classical technique, even assuming that there can be an archaeological resurrection of classical stage practice, can be but an historical curiosity at best and certainly cannot express the true classical spirit to a modern audience. Whatever style the play may have been composed in, Brahm insists that the technique must be modern. He develops this argument in the course of his review of *Antigone* as presented in the *Deutsches Theater*.[46]

[46] Schr. I, 86.

Brahm begins by praising the realistic spirit of the classical performances in the *Deutsches Theater*. Since the stage-worn Tieck version of *Antigone* had been conceived in the romantic tradition, a re-translation of style into the realism of the *Deutsches Theater* became necessary. Brahm contrasts Tieck's staging with that of the present performance. In the former, straight lines predominated, the set comprising a tall, square room running across the entire stage and surrounded by pillars; this was supposed to represent the "classical" stage. The modern setting eschews this severe and angular design. Profiting from the example of the Meininger, the application of artificial perspective has widened or narrowed the stage as required. Hard angles have been rounded off; austere and balanced proportions have been altered deliberately to create an asymmetrical and more natural effect. The static level of a single room has been changed to the varied levels of stairs and of a higher room beyond the one in the foreground. An exterior scene before the royal palace at Thebes is literally out of doors, with trees and an outside view of the palace. There is no geometrical starkness such as that of the single "classical" set upon which both interior and exterior scenes had been indiscriminately played in Tieck's staging of the play. The realistic staging in the *Deutsches Theater* thus stands in sharp contrast to the "romantic" staging of Tieck:

... alles mit einander gibt den Eindruck: hier können Menschen wohnen und sich heimisch fühlen. Die Anordnung in der alten Weise aber erreichte nur den Eindruck: hier ist eine gute Akustik, hier können Menschen Verse sprechen.[47]

The change to a realistic technique has also affected the chorus which is not placed as a single group in the center of the stage but to one side and in a natural, scattered formation. The one discordant effect which Brahm finds is the retention of Mendelssohn's music. Although the music is excellent considered as a separate composition, Brahm feels that it clashes with the Sophoclean spirit. The discrepancy of mood derives from the bright, lyrical, and at times operatic quality of the music which is artificially superimposed on the grave and minor undertones of the tragedy.

[47] Schr. I, 88.

The chorus should speak or chant, not sing. On the whole, however, the realistic note prevails.

The question arises whether these realistic innovations are
stylistically "true" to the spirit of classical antiquity. Brahm
answers this with an emphatic affirmative by showing that the
living classics themselves change throughout the years and
throughout the development of individuals, a phenomenon true of
all permanent art and therefore of stage art as well:

> Wir nennen diejenigen Dichtungen klassisch, welche eine nicht
> endende, unmittelbare Wirkung durch die Folge der Jahrhunderte
> bewahren. Sie überdauern den Wechsel der Zeiten; allein nicht ist
> damit gegeben, dass sie in der Anschauung der Lebenden stets die
> nämlichen bleiben. Anders wirkte Shakespeare auf sein Jahrhundert,
> anders wirkt er auf uns Heutige. Gerade weil er lebt, wandelt er sich
> auch, zugleich mit den Menschen. Wie es uns wohl begegnet, dass sich
> künstlerische Eindrücke aus frühen Tagen in uns, mit uns entwickeln,
> (ohne dass doch eine erneute Berührung mit den Gegenständen statt-
> gefunden hätte), wie dichterische Werke in unserem Urteil steigen
> oder fallen, allein durch die Wirkung der Zeit, so entwickeln sich auch
> jene Schöpfungen der Klassiker, wie die Menschheit selbst.[48]

Now the theatre is a peculiarly social form of art which must
make its appeal to broad groups of naïve individuals whose approach lacks the complexities of a literary background; so that, in
order to represent the true spirit of a classical play, the theatre is
best served by presenting this play in terms of the living spirit
which already suffuses its naïve audience. Brahm concludes from
this that the art of the theatre can be nothing else but modern:

> Die Schauspielkunst kann nicht anders als modern sein—gleichviel
> ob sie Shakespeare oder Schiller, Sophokles oder Kleist darstellt.
> Für alle gilt in diesen Tagen der realistische Stil; nur innerhalb dieses
> Stiles mag sie die Nuancen zwischen alter und neuer Zeit weise ab-
> wägen.[49]

Brahm continues to develop the idea of change in the attitude
toward the classics by contrasting the meaning and appeal of
Sophocles' *Antigone* to the audiences of ancient Greece and to
those of modern times. Our profoundest impressions in regard to

---

[48] *Ibid.*   [49] Schr. I, 89.

Antigone are not the same as those of the Greeks. The play, more than any other classical tragedy, makes its appeal to us because of the central conflict between the rights of the individual and the rights of the group, a conflict which is still operative today. Both forces in the conflict are equally justified; that is, the feeling of the individual is opposed to the collective necessity, yet both remain inevitably and unalterably what they are through the very nature of things. Opposed to the pious will of Antigone is Kreon's inflexible and imperious will to power as a ruler. To the Greeks, however, these two antithetical forces were not equally justified as we now conceive them to be. In the Attic drama Kreon was merely the antagonist of Antigone and thus only a foil to the heroine.[50]

A further action of Kreon, which now impresses us as tragic and sympathetic but which made him dwindle in the estimation of the Greeks, is his inner transformation and collapse at the end of the play after learning of the impending extinction of his family line. The Greek hero, according to Freytag (whom Brahm follows in this analysis),[51] was characterized by an adamant will; any indecision or wavering in a moral crisis was looked upon derogatorily and was generally relegated by the Greek dramatist to a minor character. Thus, in respect to the tragic greatness of Kreon the modern attitude is entirely at variance with that of the Greeks. And this change in the basic conception of the play, which every epoch re-translates for itself, is accompanied by a similar change in the technique of interpretation which also develops in conformity with the spirit of each succeeding era.

Stage technique, as we have seen, is always modern and is conditioned by the spirit of its own times. The actors of Goethe's day who played *Antigone* were not playing as the Greeks had played but merely as they conceived the Greeks to have played, with the statuesque poses and declamatory resonance that characterized the Weimar style. But they did not attempt to take over the mask and cothurn of the Attic theatre. Their style was modern

---

[50] Brahm supports this view by reference to Greek stage practice and by a comparison of the various Kreons who appear in other Greek plays.

[51] *Die Technik des Dramas*, Leipzig, (1863) 7. Aufl., 1894, pp. 123ff., "Der Bau des Dramas bei Sophokles."

as of the eighteenth century just as the realistic style is modern as
of today:

Die Klassiker klassisch darstellen—ist das überhaupt möglich?
Gegenüber den Griechen entscheidet sich die Frage in ihrer letzten
Folgerung von selbst: niemand will den Kothurn und die Maske der
antiken Bühne auf die gegenwärtige hinüberführen. Aber können wir
auch nur Shakespeare darstellen, in dem Stile seiner Schauspieler;
können wir einen Hamlet geniessen, wie ihn Burbadge spielte? Ja,
selbst unsere deutschen Dramatiker, selbst Goethe und Schiller sehen
wir heute nicht mehr, wie sie die Zeitgenossen des Dichters und die
nächste Generation sahen; nicht in dem Tone der Esslair und Emil
Devrient, sondern in dem der Sonnenthal und Kainz hören wir sie.
Modern waren jene, modern sind diese.[52]

Brahm concludes from this that it is impossible to play the
classics effectively on the modern stage in the style of past eras.
To do so would be to vitiate the eternal and living essence of the
classics with archaeological pedantry. Those who wish to adhere
to so-called "classical" styles of interpretation are attempting to
perpetuate obsolete convention and must, as reactionaries of the
theatre, forego even the illusion of being true to life. The realistic
style that asserted itself, if only in intermittent spurts, in the performance at the *Deutsches Theater* proves to Brahm that a modern,
realistic technique of staging and the style of classical drama are
not mutually exclusive.

I. SUMMARY

Otto Brahm's principles underlying the directorial functions of
dramaturgy and technique can be pithily summarized on the basis
of the frequently made distinction between internal and external
direction ("*innere und äussere Regie*").[53] To Brahm the problems
of theatrical interpretation, as suggested at the beginning of this
chapter, take the drama as their point of departure. The intention
of the dramatist expressed in a literary medium provides the focal
point, the *primum mobile* for the art of the stage. This particular
emphasis in directorial approach is termed "*innere Regie*" because
its dominant concern is with the poetic word which it endeavors

---

[52] Schr. I, 91.
[53] Cf. Adolf Winds, *Geschichte der Regie*, Stuttgart, 1925, Einleitung.

to infuse with life (*"Verlebendigung des dichterischen Wortes"*).[54] The antithetical approach is from without and is consequently known as *"äussere Regie"* since it envisions the drama primarily in terms of a mood-creating structurization of scenic milieu (*"stimmunggebende Gestaltung der szenischen Umwelt"*).[55] Internal direction makes its emotional appeal through the ear and the mind; it objectifies psychological conflicts and promotes ideational nuances; hence the importance of characterization, the minimization or "toning down" of light, color, and sensuous effect, and in general the relative subservience of the theatre to the idea. The converse is true of external direction: the appeal is sensuous and primarily visual; colorful settings, technical dynamics, and so-called "showmanship" prevail.

On the basis of these considerations there can be very little doubt but that Brahm's criticism, as well as his subsequent theatre practice, conforms to the ideal of *"innere Regie."* His constant emphasis on the idea and meaning of a play, his subtle analyses of plot and characterization, his excoriation of meretricious theatrical effects which tend to obscure the germinal idea of the author, all tend to magnify the principle of internal direction. However, we must bear in mind that the above distinction between two types of directorial approach merely serves to conceptualize general differences in emphasis but not differences which are so sharply antithetical as to become mutually exclusive. The pure type does not exist in reality. Only thus can we fully understand Brahm's leading concept of unity in the theatrical arts, a unity between the nuclear spirit of a play and its technical projection upon the stage. While Brahm emphasizes the interpretation of a play, he does not neglect the demands of the theatre.

An ideal sketch of the director and his functions thus emerges inductively from Brahm's criticism. The director as a literary and aesthetic critic, as an historian of the drama and stage, and as a practical dramaturgist, analyzes and interprets the play and prepares a working script. Upon the basis of this interpretation he casts the roles, designs the settings, molds the characterizations, and performs the other details essential to the staging of a play.

[54] *Ibid.*   [55] *Ibid.*

The director, of course, is not necessarily a Protean genius; he frequently enlists the aid of a dramaturgist, of scenic designers, and of the other ancillary specialists of the theatre. But he must always exert his unifying influence upon all the departments of the theatre so as to mold them into his central design. There must be an ensemble unity of style among the actors and continuity of action throughout the play. The individual tone and style of a play, its essential spirit, the peculiar atmosphere of its time, all these must be palpable in the total mood of the staging and performance. The final effect must be organic.

VIII. *The Actor and His Art*

One of the salient characteristics of journalistic dramatic criticism is its cavalier treatment of the aesthetics of the drama in its profounder aspects. Such matters as the theory of tragedy, the structure of the play, the symbolic implications of theme and character are relatively neglected in this type of criticism. What emerges to the fore is the element of reportage which is essentially descriptive rather than interpretative. In the theatre the most immediate impression is a sensuous one; there are the settings, the costumes, the actors, all exerting their direct appeal of color, proportion, stature, and voice, both to the eye and to the ear. A description of these sensuous impressions, which are frequently more vivid than the play itself, at least for the time being, thus naturally emerges in a criticism written soon after the performance. This, of course, is only one of the reasons why Brahm devotes so many of his pages to the actor and his art. We shall find profounder ones in his more abstract essays on the history of styles in acting, on the function of the actor, and in many detailed observations on the technique of acting.

Unlike Lessing, whose logical analysis of histrionic art proved too candid for the virtuosos of the Hamburg troupe, Brahm is entirely unconstrained in his criticism of personalities. Frau Ziegler, playing the role of Marfa in Schiller's *Demetrius* is bluntly termed *"eine Geschmacksverderberin ersten Ranges."*[1] Friedrich Haase (*"ein fetter Haase"*) is hauled over the coals for his lapse into *"die pure, leere Virtuosität."*[2] A certain Frau Stolberg in Kleist's *Der Zerbrochne Krug* is pilloried for disrupting the mood of the play with her *"lederne Pathetik."*[3] In Wildenbruch's *Die Quitzows* Herr Kahle receives a more extended drubbing for his pains in the role of Straussberger:

Alles, was an falschem, kreischendem Pathos, an theatralischer Unnatur und Gespreiztheit in der Bühnentradition nur zu finden ist, trägt Herr Kahle mit rollenden Gesten und hohler Deklamation in diese Rolle hinein . . . [4]

[1] Schr. I, 196.　　　　　[2] Schr. I, 201.
[3] Schr. I, 386.　　　　　[4] Schr. I, 224.

A hapless Herr Wessels in Ibsen's *Stützen der Gesellschaft* is made
the butt of withering irony:

... und selbst Herrn Wessels gelang es diesmal, wie ein Mensch zu
gehen und zu sprechen. Wirklich, es geschehen noch Zeichen und
Wunder.[5]

And even the great Ludwig Barnay, whom Brahm has already
excoriated as a director, does not escape unscathed:

Shakespeare muss sich ad usum Barnays verbessern lassen, auf
dass Spielraum gewonnen werde für den Flügelschlag einer Virtuosen-
seele.[6]

Thomas Mann suggests[7] that the primitive artlessness of the
theatre affords dramatic critics an unhampered opportunity to
display their aesthetic superiority. Otto Brahm makes frequent
use of this opportunity. Not that he abuses it, although the above
examples may seem to argue otherwise. The opinionated exhibitionism of matinee idols, the wooden incomprehension of routiniers
who remain themselves no matter what the role, goad him into
angry remonstrance. His sense of responsibility in regard to the
theatre is too dominant in him to permit of any compromise with
mediocrity. The campaign against the virtuose actor wages unabated until the star of Kainz rises on the theatrical horizon; and
with an at first hesitant, but then increasingly unconstrained,
admiration, Brahm recognizes in him the living embodiment of his
ideal of a transfigured naturalism as the supreme expression of the
actor's art.

A. *The Genesis of Realism*

Towards the end of his career as a dramatic critic (1892) Brahm
summed up his theories on the art of acting by defining them
against an historical background. The impetus to his extended
essay: *Von Alter und Neuer Schauspielkunst*[8] was provided by
Karl Frenzel's attack on the modern theories of acting which
Brahm had been advocating.[9] Brahm had enthusiastically hailed
the naturalistic drama as of invaluable significance to the art of

[5] Schr. I, 244.   [6] Schr. I, 10.
[7] Cf. "Versuch über das Theater" in *Rede und Antwort*, Berlin, 1922.
[8] Nation, 14.5.1892.
[9] Cf. Karl Frenzel, *Berliner Dramaturgie*, Erfurt, 1877ff.

acting regardless of the literary principles involved. Whereas classical tragedy in the grand manner drove the actor into declamation and false pathos and made him a stiff and ornate rhetorician, the naturalistic drama forced him to become more human.[10] Yet Brahm holds no brief for an uninspired and unrelieved naturalism in the art of acting. His use of the Goethean term *"beseelte Natur"*[11] in connection with Kainz, and his early condemnation of the naturalistic technique of the Meininger are much more characteristic of the former Scherer pupil and Goethe scholar; this is strong enough proof against any charge of pure naturalism being levied against Brahm. The fact that Brahm champions modernity against traditionalism does not in the least mean that he is committed to any narrow doctrine of naturalism. This, of course, did not prevent the critical solons of an older tradition, of whom Karl Frenzel was the archtype, from imputing such doctrines to him. In this vein, Karl Frenzel bewails the promulgation of haphazard and newfangled theories of acting in analogy to the style of impressionistic painting. He deplores the imitation of nature at all costs in order to reproduce "hideous brutality" rather than "beautiful humanity." Such is his polemically distorted conception of the new theory of acting.[12]

Brahm diffidently disclaims any pretensions to being the harbinger of eternal and immutable theories; but he does insist upon his competence to detect and to express the demands which modern times make of the art of acting. He even goes a step further by showing that although the tendency which he represents has undergone temporal changes, it nevertheless coincides in an essential sense with a permanent tendency observable and operative throughout the history of the German theatre. He recalls how out of the rigidity of the Alexandrian tragedy and the mincing poses of the Rococo drama the first great period of German acting had emerged in the brilliant Hamburg realists, Ekhof and Schröder. This North German style was brought to the South by Beil and Iffland. It came to Vienna with Schröder himself. And the same spirit of realism and naturalness in characterization expressed

---

[10] Schr. I, 292.   [11] Schr. I, 418.
[12] Summarized by Brahm, Schr. I, 421.

itself in Berlin preeminently in Fleck and in Frau Unzelmann. At
the close of the century, the great countermovement of classicism
had set in, with Goethe as the chief theoretical promulgator of the
Weimar School of acting. To Brahm, the entire drift of modern
acting and the instinctive urge of subsequent German actors has
been directed towards the supersedence and the eventual dissolution of the Weimar style.

Brahm quotes Devrient to show the inevitable contradiction
between the stage artist and the domineering poet of Weimar.[13]
Yet he does not wholly subscribe to Devrient's extreme view. He
realizes the relative historical justification of the classical movement in the theatre, the poetic transfiguration and spiritual pro-
fundity which it brought to the stage. Nevertheless, Brahm
maintains that it is the sensitive and intelligent actor rather than
the dramatist who can best envisage the problems of the theatre.
He shows how Goethe's development from the natural and pulsat-
ing characters of *Götz* and *Werther* to the more serene and typified
characters of his later works, with their submergence of individual
traits to the generally-human (*das Allgemeinmenschliche*), must run
counter to the individually characterizing spirit of the Germanic
art of acting, if it is to remain true to itself:

Goethe selbst hatte einst ausgesprochen, dass die characteristische
Kunst dem nordischen Geiste innerlich kongenialer sei als die schöne
Kunst der Antike; aber von der Besonderheit der Natur, die der
Dichter des *Götz* und des *Werther* aufzufassen gewusst, wie kein
anderer, zog es ihn fort zum Allgemein-menschlichen, zum Typischen,
das die Schlacken der Individualität ausgeworfen hatte—und diesem
Trieb musste die deutsche Schauspielkunst widersprechen, wollte sie
nicht sich selber aufgeben. Menschendarstellung musste ihre erste
und ihre letzte Pflicht sein, und durch die reich entwickelte Persönlichkeit nur, durch die feinste natürliche Differenzierung im Ausdruck
des Körperlichen wie des Seelischen konnte sie sie lösen.[14]

Brahm goes on to show that, in spite of Goethe's sensitively
conceived theory of characterization, the Weimar *Theaterdirektor*
suffered strange lapses in his arbitrary rules for the actor, whom he
wished to dominate not only on the stage but also in private life.

---

[13] Cf. Eduard Devrient, *Geschichte der deutschen Schauspielkunst*, Berlin, 1905f.,
Bd. II, p. 153.

[14] Schr. I, 422.

In place of truth and observation Goethe set up maxims of style;
he insisted that on the stage as well as in private life the actor
should speak each word with a certain gravity, should comport
himself with dignity, and even gesticulate in a stylized manner.[15]
But the most pernicious effect of the Weimar style to Brahm was
its mechanical borrowing from the allied arts of sculpture and
music: its statuesque grace and deliberate posing inevitably re-
tarded the action, while artificial and calculated dynamic effects
were practised to achieve precise timing, with Goethe's baton
serving as a sort of metronom.[16] To this highly unnatural procedure, which may have been justified in the eighteenth century,
Brahm contrasts Schröder's efforts to achieve naturalness in
characterization:

> Mit der Natur auszugleichen, zu prüfen an der Natur und das bloss
> deklamatorisch Glänzende umzuprägen, im Feuer der Menschen-
> darstellung, in das greifbar Individuelle—das ist die Aufgabe, welche
> gegenüber der klassischen Dichtung dem Modernen erwächst, so gut
> wie sie den Schröder und Fleck erwuchs; denn nicht einen Stil der
> Vergangenheit kann er in sich konservieren wollen; er ist ein lebender
> Künstler, kein Kunsthistoriker und Antiquar; und was mit den Aus-
> drucksmitteln der Gegenwart nicht kann ergriffen werden, das hat
> kein Recht, auf der Bühne zu leben, welche unserer Zeit gehört,
> keiner anderen. Für das Ehemals das Jetzt opfern und das Recht der
> Lebendigen—der Preis wäre allzu teuer.[17]

The drift towards realism and nature continues in the history
of the German theatre; and the conflict between Hamburg and
Weimar is already evident in Laube, who strove for a synthesis of
the two. Laube seemed to lean in the direction of Hamburg; Lessing and Schröder were his mentors, and the achievement of realistic
truth in characterization, his ruling aim. But, like Goethe, he
emphasized the aural at the expense of the visual in theatrical art,
and hence was more interested in elocution than in the staging of
the play. The Meininger brought realism back to the stage with
their true-to-life settings and costumes. But they failed, Brahm

---

[15] Cf. Goethe's *Regeln für Schauspieler*, 1824.
[16] Brahm bases this on the account of Goethe's pupil, Pius Alexander Wolff, who
tells of the master presiding at rehearsals like a band leader. Schr. I, 423.
[17] Schr. I, 424.

tells us, to people the stage with living human beings who could act naturally.

Brahm continues the historical exegesis of his theories of realism in acting as part of his answer to Frenzel's charge. He recalls how in the history of the theatre every step in the direction of nature had aroused hostile opposition. Quoting from Julius Wahle's work on the Weimar *Hoftheater*,[18] Brahm refers to Talma as having been the first to break with convention in the European theatre. Talma's introduction of historical costuming was a revolutionary step that met with embittered opposition. He spoke not to the audience but to the persons in the play, often stepping into the background and even turning his back to the audience. In the creation of new roles he disregarded conventional interpretations established by his predecessors. His striving for naturalness and realism revitalized the convention-bound French stage. This is precisely what Brahm urges for the modern German stage:

. . . dass der Schauspieler in den Lebensformen unserer Zeit rede, und dass er aus kräftigem, modernem Empfinden heraus das erstarrende Alte belebe.[19]

The innovation of acting technique whereby Talma turned his back to the audience is of typical significance to Brahm; it symbolizes the difference between realistic earnestness and conventional illusion. Goethe positively forbade the actor to turn his back to the audience; whereas Strindberg once expressed a wish to see the back of an actor throughout an entire scene. Lessing's general opinion in the matter was that the audience should realize that it was in the theatre for the sake of the actor and not *vice versa*. Schröder's technique also minimized the audience in this respect; he played *with* the actors and not *to* the audience. The radical difference between the Hamburg and Weimar schools of acting is exemplified for Brahm in an entry which Goethe made in his journal[20] concerning a performance in the Leipzig Theater. Goethe condemned the naturalism, the undeliberative style which

---

[18] *Das Weimarer Hoftheater unter Goethes Leitung*, Weimar, 1892, in Schr. der Goethe Gesellschaft, Bd. 6.
[19] Schr. I, 426.
[20] 1802.

gave the impression that the actors were apparently unaware of
the presence of an audience, turning their backs and speaking in a
realistic manner. What is here condemned is for Brahm and the
modern theatre in general an axiomatic principle of technique. The
players are involved in the creation of an illusion of actual hap-
penings; they react towards one another in order to maintain this
illusion. To turn to the audience, to posture and declaim are
patently destructive of all illusion.

B. *Impressionism and Acting*

Brahm pleads guilty to Frenzel's analogy between the new
theories of acting and impressionistic painting. He traces in the art
of painting the same contradictions which he has found in the art
of acting. Carstens and Cornelius correspond to the Weimar style;
they are painters who cannot paint but who are suffused with
poetic mood and who thus are reminiscent of the actors of the
Weimar tradition, who do not act but who are enchanted by the
magic of poetic declamation. Then came Piloty, who painted
realistic costumes but no real human beings, corresponding to the
Meininger. The painter analogous to the Hamburg school would be
Menzel. French impressionism as exemplified in Millet with his
intimate observation of nature, his simple, naïve, real human
beings, represents the technique which Brahm is championing.
Brahm's admonition to the actor is that he should strive to keep
close to nature in its spiritual entirety (*"in ihrer seelenvollen
Fülle"*)[21] and this will keep him from becoming superficial and
trivial. The actor should seek nature both from within and without; and the more he develops his personality, in other words, the
stronger the temperament is through which, according to Zola's
formula, he regards nature, the more profound will be his conception of life and his re-creation of this conception through his art.
Turning from the theatre to nature and from the convention of the
foot-lights to human truth, he will learn to forego false stylization
and arbitrary mannerisms. Brahm sees a higher conception of the
ideal and of the beautiful emerging from his theory of spiritual
naturalism in acting:

[21] Schr. I, 428.

Denn die Natur suche der Schauspieler, nichts darüber. Er suche
sie ganz, in ihrer seelenvollen Fülle: so wird er vor Flachheit bewahrt
sein und vor Trivialität. Er suche sie ausser sich und in sich, in der
Welt und in der eigenen Brust: und je reicher und reiner er dann seine
Persönlichkeit entwickelt, je stärker das Temperament ist, durch das
er nach Zola's allgültiger Zauberformel die Natur betrachtet, desto
tiefer auch wird er Leben fassen und Leben geben. Wie jener Riese,
wenn er die Erde berührt, wird er vom Theater zur Natur, von der
Konvention der Bretter zur menschlichen Wahrheit zurückkehrend
Kraft sich immer von neuem gewinnen; und alles Stilisieren wird er
so meiden lernen, alle willkürliche Manier und aufgeputzte Kulissen-
empfindung. Das Ideale aber, das Schöne kann er nur in Einem empfinden, das innerhalb der Sache liegt, nicht ausser ihr in Geboten des
Herkommens: er finde es in der Treue gegen das künstlerische Ganze,
dem er angehört, gegen das Ganze des Charakters, den er verwirklicht,
des Dramas, in dem er steht. Hier soll er sich harmonisch „schön"
der ökonomie des Kunstwerkes einfügen.[22]

As we have had occasion to remark previously, Brahm began his
criticism of theatrical art by pointing out both the excellencies
and deficiencies of the Meininger. He praised their historical
realism in the matter of settings and costumes and their vivid,
naturalistic handling of mass scenes, but showed how these merits
easily became demerits when the realism of individual characterization was submerged by archaeological exactness and the lack
of outstanding performers with sufficient genius and temperament
to create living human beings. The Meininger represented a decided advance when compared to the effete sluggishness of their
predecessors who were bogged in the mire of tradition and
virtuosity. From this point of view Brahm condemns the extreme
historical naturalism of the Meininger as representing a confusion
between reality and art. Although he sees the correspondence
between their historical exactitude and the general tendency toward naturalism, he charges them with bringing reality itself on
the stage instead of selected bits of reality which in an art form
create a higher illusion of reality.[23] Brahm thus reveals himself to
be decidedly opposed to an unselective naturalism in the art of the
stage. In his opinion, the indigenously Germanic art of the stage
finds its fullest expression in the creation of individual characters.

[22] *Ibid.*   [23] Schr. I, 11.

The significance which accrues to the actor from this point of view is of course vastly enhanced.

C. *The Ibsen Cure*

As in all the other departments of the theatre, it is Ibsen who in Brahm's mind exerts a revolutionary influence on the art of the actor. The transition from the Meininger to Ibsen brings with it a deepening of the art of individual characterization. Ibsen supplies the living, realistic individuals who have been so glaringly absent from the splendid scenic milieu of the Meininger. Thus, in a review of an early performance of *Ein Puppenheim,* in spite of the irrepressible power of the play, the hodge-podge of traditional acting styles affects Brahm adversely. Yet his blame does not fall too severely on the actors since they have been falsely trained. Ibsen's plays require a re-education of the actor. Hence, one of the most forceful arguments which Brahm uses in his championship of Ibsen is directed towards the actor himself:

Und darum ist den Ibsenschen Werken ein immer reicheres Bühnenleben zu wünschen, auch im Interesse unserer Darstellungskunst; sie führen, wie den Zuschauer so den Schauspieler, zu dem Natürlichen und Grossen hin, zu neuen unverbrauchten Gestalten, an denen eine nachschaffende Kunst sich bilden und reifen mag.[24]

Brahm often regards the playing of an Ibsenian role as a test of the actor. Even as great an actress as Agnes Sorma, playing the part of Nora, reveals to Brahm a certain virtuose obtuseness in regard to the inner implications of her characterization. Recalling a conversation with Ibsen regarding "roles," Brahm quotes the Norwegian dramatist's impatience with the very concept: *"Ich schreibe keine Rollen, ich schildere Menschen!"*[25] But the essence of virtuosity is that it thinks only in terms of roles which must be theatrically elaborated, embroidered with nuances and with inchoate bits of stage business that obscure the human being behind the role. Brahm is convinced that virtuosity and Henrick Ibsen are incompatible. He recommends a curative diet of the Norwegian dramatist for Agnes Sorma and others who are afflicted with virtuosity:

[24] Schr. I, 232.   [25] Schr. I, 414.

Und darum mag ihr und ihren Genossen die Ibsendarstellung eine Kur sein, ein schauspielerisches Mittel, das vom Theatralischen zurückführt zur beseelten Natur.[26]

Concerning the further education of the actor, Brahm lays a good deal of emphasis on the indispensable need for playing repertory. The evils of specialization are more evident in an actor's art than in any other field. A variety of roles is necessary in order to develop the versatility of the actor. Only in this way can the actor achieve the power of *Wandlungsfähigkeit* so as to be able to identify himself in a more real sense with each new character that he plays. The question of repertory has already been treated in connection with the technique of the theatre. The same principles of variety, of naturalness, and of modernity apply to the individual actor.

D. Genius and Temperament: *Kainz—Reicher—Rittner*

No account of Brahm's principles of acting would be complete if it did not include the intuitive and extra-rational elements in the actor's make-up for which no amount of technical adroitness and theoretical acumen could compensate. Brahm uses the terms *Temperament* and *Genie* in regard to a few great actors of his time when he desires to designate a margin of achievement which he cannot define wholly by intellectual concepts. In distinguishing between mere talent and genius, Brahm delivers himself of a homely but none the less profound truism:

Eine jede Rolle hat bekanntlich zwei Bestandteile: das, was drin steht, und das, was nicht drin steht. Das eine treffen auch die Talente; das andere nur die Genies.[27]

Hence, it is only by indirection, by metaphor and superlative analogies that Brahm can do justice to the ineffable qualities of such great actors as Kainz, Reicher, and Rittner at their highest stage of development. It is profitable, therefore, to trace in some detail Brahm's criticism and appreciation of these, the foremost actors of his time. Reicher and Rittner he discusses at length in a three-fold comparison with Adolf Sonnenthal,[28] while stages in the career of Kainz run like a recurrent *Leitmotiv* through the extensive

---

[26] Schr. I, 418. [27] Schr. I, 66. [28] Schr. I, 355ff.

course of Brahm's reviews. And finally, Brahm's commemorative brochure on Kainz provides a lyrical epilogue to that great actor's career.[29]

Surveying the history of the German theatre prior to the founding of the *Freie Bühne*, Brahm notes that the revival of the drama was preceded by a revival of the art of acting. Lacking a modern realistic drama in which to express themselves fully, it was nonetheless possible for such geniuses as Kainz and Mitterwurzer to revitalize the classical drama in their acting so as to impart to it contemporary relevance. They created out of the former *Epigonenspielerei* a living art:

> Dass der Darsteller ein nachschaffender Künstler ist, aber kein grübelnder Kunstgelehrter, dass man König Philipp und Don Carlos am siegreichsten spielt, wenn man sie nicht deklamiert, sondern neu belebt—solche einfache Wahrheit zu erweisen mussten erst zwei geniale Schauspieler auferstehen.[30]

Of Kainz in particular Brahm has a good deal to say. As far back as 1883, Brahm is critical in regard to young Kainz for his immaturity and for the fact that he does not make the most of his possibilities:

> Herr Kainz, obgleich er schon eine Anzahl von Jahren der Bühne angehört, hat sich noch wenig in seiner Kunst befestigt, er ist ein ganz wildwüchsiges Talent, das hoffentlich bei uns in ernste Schule genommen werden kann.[31]

But in the very same year Kainz's masterful Don Carlos arouses Brahm's admiration. He says that in Kainz the Berlin stage possesses a Don Carlos who might well be the envy of the entire German theatre, not excluding Vienna. He speaks of Kainz's complete intellectual and technical mastery of the role joined to an elemental uniqueness and naturalness. Brahm foreshadows a brilliant career for the young Viennese actor who has so quickly learned to constrain his natural gifts within artistic bounds.[32]

In comparing Kainz, as Karl Moor, with a Herr Pohl, as Franz, Brahm sees the superiority of the former as inherent in his pas-

---

[29] *Kainz: Geschehenes und Gelebtes*, Berlin, 2. Aufl., 1910.
[30] Schr. I, 464.   [31] Schr. I, 49.
[32] Schr. I, 54.

sionate sincerity. Both actors strive for realism, but Pohl's realism
dwells in the mind whereas Kainz's realism dwells in the blood; for
Kainz, realism is a matter of temperament, of brilliant, flaming
passion. Brahm describes Kainz's art and its effect on the audience:

... die reiche Kunst des Sprechens, über die der Darsteller gebietet,
diese wie mit natürlicher Schnelle, flüssig und doch niemals über-
hastig hervorströmende Fülle der Rede riss die Hörer fort und bannte
sie ganz hinein in die Gewalt der Szene.[33]

Brahm is an ardent admirer of Kainz for the remainder of the
actor's career. His reviews are nevertheless not always laudatory
since his appreciation of Kainz always remains critical; he will not
accept a mediocre performance from one who has such infinitely
higher potentialities. When Kainz returns from a foreign tour
bringing with him certain virtuose mannerisms, Brahm does not
hesitate to criticise.[34] But when the foremost actor of the German
stage falls into difficulties and is boycotted by leading directors
because of a breach of contract, Brahm rushes to the rescue with
an impassioned defense.[35] In the course of this eloquent bit of
special pleading, Brahm summarizes Kainz's significance in the
history of the German theatre:

Kainz ist der erste gewesen, in unserer Tragödie moderne Kunst-
forderungen zu erfüllen—das ist sein grosses, sein historisches Verdienst. Fern von aller hohlen Doktrin, ganz aus seiner Natur heraus,
aus einer nervösen, modernen Natur, hat er die Aufgaben Shakespeares und Schillers ergriffen und sie wiederum erfüllt mit warmem
Lebensblut. Was trockene Überlieferung geworden war, Schablone
und Deklamation, er gestaltete es mit einer realistischen Unmittel-
barkeit aus, die den andern verloren gegangen war; sie waren tastende
Epigonen, er ein keck Moderner.[36]

At the death of this great artist there were few who were better
fitted than Otto Brahm to write concerning Kainz's career and art.
Brahm inscribed his personal reminiscences of Kainz in a brief,
elegiac monograph which has since become a source book for
historians of the theatre.[37]

In this appreciative essay Brahm dwells on Kainz's personal
uniqueness ("*das Gefühl seiner Einzigkeit*"), but he shows how even

[33] Schr. I, 199.   [34] Schr. I, 420.
[35] *Der Fall Kainz*, Schr. I, 308.   [36] Schr. I, 309.   [37] *Op. cit.*

this genius was a child of his milieu, and how the forces of his time
and of his training conditioned his development.[38] Beginning with
the Vienna *Burgtheater*, going to the Meininger, and finally to the
Deutsches Theater in Berlin, Kainz was molded by these various
preliminary stages of his career. Certain mannerisms had been in-
culcated into his technique, particularly under the influence of
Possart in Munich, and, as a result, when Otto Brahm as the
dramatic critic of the *Vossische Zeitung* first reviewed Kainz's performances, he pointed out these virtuose peculiarities but without
losing sight of the young actor's possibilities.[39] After Vienna,
Kainz became more clear and realistic, especially when exposed to
the Berlin atmosphere:

Es fielen die äusseren Behelfe des Theaters, die geklebten Nasen, die
unwahrscheinlichen Perücken, die Fettschminke; und es ward auch
ein Vernichtungsfeldzug unternommen gegen den inneren Feind,
gegen das Theater der Psyche, zugunsten der Wahrheit, Ehrlichkeit,
Echtheit.[40]

With the rise of Kainz, the knell of the Weimar style had
sounded; the advent of realism finally completed the destruction
of Goethe's antiquated rules. Brahm goes on to show Kainz as a
reformer in his creation of new roles and in his rejection of the cant
and balderdash of the theatre. A vital element in Kainz's genius
was his re-creation of each new role.[41] Brahm conjectures that the
highest fruition of Kainz's art resulted from his playing of the
realistic roles of Hauptmann, Ibsen, and Schnitzler, and the consequent application of this new realistic technique to classical
roles such as, Hamlet, Orestes, and Tasso. (*"Hatte ihm sein stilles
Studium des Ibsen diese köstliche Frucht getragen, dass er den Tasso
spielte wie im Stile des Oswald Alving?"*)[42]

Kainz represented to Otto Brahm a theatrical anomaly: a great
actor who, except for minor aberrations, was without the sins of
virtuosity (*"Kainz ist keine begehrliche Virtuosennatur"*).[43] He was
sufficiently independent as an artist and sufficiently responsive to
the spirit of his own time to reject the style of the eighteenth
century. Long before dramatic theoreticians had settled the ques-

[38] *Ibid.*, p. 3.
[40] *Op. cit.*, pp. 7f.
[42] *Ibid.*, p. 43.

[39] 7. 10. 1883; Schr. I, 49.
[41] *Ibid.*, p. 13.
[43] Schr. I, 307.

tion of style in the enactment of classical roles, Kainz had decided
the issue in practice. He disdained the archaeological style and preferred to play as a modern human being ("*er will lieber menschlich
sein als griechisch*").[44] Perhaps the most sensitive and at the same
time most profoundly descriptive appreciation of Kainz's art that
Brahm ever penned was his review of the great actor as Orestes
in Goethe's *Iphigenie*, performed in the *Deutsches Theater*. Disregarding technical and theoretical questions, Brahm describes the
composite effect of Kainz's performance and, as a result, we have
a complete expression of Brahm's ideal conception of the actor's
art in general:

> Aber gern und freudig erkenne ich, dass über die Fragen von Stil
> und Manier hinweg eine innere Grösse aus diesem Orest spricht, eine
> seelenerschütternde Macht, die die Gestalt neben das Tiefste stellt,
> welches Kainz uns gegeben: wie er nur die Bühne beschreitet, die
> leidende Gestalt in ein graues Gewand gehüllt, das Haupt umstarrt
> von wildem Gelocke, einer Böcklinschen Furie gleich, ist Stimmung
> da; und wie er nun, von sittlichem Schauder geschüttelt, den schuldi-
> gen Blick der Grube zuneigt, der Schwester die furchtbarste Tat
> bekennt, wie er ganz Innerlichkeit und zuckende Qual, „den Strömen,
> die hier sieden, einen Weg eröffnet," wie er zerbrechend niedersinkt
> und aufsteht endlich, ein Geheilter—da empfinden wir ergriffen ganz,
> was grosse Schauspielkunst vermag, wenn sie, verbündet dem grossen
> Dichter, aus eigenem gestaltend ihm kongenial nachschafft.[45]

One of the foremost proponents of naturalism in acting was
Emanuel Reicher of whom Brahm says that he deserted the
virtuose over-acting (*Chargieren*) typical of Sonnenthal and his
school and turned his attention to the portrayal of human beings.
Reicher, Brahm tells us, is the "conscious" master of modern
realism on the stage, the first adequate player of Ibsenian roles.
His art consists of a penetrating gift for characterization, a flair
for acute observation, and a shrewd intelligence, all of which enhanced a native power of histrionic changeability. While recog-
nizing Reicher's genius, Brahm maintains that it does not represent
the highest development of contemporary acting. Reicher has
eschewed style in favor of nature, a revolutionary change at that
time. But because of the novelty of his technique, a certain element

[44] Schr. I, 439.   [45] Schr. I, 339f.

of deliberate awareness had imperceptibly insinuated itself into his acting. As Brahm explains it:

Natur ist immer schlicht, die Knalleffekte bringen erst die Menschen in sie hinein; Natur auf dem Theater aber verliert leicht ihre Keuschheit, sie bietet sich dar auf dem Präsentierteller, sie wird inne, sie zeigt, dass sie Natur ist—und hört im selben Momente auf, es zu sein. Naivität, die von sich weiss, ist nicht länger Naivität; und wenn ein Schauspieler erst zu sprechen scheint: seht her, wie natürlich ich bin! so guckt ihm die Unnatur schon grinsend über die Schulter.[46]

In order to avoid this element of consciousness in realism, the problem of following a middle path between it and a more spontaneous realism presents itself. The problem can be envisaged in all its subtle difficulty when one realizes that the art of acting presupposes the more or less conscious creation of a character. But to project this conscious creation and yet not give the effect of deliberate and preconceived portrayal is the task to be surmounted.

The art of Rudolf Rittner, in Brahm's estimation, tends towards such a delicate balance. It represents the ultimate step from a "deliberate" naturalism to a naïve or "natural" naturalism ("*der Schritt vom leis bewussten Naturalismus zum selbstverständlichen Naturalismus*"). Rittner is not at all concerned with achieving "effects" ("*Er will überhaupt nicht wirken, er will sein*"); he actually "lives" the role:

Das, was die Situation fordert, ist er jedesmal ganz: die Stärke seines Temperaments dämpft sich zur Weichheit ab, seine Intelligenz überwindet sich zur Borniertheit, und dieser Masham (a character) wird dumm, dumm bis in die Nasenspitze. Wo Sonnenthal dem Publikum liebenswürdig Honneurs erweist, zeigt Herr Rittner ungeniert seine Rückenansicht, dass Goethe sich entsetzt hätte; und wo Sonnenthal die Vorzüge seiner herrlichen Gestalt kunstbewusst ins Theater stellt, verzichtet er, der jugendliche Liebhaber, darauf „schön" auszusehen und will nur eines sein: charakteristisch.[47]

E. *The Function of the Actor*

Having considered Brahm's theories of acting from an historical perspective culminating in the exemplary influence of Ibsen and

---

[46] Schr. I, 363f.   [47] Schr. I, 364f.

in the achievements of Kainz, Reicher, and Rittner, we may now turn to a more direct statement of what he considers to be the function of the actor. First and foremost, the actor is the faithful interpreter of the dramatist's intentions ("*der treue Interpret dich-terischer Absichten*").[48] Brahm repeatedly refers to Lessing's dictum that the actor must think *with* the poet; and that where the poet has been deficient in human portrayal, the actor must think *for* him.[49] The function of the actor thus presupposes a two-fold obligation: he must be imitative but also creative ("*ein nachschaffender Künstler*").[50] The imitative function of the actor leads him to an analysis of the character as conceived by the dramatist; and the entire characterization is built up according to this analysis. The creativeness of the actor consists in his grasp of the character as a whole; he must envision a definite living being in all his indivudual facets; but all outward, physical traits must somehow be expressive of a unified spiritual substratum ("*Unter der Oberflächengestalt das Innere ahnen zu lassen*").[51] In this respect the actor must think *for* the dramatist since the problem involved is translation from a literary to a theatrical medium. No matter how many stage directions the author may include, it is obvious that these cannot be exhaustive. Hence the actor must unavoidably interpret and invent; in short, he must create.

The whole process must be controlled by a sensitive self-criticism of the actor if he is not a lapse from his imitative-creative art into the arbitrary egotism of virtuosity. Commenting on certain subjective mannerisms which Kainz displayed in his Orestes, Brahm shows the necessity for self-criticism on the part of the actor as a check against such lapses:

Hier muss die Selbstkritik des Schauspielers einsetzen, wenn er nicht aus einem grossen Künstler zu einem grossen Virtuosen werden will.[52]

Although the actor is obliged to be creative, there are certain pitfalls which he must avoid. To think for the author is a precarious task which cannot be undertaken haphazardly. There is

[48] Schr. I, 378.
[49] "Er muss überall mit dem Dichter denken; er muss da, wo dem Dichter etwas Menschliches widerfahren ist, für ihn denken." *Hamburgische Dramaturgie*, Einleitung.
[50] Schr. I, 464.   [51] Schr. I, 416.
[52] Schr. I, 439.

the danger of over-acting, of putting too much into a role. There is the danger of over-accentuating traits and ideas which should emerge effortlessly through artistic indirection or, perhaps, through mere implication. As an example of this danger, Brahm finds that Agnes Sorma, for all her histrionic genius, has over-acted Ibsen's Nora (*"wo der Dichter eins sagt, wünscht sie drei zu sagen"*).[53] The actor should penetrate into the nuclear spirit of the character in order to avoid such distortive supererogation. The art of characterization should be imperceptible in the completed projection of the character:

. . . nicht auf Kosten künstlerischer Diskretion soll die Überdeutlichkeit eines denkenden Schauspielertums das p. t. Publikum aufklären, es soll sich nicht aus dem Löwenkopf plötzlich ein Schnock der Schreiner herausstrecken und die Sache aufdringlich interpretieren.[54]

Summarizing Brahm's views, we find that the actor has a dual function of imitation and creation; he must think with the author and on occasion for the author. The actor's self-criticism acts as a check on this dual function, preventing virtuose excesses. Above all, the art of the actor should imperceptibly round out and unify his characterization so as to create a living human being behind whose physical traits a spiritual entity is made manifest.

F. *Sins of Virtuosity*

A discussion of certain details of histrionic technique, which recur in Brahm's criticism, serves admirably to round out his theories on the art of acting. Brahm's frequent use of the term virtuoso (*Virtuose*) calls for more precise definition. We have already seen his contrast between virtuosity and true histrionic art. The sins of virtuosity are manifold: for one thing, virtuosity subordinates and hence obscures the central meaning of the dramatic word, which should be primary in Brahm's conception of the theatre; for another, it precludes the ensemble idea, which is of central importance in Brahm's theory of the organization of the theatre. Individualistic efforts run counter to the collective organism which theoretically constitutes the theatre, according to Brahm.

[53] Schr. I, 415.   [54] Schr. I, 416.

Virtuosity manifests itself in countless details of acting technique. Worst of all is its disruption of dramatic illusion by a conscious catering to the audience (*"das Spielen ins Publikum"*).[55] The virtuoso is the matinee idol, the glorified star who feels himself so much more important than the play and the other artists of the theatre. His desire is to make his role stand out beyond the others rather than to merge with them, as the economy and unity of stage art would prescribe. The mannerisms which the virtuoso affects in order to make himself prominent are legion; he uses all the registers of his voice whether the role calls for them or not. He ranges from the melodramatic quaver (*"das tragische Tremolo"*)[56] to the anguished, gasping break of the voice (*"das Überschnappen der Stimme"*),[57] from the swashbuckling roar (*"den bramarbasierenden Ton"*)[58] to the low, insidious snarl (*Intrigantenton*).[59] Gestures and stage business are also employed by the virtuoso in his exhibitionistic rites. He squeezes out of the most innocent movement a host of petty nuances (*Mätzchen*).[60] He engages consistently in over-acting (*Chargieren*).[61] The result of course is an overloaded, piecemeal, and atomic, rather than organic building up of character, leading ultimately to caricature instead of human characterization. Brahm describes a typical portrait of such virtuosity in Herr Haase:

Herr Haase, ein Virtuose von anerkanntem Ruf, wird sich am schwersten, scheint es, in ein Ensemble wieder fügen lernen. Er hat mit scharfem Blick alle einzelnen Mittel und Mittelchen der Charakteristik studiert und mit ausserordentlicher Kunst sie beherrschen gelernt; seine Wirkungen trägt er sich aus jenen kleinen Einfällen und Betrachtungen zusammen, die man, wenn sie einem gefallen, Nuancen, in anderem Falle Mätzchen nennt. Sein Hofmarschall Kalb ist in diesem Stile angefasst; in ihrer Art eine bedeutende Leistung, welche den lauten Beifall und die laute Heiterkeit der Hörer weckte. Herr Haase stellt den Hofmarschall als einen Trottel dar mit dem Lachen eines Blödsinnigen; erkennt man diese Auffassung als eine durch die Dichtung geforderte an, so muss man die Konsequenz und die Wirksamkeit der Darstellung preisen. Wir anderen, die wir das

[55] Schr. I, 185, 473, et passim.   [56] Schr. I, 186.
[57] Schr. I, 362.   [58] Schr. I, 60.
[59] *Ibid.*   [60] Schr. I, 41.
[61] Schr. I, 362.

nicht tun, glauben, dass sie nur durch das Bedürfnis des Virtuosen
gefordert ist und nennen sie Karikatur.[62]

The pure, empty virtuosity which Friedrich Haase typifies (*"die
pure, leere Virtuosität"*)[63] impels Brahm to use him as a horrible
example of what the true actor should not be. We have already
read Brahm's castigation of Barnay for the same sort of self-
glorifying exhibitionism.[64] Ludwig Barnay represents to Brahm
the archtype of a theatre centered around a single factotum who is
manager, actor, director, and what not, all combined into one.
Haase typifies the same tendency concentrated in the art of acting.
External mannerism rather than spiritual characterization is the
result, so that the actor rather than the play is the thing, and the
quality of the play is immaterial just as long as it serves as a
vehicle for the self-magnification of the actor:

> Herr Haase gehört zu jenen Darstellern älterer Schule, welche einst
> als Realisten bewundert wurden, während sie uns heute nur noch als
> kluge Manieristen erscheinen. Nicht in dem schauspielerischen Er-
> fassen des innern Menschen suchen sie ihren Triumph, sondern sie
> charakterisieren zumeist durch Äusserlichkeiten, durch ein eigen-
> tümliches Behaben, durch körperliche Gelenkigkeit und die Geschick-
> lichkeit der Maske. Was nur Stütze der Bühnenkunst ist, rückt hier
> in das Zentrum der Darstellung; was nur Mittel zum Zweck sein
> sollte, wird Selbstzweck; und so vertilgt das Drum und Dran der
> virtuos erfassten Rolle zuletzt das Beste, die Charakterschilderung,
> und gerade an dem leersten Gebilde erprobt sich eine missleitete
> Kunst am eifrigsten.[65]

G. *A Summary of Acting Technique*

Brahm's negative criticism of virtuosity in all its phases and
metamorphoses has also its more bright converse side. We have
arrived at Brahm's positive principles of acting in three ways:
first, by the implications of his negative criticism; second, by his
more positive allusions to the subject; and third, from the qualities
which he praises in the great actors of his time.

The broad general principles which we can derive from the first
way is that acting is the recreation of a profounder reality through
psychological and physical characterization. The actor should ob-

---

[62] Schr. I, 41.   [63] Schr. I, 63.
[64] *Das Barnayjubiläum*, Schr. I, 303.
[65] Schr. I, 201.

jectify in his art the living spirit of a character conceived within the organic idea-action-character complex of the play in its entirety. The character must be three-dimensional and whole; in short, he must live and breathe and react like a recognizable human being. An artistic naturalness should underly the entire creative characterization. Yet the art of acting consists in the achieving of an artistic illusion of reality; and the more contemporary, that is, the more immediate the impression of reality, the greater will be the artistic effect. This, of course, precludes the virtuose sins of acting to the audience, of meretricious bits of stage business and mannerisms of voice, gesture, and general comportment which do not arise out of the total constellation of the character.

The above principles are implicit in Brahm's detailed campaign against virtuosity. However, he has also given us a more positive expression of his principles of acting. Repeatedly he insists on the necessity for an actor to be able to immerse himself completely in a role. His use of the term *"Wandlungsfähigkeit"* in reference to Edwin Booth's versatile genius for actually "living" a succession of different roles expresses this principle from one point of view.[66] With a slightly different emphasis, he evokes the same idea when he says of Pauline Lucca: *"Ein Schauspieler muss aus der Haut fahren können."*[67] In showing the superiority of French comic actors to their compatriots of the classical tragedy, Brahm again emphasizes the principle of "living" a role: *"Man deklamiert nicht mehr, man lebt die Rollen."*[68] This capacity for complete identification with a character to be portrayed is joined to the subjective capacity of the actor to "believe" in his role. Since the "playing" of a role must be replaced by the "living" of a role, very obviously an objective characterization will defeat its own purpose; in fact, to Brahm it is a contradiction in terms and is therefore not a "true" characterization at all. This is one of his chief objections to Ernestine Wegner s style: *"Selten glaubte die Soubrette an die Rolle, die sie darzustellen hatte."*[69] Conviction on the part of the actor is imperative if a similar conviction is to be aroused on the part of the audience.

[66] Schr. I, 24.
[68] Schr. I, 187.
[67] Schr. I, 64.
[69] Schr. I, 28.

In addition to living the role with conviction, the actor should
be able also to immerse himself in the situation; in other words, he
must be able to act with other actors, to subordinate himself within
an acting ensemble. This, of course, is what the virtuoso will not
or cannot do. We have already discussed the principles of an
organically constituted ensemble ("*Das Kunstprinzip eines durchgebildeten Ensembles*"),[70] the achievement of which is one of the important functions of the director. Here we see that it is also the
function of the individual actor to facilitate the broader function
by co-ordinating himself into such an ensemble. Only thus can his
individual characterization achieve the fully rounded perspective
of reality; otherwise the character, no matter how brilliantly
played, floats in an unpeopled void.

The conviction of the actor, his identification with his role, his
enthusiasm and good will, although indispensable, are not in themselves sufficient to achieve Brahm's ideal of acting. The psychological adequacy of the actor in regard to his role must also be
realized on a physical plane if it is to become manifest to an
audience. Hence, the spirit of a character should be expressed in
every limb of the body and in every physical reaction; the emotion
must involve the entire body, or at least be evident in some way
throughout the entire physical organism:

Mit ganzer Seele bei der Sache sein, ist noch nicht alles für den
Darsteller; er soll auch mit ganzem Körper bei der Sache sein. Es
sind wenige deutsche Schauspieler, die solche Beseelung „bis in die
Fingerspitzen" dem Körper mitzuteilen wissen.[71]

The observation of these principles will necessarily lead, according to Brahm, to the achievement of "*Wahrheit in der Technik*"[72]
and to the "true" interpretation of a role. The ultimate phase will
approach a kind of "*selbstverständlicher Naturalismus*"[73] in which
there will be neither exaggeration nor understatement in the playing of a role. Art and nature will merge effortlessly and imperceptibly to create a higher reality. Yet, since genius can be taught as
little in acting as in other arts, Brahm also stresses the *Temperament* and *Persönlichkeit* of the actor.

---

[70] Schr. I, 168.   [71] Schr. I, 65f.   [72] Schr. I, 183.
[73] Brahm says this of Rittner, Schr. I, 364.

CONCLUSION

The introduction to the present study implied a threefold aim: (1) the collection of scattered materials covering the entire gamut of Brahm's career as a man of letters; (2) the classification of Brahm's critical writings according to the categories inherent in them; (3) the emphasis on Brahm's significance in the history of modern German literature.

These three aims have been respectively accomplished as follows: (1) a literary biography has been constructed based on Schlenther's account and supplemented by the findings of original research in the works and correspondence of Schlenther, Scherer, Fontane, Keller, Hirschfeld, and others. All of Brahm's more extended works have been integrated into this literary biography. In addition, a detailed account of the more important subject matter (The Materials) of Brahm's collected essays and reviews has been given. (2) The leading ideas which constantly recur in Brahm's criticism of the drama and stage have been classified (The Principles) and found to resolve themselves into the problem of naturalism, the process and function of criticism, theatre history and organization, dramaturgy and technique, and the art of the actor. (3) Brahm's significance in the history of German letters emerges throughout the entire range of this study; in his relations with Scherer, Fontane, Keller, Hauptmann, and others, and in his critical theories which are brought into relief against the background of the naturalist movement.

The conclusions arrived at in the accomplishment of these aims show that Otto Brahm was a worthy continuator of the Hamburg-Berlin tradition of rationalism in dramatic criticism. He conforms to Scherer's ideal of scientific, empirical criticism in which criteria are evolved in terms of the very subject matter that it treats rather than from *a priori* standards. Brahm's identification with the movement of naturalism was at no time subsumable to the theoretical doctrine of "consistent" naturalism; he championed the movement because of its "modernity" and because of its revolutionary implications in the creative life. His own theory of "naturalism" more nearly approximates the Goethean concept of "*beseelte Natur*." In regard to the problematical dualism between drama and theatre, Brahm strove theoretically for a synthesis of the two, but in actual critical practice he emphasized the literary aspects of the drama as of greater moment than the mechanics of the theatre. In this respect, Brahm's chief contribution, as one of his commentators pointed out, was that he supplied the stage of his day with a literary conscience.

BIBLIOGRAPHY

The general style of abbreviations used below, if not self-explanatory, are in accordance with the table of abbreviations in Robert F. Arnold's *Allgemeine Bücherkunde zur neueren deutschen Literaturgeschichte*, 3. Aufl., Berlin und Leipzig, 1931 (cf. p. 21f).

GENERAL BIBLIOGRAPHIES on German *Theatergeschichte* are listed in Arnold (*op. cit.*, Dt. Thg. p. 339f); those consulted as most pertinent to the present study are: R. F. Arnold, *Bibliographie der dt. Bühnen seit 1830*, 1909; P. A. Merbach, *Bibliographie der Theatergeschichte 1905–1910*, Berl. 1913 (Schr. der Ges. f. Thg. B. 21); also the extended bibliographies contained in the histories of the theatre listed below, particularly the works of Arnold, Devrient, Rosenthal, Bab, and Winds.

COLLECTIONS AND SOURCES (cf. Arnold, *op. cit.*, p. 33). *Th. gesch. Forschungen*, 1891ff; *Materialien u. Untersuchungen, Publicationen der Ges. f. Th. gesch.* 1903ff.

THE WORKS OF OTTO BRAHM*

Das dt. Ritterdr. im 18. Jhdt., Strassburg, 1880 (Diss.).
Heinrich von Kleist, Berlin, 1884; Revised ed. 1911.
Karl Stauffer-Bern, Berlin, 1892; 12. Aufl. 1911.
Henrik Ibsen, Berlin, 1887.
Schiller, Berlin, 1. B. 1888, 2. B. 1892 (incomplete).
Kainz: Geschehenes und Gelebtes, Berlin, 1910.
Kritische Schriften, 2. B. [abbr. Schr. I & II] hg. von Paul Schlenther, Berlin, 1913–15. (For an exhaustive bibliography of Brahm's shorter essays, cf. Schr. II, p. 419.)
Letters, in *Otto Brahm, Briefe u. Erinnerungen*, Georg Hirschfeld, Berlin, 1925.

THE THEATRE: HISTORICAL AND THEORETICAL WORKS

Bab, J., Das Theater der Gegenwart, Leipzig, 1928.
Bab, J., Das Theater im Lichte der Soziologie, Leipzig, 1931.
Devrient, E., Geschichte d. dt. Schauspielkunst, 2. B., Berlin, 1905.
Gaehde, C., Das Theater, Leipzig u. Berlin, 2. Aufl., 1913.
Günther, J., Vom Wesen und Werden der Bühne, Leipzig, 1926.
Hagemann, E., Regie, Berlin, 1921.

* Henze states that Otto Brahm left no significant writings such as unpublished manuscripts or literary correspondence, according to information elicited from Brahm's closest relatives. *Op. cit.*, p. 6.

Knudsen, H., Das Studium d. Th.wsch. in Dtld., Charlottenburg. 1926.
Lebede, H., Vom Werden d. dt. Bühne, Berlin, 1923.
Martersteig, M., Das Th. im 19. Jhdt., Leipzig, 2. Aufl., 1924.
Michael, F., Deutsches Theater, Breslau, 1923.
Petersen, J., Das dt. Nationaltheater, Leipzig, 1919.
Rosenthal, F., Wesen u. Aufgabe d. dt. Th.gesch., Karlsruhe, 1928.
Stammler, W., Deutsche Theatergeschichte, Leipzig, 1925.
Winds, A., Geschichte der Regie, Stuttgart, 1925.

Periodicals

Vossische Zeitung, from May, 1881 to March, 1885.
Nation, from March, 1885 to Dec. 1889, and from Dec. 1891 to Oct. 1892.
Freie Bühne für modernes Leben (N. Rdsch.) from Jan. 1890 to Dec. 1891.
Kritische Waffengänge, hg. von H. u. J. Hart, Berlin, 1882–84.
Die Gesellschaft, hg. von M. G. Conrad, München, 1885ff.

General Bibliography

Antoine, A., Mes Souvenirs sur le Théâtre libre, Paris, 1921.
Anzengruber, L., Sämtliche Werke, 15. B., Wien, 1918ff.
Arnold, R., Das moderne Drama, Strassburg, 1912.
Arnold, R., Das deutsche Drama, München, 1925.
Bab, J., Das Theater der Gegenwart, Leipzig, 1928.
Bab, J., Die Lebenden, in Arnold, Das dt. Dr., 1925.
Bab, J., Das Theater im Lichte der Soziologie, Leipzig, 1931.
Bahr, H., Zur Kritik der Moderne, Zürich, 1890.
Bahr, H., Die Überwindung des Naturalismus, 1891.
Benda, O., Der Gegenwärtige Stand der dt. Lit.wsch., Wien u. Leipzig, 1928.
Benoist-Hanappier, L., Le Drame naturaliste en Allemagne, Paris, 1905.
Bertaux, F., Influence de Zola en Allemagne, Revue IV.
Bertaux, F., Littérature allemande de 1870 à 1928, Paris, 1928. (Eng. trans. N. Y. 1936.)
Bleibtreu, K., Revolution in der Literatur, 1885.
Bölsche, W., Die naturwissenschaftlichen Grundlagen der Poesie, Leipzig, 1887.
Butcher, S. H., Aristotle's Theory of Poetry and Fine Art, London, 1911[4].
Cheney, S., The Theatre, N. Y. 1929.
Clark, H. B., A Study of the Modern Drama, N. Y. 1925.
Conrad, M. G., Von E. Zola bis G. Hauptmann, Leipzig, 1902.
Devrient, E., Geschichte d. dt. Schauspielkunst, 2. B., Berlin, 1905.

Dilthey, W., Das Erlebnis und die Dichtung, 10. Aufl., Leipzig, u. Berlin, 1929.

Ernst, Paul, Der Weg zur Form, 3. Aufl., München, 1928.

Eller, W., Ibsen in Germany, Boston, 1918.

Eloesser, A., Otto Brahm, BJb., B. 17, pp. 119–24.

Eloesser, A., Lit. Echo, B. 17, p. 758f (1914–15).

Ermatinger, E., Gottfried Kellers Leben, Briefe, u. Tagebücher, 3B., Berlin, 1919.

Ermatinger, E., Die Kunstform des Dramas, 2. Aufl., Leipzig, 1931.

Fischer, S., N. Rdsch., B. 24 (Jan. 1913).

Fontane, T., Causerien über Berliner Theatereindrücke, hg. von Paul Schlenther, Berlin, 1904.

Fontane, T., Briefe, hg. von E. Heilborn, 5B., Berlin, 1920.

Fontane, T., Briefe, hg. von Pniower u. Schlenther, Berl. 1910.

Fontane, T., Briefwechsel von Th. F. u. P. Heyse 1850–97, hg. von Erich Petzet, Berlin, 1929.

Fontane, T., Ausgewählte Werke, 5B., Einleitung von Thomas Mann, Leipzig, 1928ff.

Frenzel, K., Berliner Dramaturgie, 2B., Erfurt, 1877ff.

Friedenthal, J., Das Wedekindbuch, München u. Leipzig, 1914.

Fritsch, P., Influence du théâtre français sur le théâtre allemand 1870–1900, Paris, 1912.

Freytag, G., Technik des Dramas (1863), 7. Aufl., Leipzig, 1894.

Gaehde, C., Das Theater, 2. Aufl., Leipzig u. Berlin, 1913.

Goethe, J. W. von, Werke (Sophienausgabe), 143B., Weimar, 1887–1920.

Gregor, J., Weltgeschichte des Theaters, Zürich, 1933.

Grube, M., Geschichte der Meininger, Stuttgart, 1926.

Gundolf, F., Shakespeare u. d. dt. Geist, 8. Aufl., Berlin, 1927.

Günther, J., Vom Wesen und Werden der Bühne, Leipzig, 1926.

Günther, M., Die soziologischen Grundlagen des naturalistischen Dramas (Diss.), Leipzig, 1912.

Hagemann, E., Regie, Berlin, 1921.

Hanstein, A., Das jüngste Deutschland, Leipzig, 1905.

Harden, M., Berlin als Theaterstadt, 1888.

Harden, M., Literatur und Theater, 1896.

Hauptmann, G., Gesammelte Werke, 8B., Berlin, 1922.

Henze, H., Otto Brahm und das „Deutsche Theater" in Berlin, (Diss. Erlangen) Berlin, 1930. (Reprinted in "Mitteilungen des Ver. f. d. Gesch. Berl.," 47 Jhrg. Hefte 3, 4, Berl. 1930.)

Heyse, P., Gesammelte Werke, hg. von E. Petzet, 15B., Stuttgart, 1924.

Hirschfeld, G., Otto Brahm: Briefe u. Erinnerungen, Berlin, 1925, (first appeared in Das lit. Echo, 1.9.1912 and 1.1.1913).

Holz, Arno, Die Kunst: ihr Wesen u. ihre Gesetze, Berlin, 1891 (Neue Folge, 1892).

Ibsen, H., Sämtliche Werke, 5B., Berlin, 1902.

Jacobsohn, S., Das Theater der Reichshauptstadt, München, 1904.

Josephson, M., Zola's Life and Time, N. Y., 1928.

Keller, G., Sämtliche Werke, hg. von E. Ermatinger u. F. Hunziker, 10B., Stuttgart, 1919.

Kerr, A., Die Welt im Drama, 5B., Berlin, 1917.

Kersten, K., Dt. Rdsch., B. 165 (1915), pp. 153–55.

Kleinberg, A., Die deutsche Dichtung in ihren sozialen, zeit- und geistesgeschichtlichen Bedingungen, Berlin, 1927.

Kleist, H. von, Sämtliche Werke, 5B., Leipzig, 1904.

Knudsen, H., Das Studium der Th.wsch. in Dtld., Charlottenburg, 1926.

Kutscher, A., Frank Wedekind: Sein Leben u. seine Werke, 3B., München, 1922–27–31.

Lebede, H., Vom Werden der dt. Bühne, Berlin, 1923.

Mann, T., Versuch über das Theater (1910) in *Rede u. Antwort*, Berlin, 1922.

Mann, T., Rede über das Theater, in *Die Forderung des Tages*, Berlin, 1930.

Martersteig, M., Das dt. Theater im 19. Jhdt., 2. Aufl., Leipzig, 1924.

Michael, F., Deutsches Theater, Breslau, 1923.

Miller, A. I., The Independent Theatre in Europe, N. Y., 1931.

Naumann, H., Die dt. Dichtung d. Gegenwart, 5. Aufl., Stuttgart, 1931.

Nestriepke, S., Volksbühnengemeinden, Berlin, 1924.

Petersen, J., Schiller u. die Bühne, Leipzig, 1904.

Petersen, J., Das deutsche Nationaltheater, Leipzig, 1919.

Petsch, R., Deutsche Dramaturgie, 2B., Leipzig, 1921.

Piscator, E., Das politische Theater, Berlin, 1929.

Richards, I. A., Principles of Literary Criticism, N. Y. & London, 5. ed. 1934.

Root, W., German Criticism of Zola 1875–93 (Diss.), N. Y., 1931.

Rosenthal, F., Unsterblichkeit des Theaters, Bonn, 1927.

Rosenthal, F., Wesen u. Aufgabe d. dt. Thg., Karlsruhe, 1928.

Scherer, W., Vorträge u. Aufsätze zur Gesch. d. geistigen Lebens in Dtld. u. Österr., 3B., Berlin, 1874.

Scherer, W., Gesch. d. dt. Lit., Berl. 1883 (Scherer-Walzel ed. 4. Aufl. Berl. 1928, mit einer Bibliographie von Josef Körner).

Scherer, W., Poetik, Berlin, 1888 (posthumous).

Scherer, W., Kleine Schriften, 2B. hg. von Konrad Burdach, Berlin, 1893.

Schiller, F., Werke, 15B., hg. von Bellermann, Petsch, Leitzmann, Stammler, Leipzig, 1919–22.
Schinnerer, O. P., Arthur Schnitzler's "Nachlass", Gc. Rev. 8 (1933), pp. 114–23.
Schlaf, J., Die Freie Bühne u. die Entstehung des naturalistischen Dramas, Leipzig, 1914.
Schlenther, P., Wozu der Lärm? Genesis der Freien Bühne, Berlin, 1889.
Schlenther, P., Gerhart Hauptmann, Berlin, 1897 (brought up to date and edited by A. Eloesser, 1922).
Schlenther, P., Otto Brahm, N. Rdsch., 24 (1913), Feb., pp. 186–201; Mar., pp. 323–38. (Reprinted in Schr. d. Ges. f. Thg., B. 40, Berlin, 1930.)
Schlenther, P., Otto Brahm: Kritische Schriften (abbr. Schr. I & II), 2B., Berlin, 1913–15.
Schmidt, E., Dt. Rdsch., 154 (1913) Jan.
See, E., Le Théâtre français contemporain, Paris, 1928.
Simon, W., Otto Brahm: Kundgebungen zu seinem Gedenken, Berlin, 1913.
Soergel, A., Dichtung u. Dichter der Zeit, 20. Aufl., Leipzig, 1928.
Stammler, W., Deutsche Theatergeschichte, Leipzig, 1925.
Stammler, W., Deutsche Literatur vom Naturalismus bis zur Ggw., 2. Aufl., Breslau, 1927.
Stanislawski, K., My Life in Art, Boston, 1924.
Steiger, E., Das Werden des neueren Dramas, 1898.
Stern, J., ZfdU., 30 (1916), 215f.
Thomas, C., Life and Works of Schiller, N. Y., 1901.
Trebein, B., Theodor Fontane as a Critic of the Drama (Diss.), N. Y., 1916.
Volkelt, J., Aesthetik des Tragischen, 3. Aufl., München, 1917.
Wahle, J., Das Weimarer Theater unter Goethes Leitung, Weimar, 1892 (Schr. d. Goethe Ges., B. 6).
Wassermann, J., Erinnerungen an Arthur Schnitzler, N. Rdsch., 43 (1932), p. 7f.
Wildenbruch, E. von, Gesammelte Werke, 16B., Berlin, 1912ff.
Winds, A., Geschichte der Regie, Stuttgart, 1925.
Witkowski, G., Das dt. Drama des 19. Jhdts., Leipzig, 1913.
Zola, E., Le Naturalisme au Théâtre, Paris, 1881.
Zola, E., Nos Auteurs Dramatiques, Paris, 1882.